HOW TO
QUIT YOUR JOB
& TRAVEL

Everything You Need to Travel Long Term
(& All the Things Nobody Tells You)

BY LIA GARCIA

How to Quit Your Job & Travel: Everything You Need to Travel Long Term (& All the Things Nobody Tells You)

Author Contact: contact@practicalwanderlust.com

Book Cover Design: Booklerk.com

Table of Contents

Acknowledgements

I could not have written this book alone. Luckily, I didn't have to: I was helped and supported every step of the way. I'd like to thank everyone who made this the existence of this book possible:

To my wonderful Book Launch team, who made it feel like I was writing this book with a huge group of friends. Thank you for gently correcting my grammar and educating me about proper punctuation; for sharing your own stories, tips, and travel disasters with me and with each other; and above all, for helping me find my voice and giving me the confidence to speak louder. You made writing this book fun — can we do it again sometime soon?

To the amazing Practical Wanderlust team, who made this book possible. To Richie, for letting me have my rambling run-on sentences and parentheticals while fixing all of my spelling errors. To Natalie, for always being willing to handle the fiddly bits, even when it's the middle of the night your time. To Melissa, who always manages to read my mind even when I forget to explain myself. To Sarah, who is possibly the only person I've ever met who enjoys a good research hole more than I do — half of this book is yours. To Katie, for tackling each new project and challenge thrown your way with poise and confidence — I would not have met a single deadline without you. And to the rest of my incredible team: you inspire me every day by chasing after your own dreams. Thank you for helping me achieve mine.

To the world's cutest dog, Mulan. Thank you for always putting your little paws on my knee when you do a big stretch. Thank you for sticking your fluffy little butt in my face while you stand on my desk and keep guard for roof squirrels. Thank you for inserting your little wet nose underneath my hand so I have to pet you instead of writing, and if that doesn't work, walking directly across my keyboard until I pay more attention to you. You are my sweetest little bear and I love you so much.

To my family, who raised me to think critically, crack jokes, and never shy away from a challenge. To my mom, who taught me everything I know about trip planning, research, and spreadsheets. To my dad, whose backpacking days are way cooler than mine ever were. To Katya, who has always cheered me along, Pat, who always makes me laugh even when he's trying not to kill me, and Everett and Elena, who I can't wait to whisk away one day for a Very Big Adventure, Liaremy style.

To my darling husband Jeremy. Thank you for supporting me in every way, for listening to me talk endlessly about book organization on long evening walks, and for jumping in whenever I needed help writing a joke (you have the best worst jokes). You supported me every step of the way as I chased after my dreams, and I hope to take every Very Big Adventure by your side.

And to Katy. My idol. I hope you knew how much you always inspired me. I am still figuring out all the ways in which my life has been shaped by yours. I like to imagine that one day my grandchildren will delight in telling ridiculous stories true about me, the way I do about you. This book is thanks to your legacy of always traveling, and living, fearlessly and unapologetically.

Foreword

By Jeremy Garcia

Since I am a major character in this book, it felt only natural that I should ask Lia if I could write the foreword for her first book. It was either going to be me or our dog, and Mulan can't type (even though she tries to while we work). She agreed and gave me one directive: "Just don't make it a whole mushy thing about how obsessed with me you are." I begrudgingly accepted. So I'm not going to tell you about how amazingly impressive Lia is, or how she knows how impressive she is and wears it with confidence (and encourages others to do the same). I won't get into the fact that she guides her team with a clear vision while making a point to make each person feel seen, heard, and valued. I certainly won't discuss how she has an unending love for her family, friends, colleagues, and herself. Obviously, it would go against her directive if I brought up the fact that my students write her letters about how inspired they are by her and how they hope to be like her.

Instead, I would like to focus on the process of the book in your hands. The phrase "labor of love" gets thrown around too often, so I dub this book a labor of anxiety. I'll try to avoid spoilers, but before this book, before Practical Wanderlust, and even before meeting me, there was a crazy idea for Lia to quit her job to travel. Since then, anxiety has been a constant fixture at Practical Wanderlust HQ. Sometimes it looks like "Are we sure we should buy these tickets?" Sometimes it looks like "Am I staying true to myself/our readers/our brand by putting this online?"

Lately, that anxiety has taken the form of her relationship with you, dear reader. There is no Practical Wanderlust without you, and there definitely is no How to Quit Your Job and Travel without you. Over the time she has spent writing this book, she has never taken her mind off of you: Will you find this useful? Is this too preachy? Will you laugh? She puts herself in your shoes and imagines your reaction to the words that are now in your hands.

So as you giggle at our (very literal) pain, dream of your own (hopefully less fraught with danger) trip, and explore the world through our (forever worsening) eyes, I hope you know it was all for you. Count yourself lucky that someone as brilliant, pragmatic, inspiring, and entertaining as Lia brought this into your life.

Introduction

Quitting my job to travel was the scariest thing I've ever done in my life.

Here's the thing: I'm generally a very practical person. Logistical. Grounded. Balanced. Spontaneity makes me nervous. Watching a movie without knowing the ending gives me anxiety; I'm one of those weirdos who seek out spoilers so I can emotionally prepare myself.

I am not the kind of person who quits her job and hops on a plane on a whim. I'm the kind of person who makes decisions using spreadsheets and knows exactly what I'll be doing for the next five years, with a detailed plan for each year.

So how did I find myself sobbing into my new husband's chest in a stuffy 12-person hostel dorm room in Cartagena, Colombia, positive that I'd ruined both of our lives and desperately trying to video call a cat?

Well, you're going to find out exactly how I got to day one of my year-long honeymoon.

This book is what I needed five years earlier, when I first started daydreaming about taking a Very Big Adventure. I was a new college graduate coming off the high of my very first two-week-long backpacking trip, still slightly burnt from the Swiss sun. I had just moved from Louisville, Kentucky to San Francisco to start my new, exciting, grown-up life at a new, exciting, grown-up job.

I sat down behind my desk (my very own DESK!) with an empty notebook, feeling exhilarated and filled with possibilities. I was earning a SALARY! With benefits! And healthcare! I'd made it. The world felt newly opened up to me; I was starry-eyed and optimistic. I wanted to make waves. I wanted to change the world. I wanted to make an impact!

But as the months and years passed, the monotony of corporate life crept in. My exciting new job felt less and less like the beginning of an adventure, and more like the beginning of the end of my life. My role was a lot less world-impacting and a lot more "soulless robot" than I'd hoped it would be. My employer had an unspoken rule that everyone was expected to take their laptop home and work on nights and weekends, and I felt guilty every time I was doing something that wasn't work-related. Worst of all, despite putting in extra hours, I often found myself hiding in the bathroom, choking down tears after receiving harsh public criticism from my boss.

Was this all there was? Was the culmination of everything I'd been working towards for my entire life just endless, meaningless work, a never-ending feeling of not being good enough, and constant guilt?

Each day felt like a fast-forward repeat of the day before: wake up, go to work, eat, watch TV, sleep, repeat. The monotony was broken only by the 14 sacred days I was allowed to either enjoy myself away from work or stay home sick (in either case, I was still expected to bring my laptop with me and stay "on call").

I found myself daydreaming of faraway places, the backpacking trip I'd taken that summer after college when the world still felt excitingly limitless, and all the adventures that awaited me outside the fluorescent-lit confines of my job. At work I secretly browsed travel websites, hidden in a tiny window behind my email to make sure my boss, seated directly next to me, couldn't see. I looked longingly at all the places I was aching to go, trying to do mental gymnastics to figure out how I could make it work with a limited budget and too-little vacation time.

As each day passed — work-eat-TV-sleep — I found myself with less energy than the day before. I had the odd sense that I was waiting for something. Waiting for the "click." Waiting to wake up and start actually living.

But I was only 23. Wasn't I supposed to be in the prime of my life? Hadn't my "real" life just begun?

I found myself adrift. When I landed my job, I'd achieved the five-year plan I'd set for myself when I started college. Now, with no goals, I had no purpose.

I needed something else to look forward to — something other than the endless slog (work, eat, TV, sleep, repeat). But everything was happening too fast. Time kept marching forward, and I was too mentally exhausted to do anything about it.

So, I set myself a new goal: I wanted to take a trip. A long trip. Not a jam-packed weekend getaway: a full-on adventure. With every fiber of my being, I was aching to take an entire year off to just do the one thing I couldn't stop dreaming about: travel long term.

Except I had no idea how.

But no matter. That was a problem for future me. I circled an arbitrary date in my mental calendar and began slowly marching towards my goal — my escape — one tiny step at a time.

The goal gave me something to look forward to, and my energy returned little by little. I started interviewing for better jobs and managed to find one that not only paid slightly more money, but didn't regularly reduce me to tears.

With a new job (which was, if not deeply fulfilling, at least enjoyable) and a goal to work towards, I felt invigorated. For the first time in my life, I started lifting weights, hiking, and camping. If I was going to go backpacking, I figured, it might help to be in decent physical shape[1]. While I worked out, I listened to travel audiobooks like Into The Wild and A Walk in the Woods. (I found that stories of adventures gone horribly wrong were excellent motivation to train harder). Visions of watching the sunrise at Machu Picchu and thru-hiking the Appalachian Trail danced before my eyes as I sweated on the Stairmaster.

As I inched towards my goal, my faraway dream felt more and more within my grasp. And then, a few years into saving for my trip, I met a charming, sweet man with kind eyes and a bright red beard, and we began planning the trip together as our honeymoon.

And at last, after five long years of saving, plotting, and planning, I finally did it! The trip I'd dreamt of for so long became a year-long honeymoon with my new husband, Jeremy. And it was nothing like I'd imagined it would be.

After traveling for a full year, the culmination of everything I'd worked towards for so long, I came back home. I settled down again. And, to my complete surprise, I found myself at another turning point.

---

1 A quick note on this point: I am a self-confident, body-positive fat woman. My goal in training for my trip was not to lose weight, but to gain muscle and strength so that I could fearlessly tackle exciting bucket-list adventures, go on long multi-day hikes, and carry a heavy backpack without destroying my knees. With that goal in mind, I took up powerlifting and hiking, both of which I found to be helpfully low-impact and accessible for a nervous, out-of-shape beginner. They gave me a sense of strength, empowerment, and athleticism that I'd never felt before in my life, and I can't recommend them enough! Now I'm a self-confident, body-positive fat woman who lifts satisfyingly heavy weights, takes flexing selfies at the gym, and climbs mountains too.

When I was planning my getaway, I hadn't spent much time thinking about what would happen after I came back home. I figured that once my travel itch was scratched, I'd be happy to settle and continue as if nothing had happened. If I was lucky, I thought, I'd be able to go right back to work and pick up the career I'd left on hold.

But when push came to shove, I just didn't want to. Instead, I took another huge risk: I started working for myself.

Today, my career revolves around the same passion that shaped and fueled me for so many years: travel. As the co-founder and CEO of Practical Wanderlust, one of the most-read travel blogs in the world, my full-time job is to explore the world and learn about beautiful places. Best of all, I help other people take their own life-changing adventures.

I wake up each day excited, fulfilled, and energized. I finally feel as though I've truly chosen the life I'm living. I am, at long last, fully present, and truly savor each day.

If someone had told me those things were possible all those years ago, back when I was sitting at my desk daydreaming and waiting for my life to begin, I would have said, "Sorry, I'm not interested in buying oils or joining your church or whatever, thanks."

Listen: I'm not saying that quitting your job is the answer to life, the universe, and everything. It's not just that I've finally found a career doing what I love that's making me sound like a walking infomercial. And it wasn't the act of travel itself, either: I didn't "find myself" on a beach in Bali, or get deeply in touch with my inner soul doing sunrise yoga in Ecuador.[2]

For me, the real difference was leaving everything behind for a year and coming back for a fresh start. It was like hitting a reset button. It gave me a chance to re-evaluate what's really important to me, and allowed me to leave behind the things that weren't working for me.

I'm not a different person from the one I was before my trip, but I have learned to make do with a lot less and to appreciate smaller, simpler joys.

---

2 I did actually do sunrise yoga in Ecuador, exactly one time. I was tired, it was hot. I never did it again.

More importantly, I gave up trying to be someone I was not; someone who takes her computer home on the weekends and is fluent in corporate buzz-speak like, "Let's circle back on that, Carol" and "To your point, Susan, I think we need to align and get some synergy." I've finally accepted that I'm not the kind of person who fits neatly into a rigid corporate office mold.[3] I stopped looking at my salary or title as the true metric of my success in life. And I've given up on small talk, which I've never been very good at or had much patience for; these days if you meet me at a party, within a few minutes I'll probably be telling you about how I stopped wearing bras after returning from my year-long honeymoon.[4]

Ultimately, the best gifts that quitting my job to travel for a year gave me were the freedom to leave behind the parts of my life that weren't making me happy, and the permission to stop trying to be someone I wasn't. I learned to ignore other people's expectations, and to stop holding myself to definitions of success that no longer served me. I learned to look inside to find what makes ME happy and to chase after it, unapologetically.

When I returned to "real" life, it was with a renewed sense of self, the courage to take risks, and the audacity to pursue my dreams.

It is my dearest hope that quitting your job to travel gives you the same gift, and that this book helps you on your journey.

About the Book

This book is divided into four sections:

- **Part One** focuses on laying the groundwork for your trip, including the preparations and decisions that take place well before you leave. You'll learn to identify and navigate fears and obstacles in your way as you develop a rough outline for your trip, set yourself a departure deadline, calculate the cost of your adventure, start working towards a specific savings goal, and turn your travel dream into an actionable plan.

---

3 After my trip, free from the confines of the corporate world, I also stopped wearing makeup, purses, heels, and underwire bras. But hey, don't be freaked out! Listen, maybe you'll get back from your trip and think, "Wow! I really missed feeling wires poking into my chest all the time!" or "You know what? After a whole year of wearing comfortable, practical walking shoes, I can't WAIT to have sore feet again." Everyone's different!

4 Listen: spend a year free from the restrictive shackles of underwire bras and you will know exactly what I'm talking about. It is LIFE CHANGING. You will NEVER GO BACK.

- **Part Two** takes place in the months before your trip, as you finalize your plans, pack your bags, book your itinerary, and tie up loose ends at home. You'll learn how to effectively plan a long-term trip, tackle each piece of the logistical puzzle of placing your life on hold, find out what to pack (and what to leave at home), and take off on the adventure of a lifetime.

- **Part Three** prepares you for the trip itself, including all the things that nobody tells you about long-term travel, how to stay safe and prevent theft, and what to do if you find yourself running out of funds. You'll learn about the many challenges of long-term travel, the beauty of "travel magic," and how to overcome challenges while you're on the road.

- **Part Four** occurs after the trip, as you return home and attempt to reintegrate back into ordinary life. We'll cover how to prepare yourself for the most difficult part of long-term travel, including picking back up where you left off with your career (or choosing not to), and how to use the skills you learned during your travels to identify your needs and adjust to the life you've returned to.

In each part of the book, you'll find specific, actionable advice interwoven with stories and mishaps from my own year-long honeymoon.

At the end of the book is a reference section containing all of the websites, apps, businesses, academic studies, and tools I've mentioned or recommended, as well as tables organizing information you'll need as you plan. You can also visit our website for a digital and printable version of the "Reference" section.

I like to imagine that you may find yourself revisiting this book many times over the coming years as you work towards making your dreams a reality. I would love nothing more than for you to bring a battered, dog-eared copy along with you on your journey, and perhaps leave it in a hostel lounge somewhere very far away for someone else to find and enjoy.

PART ONE:
THE DREAM

A Radical Act

In many cultures, taking time off to travel is an important rite of passage. In the United Kingdom, it's known as a "gap year," a year-long trip traditionally taken before or after college which rose to popularity around the '60s.

The Australian "walkabout" originated in Australia's Aboriginal community as a six-month long spiritual journey that transforms teenagers into young adults. Today, you can meet attractive, incredibly fit Australians in their 20s in hostels all over the world on their version of a walkabout.[5]

New Zealanders typically take an OE, "Overseas Experience." In Israel, a "post-army trip" is customary before beginning college. Belgium's government goes all-in and pays for a year-long sabbatical from work, which I can only assume also involves state-sponsored beer delivery.

But in the USA, taking time off from work (or education) to travel, even just for a few weeks, is not only uncommon — it's downright counterculture. Go on, put on your favorite pleather jacket and your angriest eyeliner: you're a rebel.

Long-term travel runs contrary to several of the USA's most beloved societal norms:

- **We are taught to prioritize work and career above all else.** But long-term travel means putting career development on hold and prioritizing personal enjoyment over work. How dare you? You can't just go *enjoy yourself*. Get back to work!

- **We have a deep-seated fear of the unknown and the "other" in U.S. culture.** But travel inherently embraces foreign people and cultures. You might even find that countries you'd been taught to think of as "third world"[6] are actually wonderful, thriving places — the horror!

---

5 And, at the risk of kicking things off with an overgeneralization, they are THE MOST fun. Seriously, you must spend a night out on the town with the Aussies you'll meet at your hostel. They are a blasty blast.

6 "The term "Third World" is a vestige of the Cold War, when the U.S. and its non-Communist allies were considered the First World, the Communist Bloc was defined as the Second World, and nonaligned nations, which were predominantly poor, were designated the Third World. Later, it became a dismissive term broadly associated with poverty and colonialism. Today, it's widely considered both offensive and out-of-date. The term "developing world" is preferable, although it still implies superiority and hierarchy between countries.

- **Our culture prioritizes achieving material comfort.** Acquiring lots of shiny, expensive "stuff" in a fancy house with a well-manicured lawn equals success. But living out of a suitcase means rejecting both "stuff" and comfort — nobody in the history of backpacking has ever described a hostel dorm room as "comfortable."

Simply put, the reasons why most people want to embark on long-term travel — the pursuit of happiness, personal growth, spiritual fulfillment, and a desire to experience and learn from other cultures — are downright un-American. Cue horrified pearl-clutching.

It turns out that the fears that have been ingrained in us since birth now live in the back of our minds, keeping us trapped in our daily reality to avoid taking a gamble that could cause us to lose everything we've built.

The fear whispers nightmare scenarios to us even as we dream of escape. In the back of our minds, it whispers things like: if you quit your job to travel, nobody will ever want to hire you again. You'll have an unexplainable gap on your resume. You'll have to spend years trying to make up what you threw away. You'll spend all your money and never earn it back again because nobody will ever hire you. You'll never be able to retire!

Sometimes the fear takes on the form of a well-meaning parent or loved one: Long-term travel is dangerous — you're going to end up dead on the side of the road somewhere! Or worst of all, you might never come back. You could end up a nomad, a drifter, someone who floats on society's outskirts, flitting from place to place and rejecting the very core tenets of the American Dream. Shameful!

If this logic holds true, then quitting your job to travel is not just a terrible idea, it's an utterly life-ruining one.

Before I took the leap — and during, and after — these fears played in my head on a never-ending loop. I was terrified that I'd ruined my life, and even worse, I'd ruined my husband's life, too, since this whole crazy thing was my idea. Every step of the way — while we scrimped and saved, as we booked our plane tickets, as I fell asleep each night in various hostels, and as we boarded a plane back home again — anxiety hummed in the back of my head. Would we ever be happy again? Had we made a huge mistake by throwing away perfectly good lives and jobs? Would we ever be content to settle down again and return to "normal" life?

Years later, I can now finally answer those questions.

Taking a sabbatical did not ruin my career; I wasn't damned to a life of eternal misery. And my job, salary, and material possessions weren't the only thing that determined my happiness.

If you're thinking I'm getting ready to tell you that travel is the answer to all of your problems and the secret to lifelong happiness, let me stop you right there. Long-term travel isn't the answer to anything.[7] And much like material success, it comes with its own fair share of unrealistic expectations.[8]

But what long-term travel can help you do is reject some of the trappings and claustrophobic expectations placed on you by living in a society that values work, money, and status above all else.[9] With that gift of stepping beyond those boundaries, paired with the eye-opening and perspective-shifting learning that comes from interacting with other people and cultures, you'll have a potentially life-changing opportunity: to redefine your own standards of happiness and success.

Taking a gap year or a sabbatical or traveling long term is like pressing "pause" on the rat race. It gives you time to stop, take a few deep breaths, look around, and reassess what actually matters to you.

Or, to put things into a more modern perspective, it's like Marie Kondo-ing your entire life: taking it all out into the open and then going through every single part of it to figure out what brings you joy.

It's not just that you'll be doing that for your belongings or the things you'll be packing away or taking with you; you also have a chance to do it for your career, your friends, your lifestyle, and your values. And you have the opportunity to

---

7   I mean, personally I was at least hoping it was the answer to finally becoming a Morning Person, which is my ultimate goal in life. But I spent the entire year of my year-long honeymoon sleeping until 10am (except, of course, for the single day I managed to wake up at 5am for sunrise yoga in Ecuador, which was emphatically not worth it).

8   Before my Very Big Adventure, I liked to imagine the "travel" version of myself and all of the fabulous adventures she'd have, lying around on beaches and summiting mountains and befriending llamas and being completely and totally satisfied every second of every day. But in reality — hang on, we're still in Part One. Enjoy your daydreams for now, and I'll tell you what actually happened until Part Three.

9   See also: marriage and having children. Maybe you don't want children! Maybe you're perfectly happy on your own without a romantic partner! Maybe everyone should mind their own business! Maybe getting a really cute dog is the solution to all of your problems and the secret to happiness! Wait, what? Mulan, please get off my keyboard.

make a clean break with the things that no longer bring you joy, wish them well, gently chuck them in the trash, and walk away.

When you return home again, you'll have a cleaner slate than when you left. You'll feel more grateful for things you once took for granted and less fear about abandoning things that no longer serve you. Since, after all, you've already been without them for a time.

Although quitting your job to travel is a radical act that goes against some of the core values that U.S. society has drilled deep into our collective psyche, and even though travel won't solve your problems or give you all the answers — it is a gift. And that gift is worthy of taking a huge, terrifying risk.

Of course, it's still a risk. And as a risk-averse person who has a lot of anxiety, I'll be here to guide you every step of the way.

So let's sit down together and I'll tell you all about the many, many mistakes I made during my year-long trip. Like defaulting on six figures of student loan debt. Or getting rescued off a waterfall in Colombia. Or getting robbed at a bus station in Peru. Or failing to complete the Inca Trail trek to Machu Picchu that I'd trained so hard for.

And that's barely even scratching the surface!

Throughout it all, I want you to remember this: every misstep and mistake along the way, every expensive failure and disastrous screw-up, was each a crucial part of the adventure I needed — a wonderful twist in my ridiculous story.

I wouldn't change the life I have today for anything. Taking the massive risk of pressing "pause" on my life, quitting my job, and traveling the world was completely, entirely, totally, and without a doubt, totally freakin' worth it.

So it's going to be OK. You're going to be OK. You can do this.

Now take a deep breath, and let's get started.

Laying the Groundwork

Let's start at the very beginning: before you book a single hostel or buy a plane ticket, before you're even sure when or where you're going. Part One of this book focuses on the preparations and decisions that should take place well before you leave for your trip — ideally, years in advance. (I'm so glad we'll be able to spend so much time together!)

Think of this part of the process as the "dreaming" phase. You're still figuring out when you'll be able to make your dream a reality, laying the groundwork to put your career on hold, and pinching every penny you can to save up funds for your trip.

I'm not going to sugarcoat it: Part One takes the longest. In fact, there's a pretty good chance that you've already been in this stage for a while now: saving inspirational photos on your phone, depositing extra quarters in a jar, and dreaming of the day you actually pull the trigger and go. You may not even be entirely sure you're going at all.

I know exactly how you feel. For me, this agonizing phase lasted for five long years.

Five years of wishing, waiting, and saving. Five years of dreaming and hoping. Five years of thinking, "Maybe I'll leave next year — or maybe the year after that."

I wasn't dragging my feet intentionally, exactly; it just never felt like the right time. I didn't have enough money. I wasn't sure I wanted to go alone, and I hadn't met anyone I wanted to go with. I had just been promoted, or started a new job, or things were going really well at my job, or I was finally feeling really settled in my apartment and I had a lot of things coming up on my calendar and … it was just never the right time.

It wasn't the right time for four years in a row.

Until finally, one year, I'd had enough of waiting. I set myself a deadline and while it may have been tentative, it was a deadline nonetheless. It was happening! I opened a savings account, borrowed some library books on backpacking and traveling, started going hiking on the weekends, and asked for travel gear for Christmas. I was so ready!

My deadline came … and went. I've never been any good at sticking to deadlines.

So, I set myself a NEW deadline. And this time, I set it with someone else: a guy I'd barely met, on our second date. It wasn't a particularly special moment; we were having drinks in a loud, crowded bar somewhere in San Francisco and I shouted, "I'm probably going to be leaving for a really long trip next year" and he shouted back, "Cool, that sounds really fun" and I yelled, "You can come if you want to" and he yelled back, "Ok then."

One year later, we were engaged. We planned our wedding at the same time as planning our year-long honeymoon (a terrible idea which I would highly discourage anyone from doing). This time, there was no pushing back our deadline. It was time for Phase Two.

If you're smack-dab in the middle of Phase One, I know how agonizing it is to wait. I know how painful it is to have a dream that feels frustratingly unachievable, how obnoxious it is every time you hop on social media and see other people, who are somehow almost always ridiculously attractive, making it look easy.

It's not easy. It's really, really freaking hard.

But I can promise you one thing: no matter how long it takes you, no matter how many years you spend biding your time and waiting for the right moment to finally come, it will be worth it. Achieving your dream of long-term travel will be one of the most satisfying, exciting, and exhilarating things you ever do. So have patience: it will all pay off.

And now, let's get working on setting that deadline, shall we?

Where Are You Going?

Figuring out where you might want to go is the most fun part of planning a long-term trip. If you've ever planned a wedding, this is like the part where you're just collecting inspirational photos on Pinterest and dreaming about your big day — before you have to call a zillion people and talk about things like the length of your tablecloths while juggling a massive budget and realizing how expensive everything on Pinterest actually is.[10]

---

10 Planning a year-long honeymoon is *much* more fun than planning a wedding, and also it's a terrible idea to plan them both at the same time. Our wedding vendors would be like "how long would you like your table runners to be?" And I'd be like "HOW CAN YOU EVEN ASK ME THAT WHEN I AM LEAVING FOR COLOMBIA IN 5 MONTHS?!?!? WHO EVEN CARES, SUSAN?! PICK SOMETHING." Just don't do it.

So, where do you want to go? The world is your oyster. You could go anywhere!

… Which, personally, I find incredibly overwhelming. The world is an ENORMOUS place. Where to even begin?

I have three tried-and-true methods to help narrow it down.

Method One: The Bucket List

The Bucket List method is for big dreamers who want to go everywhere — and just need a little help narrowing things down.

Start by compiling a list of all places that you'd like to visit (and yes, I give you full permission to go totally nuts on social media). Take your time pulling this list together; you're in no rush!

Personally, I like to find inspiration for places I want to go by looking at photos or videos online, reading travel books, or watching scenic TV shows and movies.

And of course, your favorite travel blog is also a fantastic source of inspiration — and I'm not just saying that because I'm a travel blogger. When I was planning my year-long trip, blogs were my primary source of both inspiration and logistical information. They're the reason I was inspired to create a blog of my own!

Once you've got a healthy list of places going, it's time to narrow things down a little bit. Get out a map and circle everywhere on your list, or create your own digital version — you can make your own custom map using the Google MyMaps[11] tool.

Eventually, a pattern may begin to emerge. You might notice a number of places on your bucket list are focused in one corner of the world — or at least, within one general area, like a continent.

Once you've figured out that your list is concentrated in a few specific areas, it's time to hone your research to find more points of interest nearby. For instance, if you've got five cities or countries you'd like to see in South America, do some sleuthing to find suggestions for popular tourist or backpacking destinations.

---

11   Throughout this book, I will be recommending specific businesses, websites, and tools that can be found online. To make things easier, I've included a list of all of these resources, organized by Part, at the end of the book. You can also find a digital, clickable version online at practicalwanderlust.com/quit-your-job-book/ with the password *verybigadventure* .

Now a plan is coming together.

If you're having difficulty narrowing things down, perhaps move on to method two: following the well-trodden paths of decades of intrepid backpackers before you.

Method Two: Following Well-Worn Paths

Long-term travel is not a new concept, but modern backpacking does have relatively recent roots. It was the '60s, and adventurous, counterculture young people were donning a new invention called a "frame backpack," hopping onto shiny passenger airplanes, and hitch-hiking or bussing their way across Europe, the Middle East, and Southeast Asia. They stopped at newly popular hostels along the way to hang out with fellow travelers, with what I imagine included lots of acoustic guitar-playing, drug-doing, long-hair-having, and deep discussions about "the man."

At the time, this route was known as the Overland. Today, it's referred to as the Hippie Trail, and evidence of it can still be seen in places like Kathmandu, Nepal, where a certain part of town is still known as Freak Street.

One of those intrepid hippies was my dad, who bought a cheap van with a couple of friends one summer in grad school and gallivanted all over Europe and Southeast Asia. (He was living in his car on a scholarship anyway, so I imagine that the van was a step up.)

I once stayed at a hostel he frequented in Vienna, and it was fun (and super weird) to imagine him partying there in the '60s with his bright red beard, blonde mustache, and dark curly Jewish 'fro, hippie travel van parked outside.

He tried to give me some travel tips, but I've realized that a *lot* has changed since his travel heyday — not a single one of his suggestions was helpful. It's far easier to travel through these well-worn paths today than it was back in his time. But that wave of early backpackers gave rise to an entire industry catering to and relying on tourists, including public transit between popular destinations, English-speaking guesthouses and restaurants, and easy-to-access internet and phone service.

But the legacies of those well-worn paths remain. Certain parts of the world have developed a strong backpacker culture over the years, and still play host to today's backpackers. Sure, we tend to have fancier luggage and rely on cell phones instead of maps or heavy travel books, and those old hostels have been updated with WiFi, but the original vibe of a multicultural melting pot is still alive and well.

You can still step into one of these hostels after a long day of padding down dusty roads and feel the same warm, welcoming feeling as you could all those decades ago, complete with a shared kitchen and lounge filled with travelers drinking, playing games, listening to music, and conversing in several languages. Most of those travelers have either been where you're headed or are headed where you're going, and the sharing of experiences makes for wonderfully easy conversation.

So if you're not sure where to go on your trip, or are having trouble narrowing it down, take a look at one of these popular backpacking routes:

The Gringo Trail

The Gringo Trail in Central and South America is named after the local slang word for a foreigner, where everyone who isn't local is a gringo.[12]

The route loosely follows a portion of the Pan-American Highway that stretches from Mexico all the way down the western coast of South America to Chile, crisscrossing through giant volcanoes, gushing hot springs, lush tropical jungles, towering snowy mountains, and tracing the footsteps of several ancient and powerful cultures.

Generally speaking, the route is split into two parts: Central America, including Guatemala, Honduras, Nicaragua, El Salvador, Costa Rica, and Panama; and South America, including Colombia, Ecuador, Peru, Bolivia, Chile, Argentina, and Brazil. Every part of the route is connected by bus, although the countries in Central America are much closer together than in South America.

One crucial bit of information to know before considering the Gringo Trail is that English is not as commonly spoken along this route as it is in Southeast Asia or Europe. English proficiency tends to vary by country, and you will likely struggle without a basic grasp of Spanish.

But the good news is that if you do speak some Spanish, you'll have no trouble along most of the route — barring Brazil, which speaks Portuguese rather than

---

12 One can only assume that a pasty white girl from Kentucky with a giant backpack, like me, is *extra* gringa.

Spanish, as well as regions where Indigenous peoples have managed to preserve their culture despite Spanish colonization.

I chose the Gringo Trail as the first stop on our year-long honeymoon. The trail appealed to me not only because of my ability to speak Spanish (thanks to years of classes at school), but also for its proximity to home, just a few hours away by plane. Also, I'd visited Colombia once before, which made it feel slightly less terrifying.

Our route snaked down through Colombia into Ecuador, Peru, and Chile, and then wound back up again into Argentina. I was aiming for about a month in each country — enough time to travel to 3-4 destinations in each.

To my delight, we found that getting around South America is both easy and affordable, if you don't mind a few long bus rides (heads up: the buses will either be very hot or very cold, there will usually be a movie playing at top volume, and you're gonna want to take dramamine and sit by a window). That said, we did take a few shortcuts by plane to skip particularly miserable multi-day bus rides (which was well worth the extra expense), but overall we were impressed and surprised by how interconnected much of South America is.

In terms of cost, $1,000 per person per month (or around $25-35 per day) is reasonable for most of this route except for Costa Rica, Panama, Chile, Brazil, and Argentina, which are pricier.

But even traveling cheaply won't feel uncomfortable on the Gringo Trail. I found that the hostels in South America are some of the best in the world! For under $30 a night, you can dine on a delicious complimentary breakfast while overlooking the tangled jungles of Colombia and listening to birds chirping and the gurgling of a private waterfall pool.[13] Or for under $50, you can sleep in a hostel tucked high in the foggy Andes Mountains of Ecuador, complete with a glass dome hot tub overlooking a snow capped volcano, never-ending baskets of banana bread, delicious family-style meals, and several sassy resident llamas.[14]

---

13 This phenomenal hostel is called Eco Hostal Yuluka and it can be found right outside the entrance to stunning Parque Tayrona on Colombia's northern coast. When we visited, a bed in an 8-person dorm room was a jaw-dropping $6 per night — although prices have since risen to a more reasonable amount. If you're curious to learn more, we have a blog post about our stay, which you can find at practicalwanderlust.com/parque-tayrona-colombia/

14 This hostel is called Secret Garden Cotopaxi, and yes, we totally splurged on a hobbit hole.

Truth be told, the hostels in South America are almost unfairly amazing and set an unreasonably high expectation for hostels in general.

The Banana Pancake Trail

This Southeast Asia route has a tongue-in-cheek name dating back to its early days as a destination for backpackers, which refers not to travelers strumming Jack Johnson songs on their acoustic guitars, but to the hostels and cafes that catered to the sudden influx of Western travelers back in the '60s by serving Western comfort foods, like banana pancakes. Finding a place that served these foods was a clarion call that other travelers had been here before. In the absence of online forums, perhaps that evidence — along with a battered old copy of Lonely Planet left in the lounge — was a comforting sign to young people far away from home.

Learning about this trail actually drew me to the idea of long-term travel more than the route I eventually ended up taking. And while I didn't get a chance to travel through Southeast Asia during my year-long trip, I'm hoping it will be the starting point of my next long journey.

Although there is no one specific route, the Banana Pancake Trail generally includes Thailand, Laos, Cambodia, and Vietnam, all easily accessible overland by train and bus. Some travelers also connect to island destinations nearby, including Indonesia, Singapore, and the Philippines — although they tend to be a little more expensive. Backpackers along this route can be found lying on tropical beaches and attending Full Moon parties on islands in Thailand, exploring the lush green hills and floating markets of Vietnam, and visiting ancient temples in Cambodia and Laos.

Popular among both Australian and European travelers, this region has been a hotspot for backpackers for decades, and English speakers are fairly easy to find. The weather is generally warm and sunny — just be sure to account for annual rainy seasons when planning your trip. You'll be exploring some of the most beautiful countries in the world with ancient, rich cultures — and *incredibly* delicious food.

Also, and this is no doubt part of why the route is still so popular: it's extremely inexpensive by Western standards. You can travel comfortably along most of the Banana Pancake trail for about $1,000 per person per month, or around $25-35 per day.

Honorable Mentions

While the Gringo Trail and the Banana Pancake Trail are generally considered the two most popular backpacker routes, there are a few other options worthy of an honorable mention and a spot on your itinerary. The places mentioned below are good options for backpackers due to their ease of transportation and tourist infrastructure.

Europe

Spanning from the Russian Ural mountains in the east to the island of Iceland in the west, Europe is an incredibly diverse and culturally rich continent which you could spend years exploring and still barely scratch the surface.

Europe is an endless highlight reel, and honestly, you can't go wrong no matter where you decide to visit. The medieval castles of Poland and Scotland, the Roman ruins and alpine lakes in Slovenia, the sunny islands of Spain, the rolling vineyards and medieval hilltop towns of France and Italy, the Bavarian charm of Germany, the Northern Lights of Norway and Finland, the gushing waterfalls of Iceland, the mountain meadows of Switzerland — it's impossible to narrow it down.

That said, there is one consideration that will limit your options considerably: finances. Europe is one of the priciest places to go backpacking in the world — but your budget will vary greatly depending on where you are in Europe. In Scandinavian countries, expect to spend a whopping $120 or so each day, but you'll get by happily on less than $50 per day in eastern European countries.

For this reason, many backpackers are drawn to Eastern European destinations, where their budgets stretch further. These countries are often considerably less crowded and expensive, but they're just as rich in history, cultural activities, and culinary delights as Western European countries. Slovenia, Croatia, Hungary, and Estonia are particularly backpacker (and digital nomad) friendly.

Despite its price, one of the major benefits to traveling through Europe is the relative ease of doing so, even for a novice backpacker or traveler. You will find that most people will speak at least some English (and in some countries, they'll speak English even better than you, along with eight other languages). As with other backpacker trails, there are superb and affordable public transportation options crisscrossing the continent, but unlike South America or Southeast Asia, they're relatively easy to figure out.

Another huge plus is that there are no border controls across most EU countries — meaning you won't have to keep track of tiny pieces of paper, or spend hours waiting in line at customs telling your life story every time you enter a new country.

You will, however, want to keep visa limitations in mind: U.S. passport holders can only stay in the 26 countries known as the Schengen Area for 90 days out of every 180 days. But in theory, you could stay in Europe indefinitely on a tourist visa as long as you timed your visits carefully, breaking up your travels with trips to non-Schengen countries such as the United Kingdom, Ireland, Croatia, Albania, Romania, or Bulgaria.

The Golden Triangle

The Golden Triangle in India is a popular route for discovering northern India's most popular and stunning attractions. The route is called the Golden Triangle because its three major cities form a near-perfect geometrical triangle: the bustling capital of Delhi, the historic Pink City of Jaipur, and Agra, India's former capital and home of the Taj Mahal.

Backpackers tend to choose this route because it includes some of India's most well-known highlights, it's budget friendly (around $38 per day for accommodation, food, and sightseeing), and it's a good starting point before exploring the rest of India or Southeast Asia. Also, the food is *amazing*.

Most backpackers start in Delhi and stay there for at least a week to orient themselves, enjoy the rich cuisine, and take in all the cultural sights. Delhi's highlights include Humayun's Tomb, Jama Masjid, and the Red Fort, a sprawling complex constructed in the 1600s as a seat of power.

The next stop is Jaipur, known as the Pink City, which is a colonial city dating back to the 1700s and is full of (pink) architectural delights, including the Hawa Mahal and the old Amber Palace just outside the city.

Agra, the last city, is known for the Taj Mahal but also has a range of other equally stunning sights, such as Agra Fort and the Tomb of I'timād al-Dawlah.

You'll only need about two weeks to complete the Golden Triangle, after which you can head to southern India or further north to hike in the Himalayas (check out Shimla and the mountain villages of the Spiti Valley if you do!). Many travelers choose to continue into nearby countries historically popular among backpackers, such as Nepal, Turkey, Jordan, and Iran, all of which are part of the historic Hippie Trail.

Southern Africa

Soaring dunes, white beaches, red wine, and great plains filled with wildlife: welcome to the southern region of Africa! South Africa, Namibia, Botswana, and the two smaller nations of Lesotho and Eswatini (formerly known as Swaziland) make up this vast and diverse region, popular due to the relative ease of overland travel and backpacker-friendly infrastructure.

Some of the highlights of this route include Eswatini's Mkhaya Game Reserve, Lesotho's Kome Cave Dwellings, the world's largest sand dunes in Namibia's Sossusvlei desert, South Africa's scenic coastal Garden Route, the beaches and vineyards of Cape Town, and the art and museums of Johannesburg.

Speaking of vast, while just a small part of the enormous and diverse continent of Africa, southern Africa is still bigger than all of Europe combined. Make sure to keep the longer distances between destinations in mind while planning your travels!

Depending on your travel style, you can travel overland through southern Africa via local buses or hired drivers. Budget between $45-80 per day for accommodation, food, transport, and activities if you are traveling by local transport. You might also consider traveling with a group. Prices for a tour package start around $115-150 per day and include accommodation, transport, and most food and activities.

Method Three: Throw a Dart at a Map ...

I've got one last suggestion to help you figure out where to begin your trip.

By now, you can probably tell that I'm too much of a pragmatic worrywart to tell you to spin a globe and buy a plane ticket to wherever your finger lands. But the modern equivalent of throwing a dart at a map is buying a cheap one-way plane ticket to wherever Google tells you.

Here's what to do: pull up Google Flights, don't put a destination in the "where to?" field, and set the price limit to something unreasonably cheap for your planned departure date. Then, just scroll through that world map and figure out where the Universe — or in this case, the tech overlords at Google — wants to guide you. Can you find an affordable flight that lands somewhere along the Gringo Trail or the Banana Pancake Trail? Fantastic! You can use that as a starting point for the beginning of your trip.

Another option is to plan a starting point for your trip where you can stay somewhere free for a while, like visiting a friend who's living abroad, house sitting, or participating in a work program. It's a great, low-cost way to get your feet wet before you hit the road, and it solves the problem of "Where to first?" We've got a whole chapter full of suggestions for ways to find work during your trip, either for pay or in exchange for accommodation, in Part Three.

Who's Going?

Once you've got a rough idea of where you're headed, the next step is to figure out who you'll be traveling with or whether you'll be embarking on a solo adventure.[15] Each has its advantages and disadvantages, and can be a critical part of your enjoyment. Don't leave this one up to chance: spend some time figuring out your travel preferences in advance. Below, we've included benefits and downsides to consider when you're deciding whether to go it alone or travel with a companion.

In either case — and this may just be my anxiety talking — you may want to mull over a few worst-case scenarios. What if things don't work out with your travel companion? Will your relationship recover? Is it worth putting your relationship to that test? What if they're ready to go home but you're eager to continue traveling?

If you'll be traveling solo, what will you do if you find yourself missing companionship? How far out of your comfort zone are you willing to go alone? What safety considerations should you account for, and how can you prepare?

But before you commit to either solo travel or traveling with a companion for your trip, it's important to test the waters first. Have a few frank conversations about travel styles with your prospective travel companion (or yourself), and then take a trip — or three — to work out a few kinks before you hit the road.

Whatever you decide, one thing is for sure: travel will strengthen your ability to rise to new challenges and overcome obstacles. Traveling, by its very nature, strips away the things that you're used to, pushes you well out of your comfort zone, and leaves you with no choice but to adapt. Travel is like a muscle that you'll strengthen every single day as you problem-solve a constant stream of challenges: from figuring out what to order off a menu that you can't read full of food you've never heard of, to attempting to use a "squatty" potty (a skill I will probably never master), to trying to get literally anywhere.

---

15 What about traveling with a group? Traveling with a group of friends (or strangers) can be a lot of fun and a great option for a vacation or a few weeks at a time, especially if you're nervous about venturing out alone — but I'd suggest leaving yourself some opportunities to explore alone or with a companion. The notable exception is family travel. Whether you're traveling with siblings or with your partner or children, traveling as a family can be a wonderful experience that creates lifelong memories and strengthens deep, impenetrable familial bonds. Although Jeremy and I aren't parents yet, we often daydream of seeing the world with our kids on a summer or year of adventure. While we can't give specific advice in that department, there are loads of family travel blogs full of fantastic advice for long-term travel with children of all ages.

You will quickly develop ways of adapting to unfamiliar and confusing scenarios and master skills that you didn't even realize you were lacking (like speaking in conversational Spanish to taxi drivers, which was one of my crowning achievements after six months of backpacking through South America). And whether you're tackling the challenges of travel on your own or with a companion, you will grow stronger, more independent, and more capable.

Traveling Solo	Traveling with a Companion
Benefit: Independence You'll never need to make compromises: everything you do on your trip is entirely up to your own personal preference. You'll get to pick where you eat, where you go, what you do, and absolutely everything else. You'll be in control of your own destiny: you'll be able to craft your dream trip!	**Benefit: Relationship Strengthening** Venturing outside of your comfort zone and navigating unfamiliar challenges together can bring you closer and improve your communication and problem-solving skills.
Benefit: Personal Growth Relying on yourself, navigating unfamiliar places, and tackling challenges as you go can have a phenomenally positive impact on your self-confidence, pride, and autonomy. Never again will you question whether or not you can do something once you've mastered the art of venturing way outside your comfort zone and figuring out extremely confusing things as you go — which is pretty much travel in a nutshell.	**Benefit: Comfort & Familiarity** Leaving your comfort zone to embark on adventures in unfamiliar places can bring on anxiety and be overwhelming. Having a close companion by your side brings a little piece of home with you wherever you go, which can help you feel more grounded.
Downside: Isolation Traveling solo can feel isolating; relying on yourself to resolve every single setback and challenge can become exhausting. But it doesn't have to be lonely: solo travelers typically find travel companions as they go, meeting new friends on the road at hostels or on travel activities. Often, and especially on common backpacker trails, routes will overlap and you'll find yourself traveling for a few days or weeks with a new travel companion. Lifelong friendships and even relationships can form on the road, built on the foundation of shared adventures and those long, deep conversations that travel tends to invite.	**Downside: Frustration** Traveling with a companion can end up in arguments or misunderstandings, particularly when there are mismatched travel styles, differences in expectations, or communication gaps. Nothing illuminates cracks in the foundation of a relationship like traveling together, because it's a constant series of problem-solving while dealing with feelings that go hand-in-hand with travel: overwhelm, exhaustion, hunger, confusion. But where it can highlight those problems, it can also help you to develop the tools to resolve them. Jeremy and I quickly realized that almost all of our arguments on the road could be attributed to one of us feeling hungry, tired, or overwhelmed, and learned to communicate those needs to one another — and to not take hunger-induced grumpiness personally.

Although I spent the first few years of my trip preparation mentally preparing myself to take the journey of a lifetime solo, the idea absolutely terrified me. I'd consider myself a smart, capable person — but when it comes to common sense or very simple, easy things, I'm a complete idiot. Like, I'm the kind of person who gets lost driving home from work — even though I've taken the exact same route every day for years. I'm also very easily overwhelmed: give me two things to hold and I shut down like a robot, completely unable to function because both of my hands are occupied.[16]

I was fully prepared to travel solo, but truth be told, I was incredibly relieved when I didn't have to.

Jeremy and I found that travel strengthened our relationship and our communication skills in ways that have lasted long after our trip ended. Which is lucky, because we left for a year of travel together right after getting married. We (half) joke that the honeymoon was the ultimate relationship test, and we were fully planning on making it home in time to get an annulment.

But traveling together for a full year only confirmed what we already suspected: we're freakishly, disgustingly, and unrealistically compatible. Other than a few days when we each needed a little break to spend some time alone, we didn't even get sick of each other: we soaked up every moment together — all 31,536,000 of them[17] — like they were a treasured gift (though we won't admit to that without some heavy eye-rolling).

If we'd had any doubts about the longevity of our relationship before our year-long honeymoon, they were long gone by the time we returned home. Traveling together may be the ultimate relationship test, but it's also an incredible opportunity to spend plenty of time together (so much time). It's an opportunity to see the world and experience new things together, and return home with stories and experiences that only the two of you will ever fully understand. And it's a wonderful way to cement your relationship so that it will truly stand the test of time.

We were lucky enough to overlap on almost all of our travel preferences, except for one: it turns out that Jeremy is much more of an adrenaline seeker than I

16 This is also Jeremy's favorite way to hit the "off" switch when he wants me to stop talking about something. Annoyingly, it works every time.

17 Technically, this isn't mathematically accurate. I'd estimate that we spent maybe a total of 24 hours apart during the entire year, which means that we only had 31,449,600 treasured moments together. Either way, barf.

am. Figuring that out and making peace with it was no simple task, though. It took a series of misadventures, beginning in the first month of our trip with me needing to be rescued off a 200-foot-tall waterfall on what should have been a fun rappelling excursion in Colombia,[18] and ending just three days before flying back home, when we had to extend our trip due to me having a panic attack quickly followed by the worst ear infection of my life on what was supposed to be a relaxing white water rafting trip.

You'd think that 12 months of traveling together would have helped us figure this one out, but it wasn't until I was lying on a hospital bed in San Jose, Costa Rica, crying and getting injected with steroids in my butt, that we both finally accepted that maybe adventure sports just weren't my thing.

These days, Jeremy goes on high-adrenaline adventures alone — and I look forward to hearing all about them after a relaxing day spent alone in complete safety.

Travel Companion Compatibility Discussion Points

Here are a few talking points to discuss with your prospective travel companion (and, if you're going solo, anyone you might meet along the way that you're considering traveling with):

- **Are you a planner, or do you enjoy spontaneity?** Do you prefer to map out your itinerary in advance, or do you like to leave the door open to figure things out as you go and allow suggestions from locals or other travelers along the way to determine your next move?

- **How do you feel about traveling off the beaten path?** Do you prefer to visit well-known destinations and check popular attractions off your bucket list, or do you seek out off-beat excursions to lesser known places, even if it means there may be few other travelers and a lack of certain

---

18 I got about 3 steps down the waterfall before I was so gripped by panic that my hands turned into frozen gargoyle claws and I found myself unable to do anything but scream at the top of my lungs. I ended up stuck in the fetal position in a tiny cave behind the waterfall about 197 feet up, until Jeremy made it down and asked someone to rescue me. The rappeler told him "tranquilo" and calmly sent someone to carry me down on their lap while I shrieked with terror. Once I regained my composure, I asked the friendly guide if this kind of thing happens a lot – having to rescue people, like me. He very nicely said, "No. Never."

amenities? Do big cities excite you, or do you prefer small towns or rolling wilderness?

- **Are you risk-averse, or an adrenaline seeker?** Are you into adventure sports and challenging hikes, or do you prefer to take things easy? Does venturing into dangerous and unknown territory excite or terrify you? And if your preferences don't match up, are you comfortable going on a few adventures separately?

- **What are your financial limitations?** Are you a frugal budget traveler, more of a luxury traveler, or somewhere in between? Will you need to carve out time to buckle down and work during your trip for hours, days, or weeks at a time? Is it important to you to have the trip of a lifetime, even if it means being a little more spendy? What specific things are you — or are you not — willing to spend a little more on, such as food, certain activities/tours, transportation, or accommodations?

- **What is your preference for accomodations?** Do you prefer hostels, inns, Airbnbs, or hotels? Are you willing to splurge on a nice hotel, or do you see accommodations as nothing more than a place to sleep? Is budget your highest priority, even if it means sacrificing luxuries like privacy and comfort? Are you willing to sacrifice amenities and/or pay extra for one-of-a-kind experiences, like a jungle lodge or an Indigenous homestay?

- **Are you an extrovert or an introvert?** Do you enjoy spending all day long hanging out and chatting, or do you need a few hours of quiet or alone time? Are you excited to meet new people and enjoy socializing on your travels, or does that sound a little exhausting? If you differ on these preferences, are you comfortable taking some time apart in order to get your socialization or alone time needs met for a few hours each day?

- **Do you have daily routines?** Are you an early riser or a night owl? Do you like to do sunrise yoga, or are you entirely unable to function before your first cup of coffee? Do you like to spend quiet time each day journaling, meditating, reading or drawing? Is a nightly Netflix binge-watch a critical part of your evening routine (also me)?

- **What are your food preferences?** Do you like to try street food and local delicacies? Do you want to cook all your meals at the hostel or only eat in Lonely Planet approved places? How often do you want to splurge on a nice meal? Do you have any dietary restrictions?

Discussing each of these needs will help set expectations before your trip, and make it easier to identify problems, understand underlying differences, communicate needs, and problem-solve along the way. Of course, that all takes lots of practice — but traveling together will give you plenty of it!

When Are You Going?

There may never be a perfect time to put your life on hold and take off on a thrilling adventure, but there are definitely times that are better than others! The trick is finding the balance. You're looking for a window of opportunity when you COULD potentially go on a life-changing long-term trip, and then clearing away the obstacles standing between you and that very first flight. If you're traveling with a companion, you'll need to work together to establish your trip timeline.

A few of the things you'll want to take into account when figuring out when to take your trip are your career, your age, your health, your dependents, your legal obligations, and of course, your finances. Let's start from the top.

Career

I made up my mind to take a year-long trip almost as soon as I'd sat down behind a desk at my first job out of college. But even though it was infinitely more enjoyable to daydream about faraway places than read reports or answer emails, I was afraid that if I left, I would run the risk of slowing down or halting my career trajectory. After all, fresh-faced recent college grads eager to bend over backwards in order to prove themselves are a dime a dozen; I felt incredibly lucky to have landed a job out of college at all.

So I swallowed my wanderlust, made do with traveling on as many weekends and holidays as I could, and decided to wait. My goal was to get a few promotions under my belt so that when I came back home, I'd have a solid career to return to.

I ended up waiting for five years, and by the time I left, I was ready to move into a role with more responsibility. When I returned, my decision to wait paid off: I was able to interview for a more senior-level position. I may not have taken the risk to interview for the next rung on the career ladder if I'd stayed behind at my old job, waiting for someone to recognize my skills and hand me a promotion.

My experience is a best-case scenario. Although it ended up working out well for me, perfectly timing a career break is, frankly, pretty much impossible, and you won't know how well you've done it until you come back again. There's always a good reason to stay at a job. The best you can hope for is finding a balance between when you've been hired and when you're ready to take on a new role.

If you've just taken a new job or accepted a new position, I would wait for about 1-2 years before quitting. That's plenty of time to plant a few seeds of goodwill that can get you rehired when you return.

Likewise, don't be afraid to leave when you're on the cusp of a promotion. Trust me: if your employer values you enough to promote you now, they'll still value you when you return. And even if they aren't interested (or hold a grudge), you'll know that you have the skills and experience ready to take a jump to the next level in your career when you return. Besides, post-sabbatical is the perfect time to make a switch to a new company or industry (more on that in Part Three).

If you're concerned about the impact that a career break might have on your potential re-hireability, you might be surprised: sometimes a sabbatical is exactly what you need to help your career. Taking a break can reinvigorate your enthusiasm for your work, or it can illuminate your utter lack of passion for it — and create the perfect pathway to a new career which is better suited.

Likewise, a long-term trip can be spun into a benefit for any concerned interviewer: you can talk about how taking a sabbatical cemented your love of [insert job here] and gave you the clarity and time you needed to really think about how you can make improvements on [insert job function here].[19] Or, if nothing else, it gives you a great story to tell potential employers and makes you a unique and memorable applicant.

If you work during your trip — and we've got a whole chapter of suggestions later on in the book — you can spin it into a valuable opportunity to build skills and experience. Your time volunteering at a hostel may have polished up your customer service skills. Perhaps the business you ran on Fiverr taught you the

---

19 You'll find more tips on spinning your career break into a positive for hiring managers in Part Four.

fundamentals of marketing. Maybe helping a farmer make cheese in Italy taught you about patience, quality, and craftsmanship.

If you're concerned about how you'll be received back in your old job, take time to plant a few seeds before you go that you can harvest upon your return. You could talk to your boss about a skill that would be helpful to develop, and then commit to spending time during your trip taking an online class or practicing that skill. When you return, surprise! You're ready for that promotion!

Or, just spend the time before your trip really shining in your job. Making yourself seem invaluable, a core part of any team, the go-to expert for a few specific topics, or even just the fun, kind coworker who brings everyone donuts and cracks jokes during awkward silences.

If you become the model employee for the year before you leave and depart in a blaze of incredibly valued and useful glory, the likelihood of being invited back into your old job will increase. Or, at the very least, you'll have a network of appreciative coworkers who would be happy to help you find a new job.

And remember: you're more valuable than you might think. Good employees are hard to find, and training new employees takes a lot of time, effort, and money. If you were able to snag the job you have now, you'll be able to get a job when you return. Either you'll be at the same level as you are now and nothing has changed, or you'll be able to move up on the career ladder. Worst-case scenario, you'll take a temporary demotion while you get your bearings again — and that will be well worth the adventure of a lifetime.

For us, it was an even split: my husband returned home from our year-long trip with a renewed excitement to return to his teaching career and was rehired for his exact same position.

But I came home with a pit in my stomach: I didn't want to go back to my old job. I interviewed for a few roles that were a step up from my former position in companies that were a better fit for me, but ultimately I just couldn't bring myself to return to corporate life again.

Instead, I took a temp contract role to earn some money doing a job that was easy enough not to demand my full mental attention (essentially, a temporary demotion) and struck out on my own as a self-employed small business owner, which ultimately became my full-time job.

Years later, both of us are happy with our career decisions. Our year-long trip didn't negatively affect our career trajectories or re-hireability, and it actually helped us to clarify what we wanted from our jobs and gave us the space and focus that we needed to pursue our true passions.

We'll cover our return in much more detail at the end of the book, but for now, rest assured: you don't need to put off chasing your dreams just for the sake of your career!

Age & Health

Finding the perfect window of time when your health is up for the physical challenges of a long trip doesn't necessarily have to do with the age you'll be when you take off. Here's a rule of thumb to follow: if you feel up for a trip right now, you are within that window! Take advantage of it while you can, because you never know what might happen in the future.

Although many people take a gap year while they're young, I've met just as many long-term travelers in their 40s, 50s, and 60s. Their concerns are typically a little different and their travel styles may account for varying levels of comfort, but there's no arbitrary rule that says the "best" time to travel is when you're young!

There are certain advantages to traveling at any age. In your 20s, you're able to handle physical discomfort like a champ, leaving you able to make sacrifices to account for a limited budget. In your 30s and 40s, you're still up for a few worthwhile demanding physical challenges — but you're more in touch with what your body needs to recover and prepare for those challenges, and better equipped financially to account for them. In your 50s and beyond, you're fully comfortable with traveling exactly the way you like and don't hesitate to give your body what it needs to take you along on the adventure of a lifetime.

I started dreaming about taking a round-the-world trip at age 21 and left for my year-long honeymoon at age 26. I had all the energy in the world! I didn't mind taking a 24-hour overnight bus ride, especially if I could save a few bucks on accommodation and eat free (albeit disgusting) bus food, even if it also meant I'd spend a sleepless night freezing in sub-arctic A/C and trying to drown out the noise of a horror movie playing at full volume while careening at top speed over death-defying cliffside roads and trying not to throw up. (That said: after a handful of those miserable long-haul bus rides, I refuse to ever go on one ever again. That chapter of my life, happily, is over.)

As a spry young 20-something, uncomfortable dorm beds didn't bother me; multi-day hikes on high-elevation peaks sounded like a thrilling challenge, and lugging around a 30lb backpack was no big deal. I didn't give a second thought to discomfort in the name of a few dollars saved. I was in good health and peak physical fitness — I even trained for the trip in the gym, with that heavy bag and those difficult hikes as my goals.

Now in my 30s, my travel style has changed. Although I still love staying in hostels, I'm no longer as willing to stay in a dorm if there's a private room available — and I'm happy to pay for the extra comfort of privacy, quiet, and a larger bed. I avoid "party" hostels — I have no interest in nightlife past 10pm, and I'm also not shy about asking a room full of strangers to keep it down if I'm trying to sleep (especially if it's 2am and they've been playing thumping house music at top volume for the past five hours).

I've also learned to slow down my travel pace, plan fewer activities each day, and to schedule a day of just doing absolutely nothing at regular intervals. And I no longer suffer from the delusion that I'll be up for exploring after hopping off a plane, train, or bus and dropping my bags off — travel days are now also recovery days.

By contrast, when I travel with my mom, who's in her late 60s and in the prime of her life, I can barely keep up. She's up by 5am and out the door on an adventure (binoculars in hand, no coffee needed) before I can drag myself out of bed, then she runs around all day long sightseeing and goes to bed when I'm just starting to turn on Netflix at night. Whenever I try to invite myself along on whatever fabulous trip she's planning, I tend to get a motherly side-eye. "You slow me down," she once told me, as I tried to weasel my way onto a trip to visit a friend of hers in southern Italy. "You wake up so late! By the time you've had your coffee, half the day is gone." (She's not wrong, but I'm still waiting for my genetic ability to wake up at 5am to kick in).

Both my mother and I learned to travel from my grandmother, Katy, an intrepid backpacker and adventurer who traveled her entire life. She taught English in Vietnam in her 40s, hiked the Annapurna Trek in Nepal in her 50s, tackled the Inca Trail to Machu Picchu in her 60s, spent the entirety of her 70s gallivanting around the globe ticking places off her bucket list, and only slowed down in her late 80s when she fell in love with a man in his 90s, moved into his assisted living facility, and promptly started a hiking club. Katy has always been my idol, and she's the reason why I have no intention of ever letting age slow me down.

So take your lessons from the women of my family: don't spend too much time worrying about whether you've already passed the "best" age for long-term travel. The fact that you're reading this book means you're up for it! Just remember to listen to your body, and always advocate unapologetically for what you need to manage your health and wellbeing. Even if it means going to bed by 10pm...and waking up at 10am. (Yep: I spent an entire year getting a wonderful, luxurious 12 hours of sleep every single night — hostel dorm rooms and my mom's side-eye be damned).

If you're concerned about physical challenges that may affect you during long-term travel, I suggest talking to your doctor about ways you could incorporate your needs into your trip, such as visiting major cities where hospitals are close by, crossing certain adventure sports off your itinerary, researching whether transit and attractions are wheelchair-accessible,[20] or limiting the time you'll be away from home to account for check-ups and medications.

Dependents

Timing your trip around dependents is, in my opinion, one of the trickiest things to account for. If you don't have any dependents, you're in a window of opportunity! Go forth and take advantage of it.

But if you're concerned about leaving behind children, aging parents, or pets, it's important to plan around their needs. Some of the logistical quandaries you'll want to add into your considerations are whether you'll be able to financially account for your dependents' needs while you travel, what care will be in place in your absence, how you'll deal with any issues that arise while you're on the road, how frequently you'll need to be in communication, and how you can emotionally prepare your dependents for your temporary absence.

---

20 The blog Curb Free with Cory Lee is a fantastic resource for wheelchair-accessible travel.

If you're torn between feeling an obligation to stay and the call to leave, I highly suggest discussing your concerns with a counselor or therapist.[21]

Ultimately, your decision will be unique to your situation, and only you will be able to determine when is the best time for you to leave and how long you feel comfortable being away for.

Legal Obligations

It's important to account for legal obligations when planning your trip: breaking a lease or contract can be an expensive decision, and leaving in the middle of a legal battle can have consequences that last long after you return from your trip to face the music.

You'll also want to plan around anything that might require your physical presence in court, or even your physical signature or documentation — finding a printer and shipping documents internationally is not always an easy task.

Depending on your situation, you may be able to find someone who can help take care of legal proceedings in your absence, like a lawyer. Be careful of leaving any important legal obligations to someone who isn't a professional, or who isn't directly involved: a missed piece of mail or an absence in court can have costly ramifications.

---

21 Frankly, much of the mental and emotional work you'll be doing when preparing for this trip is best done with a professional to help guide you and give you the tools you'll need to process and work through intense feelings like trepidation, anxiety, guilt, and fear. I can't recommend therapy enough, and I personally have years of counseling to thank for many of the tools I'm sharing in this book.

Finances

There's no way around it: finances are probably the biggest determining factor for your long-term trip. Your financial situation will determine everything from where you'll go to how long you'll be able to travel to how much "roughing it" you'll do to whether you'll need to work on the road.

That said, there is a common misconception that bears dismantling: long-term travel is widely assumed to be inaccessible to all but the most wealthy and privileged members of society.

There are a few specific cultural assumptions at play here. First, there's the way that many Americans view "travel." For most, travel is equivalent to taking a vacation, and a vacation is something luxurious, something that you save up for a long time so that you can fully enjoy yourself — and something that most people are only able to do infrequently.

For many people, a vacation means relaxing at a resort on a beach somewhere tropical, drink in hand, or maybe taking a cruise, or a romantic trip to Paris. It's expensive, but it's worth the expense: if a vacation is a luxury you can only enjoy infrequently, you'd better believe you're going to splurge on that pricey but oh-so-fancy all-inclusive resort.

So if you announce that you'll be traveling for a year, to many people that means you'll be taking a year-long vacation — an expensive and luxurious concept that surely only the wealthy could afford. A hotel is what, $250 per night? For 365 days?! That's nearly six figures spent just on accomodation alone.

Those same people may not realize that there are beautiful boutique hostels in South America or southeast Asia with private rooms for under $20 a night — breakfast included.

Or perhaps they do realize but don't care, because the word "hostel" is unfortunately associated with a slasher movie, and as a result now holds a permanent place of fear and disgust in US pop culture (thanks a lot, Eli Roth!). Too many U.S. travelers assume that a cheap hostel is full of filth and crime — and sure, in some cases, that may be true. But spend about three seconds looking at reviews online, and you'll easily be able to avoid those places.[22]

More often, I've found that hostels are lovely places to stay, full of fascinating and friendly travelers, often deeply embedded into local culture, and usually have the best recommendations for things to do and see in town. On many occasions, the hostel I've stayed at has been the highlight of my trip (one in particular, located in Minca, Colombia, is so magical that I've been back to visit five times!).

The concept of traveling on a shoestring budget for less than, say, $25 a day — including accommodation — is similarly uncommon for many US travelers. It's difficult or downright impossible to do in the most popular vacation destinations for those from the USA — think resorts on Caribbean islands, Western European cities, Disney theme parks, and so on. Without experiencing just how inexpensive travel is in certain places, it can be hard to imagine.

When my husband and I were planning our trip, we encountered a few well-meaning but incredulous coworkers and friends who assumed we had a zillion dollars lying around. But once we explained that hostels are not hotbeds of murder — and showed a few photos of the beautiful hostels we'd found in our planned destinations — their perspectives shifted.

It turns out that, for most people, the difference between a luxurious vacation and an inexpensive backpacking trip is just a difference in expectations and preferences for comfort. After all, a vacation is a luxury, so why wouldn't you want to be comfortable?

But for a long-term traveler, comfort and luxury become relative. "Luxury" could mean in-room A/C, drinkable tap water, a beautiful view outside your window, beach access, or the blissful quiet of a private room. And you may find that a few comforts or luxuries are worth forgoing if it means traveling for an extra month, or being able to afford a once-in-a-lifetime experience, like a guided trek through the Himalayas or a week in the Galapagos Islands.

---

22 A few tips on avoiding shady hostels: we always look at reviews on Hostelworld, which include the demographics and travel style of reviewers so we can compare that to our own travel style. We look for a few key things that let us know that if a hostel is our style. Personally, we avoid hostels with photos of crowds of people drinking and reviews mentioning things like "party," and "a great social vibe." We run far, far away from those hostels in favor of hostels described as "super chill" and "quiet" and "devoid of fun parties".

So if you've made the mistake of assuming that long-term travel is only for the very wealthy, think again! But you do need to be honest with yourself about your comfort level and your expectations.

How Much Money Do You Need?

Before you open up a spreadsheet and start planning your trip budget — although I can understand your enthusiasm, because that's my favorite hobby — you'll need to do some soul searching to figure out what kind of traveler you are when it comes to cost. You'll want to figure out what you need to feel safe and comfortable — the things you can't do without — and what is less important to you.

If sleeping in a hostel or on an overnight bus makes you a little uncomfortable, that's okay: change is uncomfortable, and it's also a sign of growth. Don't worry — I adapted quickly, and you will too — although I hope that a sense of gratitude for those small luxuries sticks with you, as it has for me. Or you may decide that you're not willing to compromise. After all, it's your trip, and your budget!

What's Your Budget Travel Style?

Before I stayed in a hostel for the first time, I wasn't sure how I'd feel about sharing a bathroom with strangers. Frankly, it sounded annoying and honestly, kind of gross. But once I gave it a try, I realized that the things I'd come to take for granted in my life back home had been luxuries all along; expectations that came hand in hand with a Westernized standard of life I'd never questioned or been without. It turns out that bathrooms in hostels worldwide (and shared rooms, lounges, and kitchens) are cleaned regularly — and if they aren't, it's usually apparent in reviews online.

I learned that being able to leave your own toiletries scattered around was a luxury I was comfortable doing without. I also made my peace with sleeping in shared rooms, so long as there was a secure locker near my bed that I could store my belongings in.

Honestly, I think hostel dorms are probably the biggest benefit to my superhuman ability to sleep through literally everything (even if it means being permanently disinvited on my mom's early-morning birding capers).

But while I liked to consider myself a strict budget traveler, once I arrived I found myself willing to spend more money on certain things — most of which involved food. I spent an entire year saying "yes" to every hard-to-pronounce dish on every menu, and Jeremy and I even spent a few romantic evenings dining at some of the best restaurants in the world, which it turns out are surprisingly affordable when compared to U.S. prices. (In preparation for one particularly incredible dinner at the extremely fancy Central in Lima, Peru, I quietly crept into a department store to put on a full face of makeup using only free testers in the beauty department. I have no regrets — that was the best meal of my life.)

For Jeremy, adrenaline-inducing activities were worth the extra expense: he took up scuba diving, white water rafting, canyoning and horseback riding. (Luckily for our budgets, I discovered that I hate all of these things).

So, we became mid-range budget travelers: we balanced our appetite for fancy food and pricey adventure sports with our willingness to sleep in inexpensive hostel dorm rooms, fill up on free breakfasts in order to skip lunch, and take extremely long overland journeys by bus.

We found as traveled, our needs and preferences — and what we were willing to spend — changed. When we were fresh-faced and new to long-term travel, we cheerfully considered ourselves frugal, or perhaps mid-range budget travelers. We'd do just about anything to save a buck, save a few fancy restaurants here and there and the occasional adventure tour.

But by the end of our trip, we were sick and tired of unappealing free breakfasts and long, miserable bus rides. We resented our hostel dorm-mates and their annoying habits, and all we wanted was to be able to wear a towel back from the shower — and leave our toiletries behind (the luxury!). We started booking trains, planes, and Airbnbs, staying in private rooms in hostels rather than dorms, and off-setting our expenses with long stints of house sitting.

In less than a year, we had evolved from energetic, frugal young backpackers into "flashpackers," a term used to describe "fancy backpackers" who are willing to spend more in exchange for added comforts. (These days, we are quite firmly in the "flashpacker" category.)

Ultimately, only you will know what you're comfortable with. So take whatever you're unwilling to part with (Privacy! Great food! Good WiFi!) and work that into your budget. You may need to save up longer to accomodate for your personal preferences, but it will feel worth it to have the trip of your dreams.

Below are three common budget travel styles. You will meet all of these travelers on your trip (and a whole lot more! There are many, many different kinds of travelers). Do any of them sound like you?

Frugal Traveler	Mid-Range Budget Traveler	Flashpacker
Accomodation		
Permanent fixture of a 10-bed hostel dorm room. Offsets budget with couchsurfing or work-for-stay.	Bounces between shared accommodations and the occasional private room, depending on the price and location.	Only books private rooms in hostels. Also enjoys budget-friendly boutique hotels and Airbnbs.
Food		
Fills up on free hostel breakfasts to skip lunch. Grocery shops regularly and cooks most meals; is a hostel-kitchen pro. Occasionally enjoys the luxury of street food or a set lunch at a local hole-in-the-wall.	Never passes up a free breakfast, but generally eats out for lunch and dinner. Cooks a few nights a week and buys snacks on the street or in local markets to save money. Wishes they were as good at hostel kitchen cooking as frugal travelers.	Dines out for most meals. Occasionally shops at local markets and cooks meals.
Transportation		
Can usually be found riding on a crowded local bus. Has totally considered hitchhiking. Only takes a taxi when it's shared with other travelers. Considers the journey part of the destination.	Rides local buses on occasion, but only for short distances. Occasionally books overnight buses or trains, but upgrades to lie-flat seats or sleeper cars. Frequently checks budget airline websites — just in case.	Books the shortest possible method of transportation. Believes that only really scenic rides are part of the destination. Downloads the local taxi app in each country; is a big fan of motorbikes.
Activities		
Can you do a self-guided tour by taking public transportation? No? Then no, thank you. Besides, getting lost is part of the fun!	Is willing to do the occasional self-guided adventure, but usually springs for the guided tour — it's much easier, and you learn more, too.	Never gets tired of comparing how much similar activities would cost back at home and feeling like it's well worth it. Happy to pay extra for a guide in order to avoid getting lost.

Calculating the Cost of your Trip

Now that you have at least a rough idea of where you'd like to go on your trip and the style of travel you're comfortable with, it's time to start calculating. This is where things get *sexy*. Go on — put on your favorite pair of computer glasses, pop open a bottle of wine, and open up a nice, blank spreadsheet. Maybe throw in some conditional formatting if you're feeling a little naughty. Is it getting it hot in here, or is that just budget planning?

1. **On your spreadsheet, map out a very rough idea of your itinerary and route.**

You don't have to get specific — you can be as vague as "six months in Southeast Asia" or "one month in Colombia[23] and one month in Ecuador[24] with a week in the Galapagos Islands[25]," and so on. That said, the more specific you are, the more accurate your budget estimate will be.

2. **For each destination, figure out the average daily cost.**

I like to use BudgetYourTrip.com, which has up-to-date cost estimates for destinations all over the world submitted by travelers for everything from food and accommodation to bottled water and transit. You can even select your budget travel style to get an estimate tailored to your comfort level.

3. **Add in the cost of transportation between destinations.**

Don't skip this step! Flights, trains, buses, and other methods of transportation will add up, even if you're traveling slowly or overland. To estimate transportation costs, I like to search on Rome2Rio.com. Put in your "to" and "from" destination and the site returns all of the transportation options, how long each option takes, and how much it costs.

4. **Add in any special activities that you'll need to budget extra for.**

From multi-day guided treks like the Inca Trail to pricier destinations like the Galapagos Islands, certain bucket list activities are worth the extra cost — if your

---

23 Hey, I've got a travel guide for this exact topic: Colombia Itinerary: Ultimate Guide to 1 Month of Backpacking Colombia

24 Oh, I've got this one too! Backpacking Ecuador: Itinerary for 1 Incredible Month

25 It's the darndest thing — this one, too: How to Visit the Galapagos Islands without a Cruise: A Complete Guide. How'd that happen? What a crazy coincidence.

budget allows for it. You'll want to account for those extra costs in advance so you don't miss out.

5. **Add a little padding**.

Throw in a line item for your travel insurance (we've got a whole chapter on that later). Do a quick Google search to see whether you'll need to pay for visa costs for your target destinations — those can add up[26]. Budget a few hundred extra for medication, vaccinations, and purchasing any gear that you'll need to get sorted before your trip — including getting a passport if you don't have one yet — and then throw an extra 10-20% in there, just to be safe and soothe my anxiety.

This is also a good time to add in a cushion for when you return. Set aside a certain amount as emergency money — you may well need it during your trip, but hopefully, you'll be able to save it until you come home. If you don't touch it at all, it can help build up your emergency fund and replenish your savings after you return from your trip.

Voila! You've now got a rough estimate of what your dream trip will cost. If that number looks daunting, you might want to play with your itinerary, the length of your trip, or your destinations until things look a little more doable.

Now the real question is: how long will it take you to save up for your trip? In order to figure that out, you'll need to work backwards: divide your target budget by the number of years or months you might feasibly be planning your trip, and you'll have an estimate of how much you need to save each year or month.

So: is that doable? Before you answer that, let's take a quick side-trip into the titillating world of financial planning.

Budgeting & Saving

Before I dive into how to create a budget to save for a round-the-world trip, I want to first begin by acknowledging my financial privilege.

I was fortunate enough to grow up comfortably, in an educated family with strong financial literacy. I learned about budgeting and saving from an early age. My

---

26 U.S. residents can search for tourist visa requirements and limitations by country at travel. state.gov

grandmother gave me stocks and bonds as birthday gifts growing up (not exciting as a kid, extremely exciting as an adult) and my parents were able to provide me with the incredible gift of graduating from college debt-free, thanks to their diligent savings and investments. They even opened a credit card in my name for me when I was a teenager so that by the time I graduated college, I had a near-perfect credit score and was able to immediately begin racking up credit card rewards, which helped pay for parts of my year-long honeymoon (more on that shortly).

All of this served to give me a huge leg up. I did not pull myself up by my bootstraps, and I am not self-made. I owe my privilege and the fortunate life in which I now find myself to not only the family who came before me and carved out the life that I now enjoy, but to a series of systemic benefits that served to boost me up every step of the way. The fact that I was able to save for a year of travel in five years is not due to my own cunning brilliance: it's due to a series of fortunate events working in my favor since the day I was born.

If you didn't experience the same financial privileges as I did growing up, I'm not going to tell you that it's possible to pay for a long-term trip just by giving up a daily $5 cup of coffee that you might not even be able to afford in the first place. And I also don't want to give you empty promises or mislead you into thinking that anyone can save up for a year-long trip — no matter how cheap hostels are, a year of travel still costs a whole lot of money.

What I can do is share the financial tools I've learned over the years to help you set a budget, which will tell you whether saving up for this trip is feasible.

If the numbers aren't working out in your favor, I can also assure you that saving up in advance is only one way to pay for a long-term trip. I've also included a chapter on working during your trip, including finding job opportunities or remote work while you're traveling abroad, and working in exchange for free accomodation. If you can't save up for your trip in advance, it's okay: try to save as much as you can, and plan to work during your trip as you refill your coffers.

Now that we've got some context, let me tell you about the five years I spent saving up for my year-long trip.

My initial savings target was $15,000: enough for 12 months of budget backpacker travel in South America or Southeast Asia, plus a little extra cushion. I had a salary and no student loan payments. It seemed doable to save up that amount in around 3 years if I was able to sock away $500 per month. Not bad!

In order to cut my expenses, I moved into the tiniest apartment I could find to save money on rent, brought my own lunch to work each day (usually some variation of stew made in my crockpot — I am not much of a cook), whipped up my own boring coffee each morning and drove as little as possible. And, since I was 22, I continued a hallowed college tradition of pre-gaming before a night out and sneaking my own flask into bars. You know, to save money.

I also ran a few side hustles, like mystery shopping (which is, weirdly, a lot of fun) and running an online handmade jewelry business (truth be told, it was more fun than profitable), and credit card churning (which I highly recommend to anyone with a lot of free time, an affinity for spreadsheets, and a high credit score).

But when I met Jeremy, things changed. For starters, my trip savings target had to double to $30,000 to account for the dead weight (I'm kidding of course; if anyone's the dead weight in our relationship these days, it's our dog, Mulan).

Jeremy's financial situation was very different from mine. For one thing, he kept getting shady calls at all hours of the day that he refused to answer. When I finally worked up the courage to ask him why, he told me they were debt collectors. (I'm not sure whether that was a relief or not).

A few months into our relationship, we were getting ready to move in together — and I started to piece things together. My handsome, charming new boyfriend was a barista with a degree from a for-profit art school, and yet, every time he took me out, he insisted on paying. It was incredibly sweet, but it didn't really make sense. And if we were going to get serious about things (and share my extremely small apartment), we needed to be honest with each other about everything. I needed to know the most intimate detail about him: his credit score.

Let me be honest when I say: I did not know that credit scores could go that low.

We had a few honest conversations, and I realized that Jeremy's financial literacy and background was very different from mine. I came from a background of financial privilege and education; Jeremy was the first in his family to go to college and had been living paycheck to paycheck for his entire life. And while I grew up taking family vacations, Jeremy had never been able to afford much travel: in his entire life, he'd never left the West Coast.

We had a lot of work to do.

Jeremy got started right away, going through every negative mark on his credit score. He called each and every debt collector to contest, renegotiate, or pay down his debt. He set up a budget and stuck to it.

He also quit his job at the coffee shop to pick up better paying part-time work as a substitute teacher, a job he found himself enjoying immensely.

Moving in together meant we could split our variable costs and save more money. To save money on food, our biggest expense after rent, Jeremy worked on improving his cooking skills (I'm still only able to cook with a crockpot). We replaced nights on the town with hiking, camping, picnics in the park, or riding bikes together. We were making great progress!

And then, in a weird twist of fate and luck, just six months into dating, Jeremy totalled my car on a camping trip while driving on a windy mountain pass in the high Sierra Nevadas.[27]

To my complete shock, I wasn't even mad. I was just glad we were okay. And even more surprisingly, I found the whole thing pretty amusing.

It was in that moment that I realized we were destined to be together: I would have murdered anyone but my true soulmate.

Even though we did receive some insurance money to cover the loss of my car, we decided to go car-free for the next few years, which ended up being a great way to boost our savings since we were suddenly forced to walk, bike, and transit everywhere.

We hit our savings target on time. And thanks to the insurance money from our poor totalled car (RIP), we even managed to scrounge together a few thousand extra to pay for a beautiful, intimate wedding in the Berkeley redwoods.

Today, my wonderful husband not only has a near-perfect credit score, but he even teaches budgeting and personal finance as part of his 12th grade Life Skills class. (Oh, and he's an *excellent* cook).

---

27 I'd love to say it was a freak accident that nobody could have seen coming, but it was entirely avoidable: he ran over a giant rock which tore the oil pan out from underneath my car, and then continued driving as alarm lights lit up on the dash until the car just gave up and died. It was only the beginning of a car curse that haunts us to this day. You can read the full story on practicalwanderlust.com/mono-hot-springs-incident

In fact, I ripped off one of his lesson plans to write the rest of this section. So, technically, here's Jeremy's guide to creating a budget.

How to Create a Budget

First things first: you'll need to figure out how much you're spending each month. You'll need to know both your fixed costs and your variable costs. Fixed costs are specific amounts you have to pay, like rent, utilities, and bills. Variable costs cover everything else, from food (both groceries and dining out) to shopping and entertainment.

There's a good chance that your estimates of your variable costs are completely inaccurate. Don't take it personally — it's a universal truth. (Jeremy and I like to pretend that we spend a lot less money on eating out at restaurants each month than we actually do, for instance.)

To get an accurate estimate of your variable costs, I recommend tracking your expenses. You don't need to write down everything you spend (unless you pay for everything in cash): Mint.com is a fantastic free resource for tracking your spending, setting a budget, and helping you manage your finances.[28]

Once you've accurately tracked your expenses for a few months, you'll have a pretty good idea of what you're spending compared to what you're earning, the difference of which is how much you're able to save each month. Take that savings amount and do some quick math: if you divide the amount of money you think you need for your long-term trip by the amount you're able to save each month, how long will it take you to save up for your trip? (Divide by 12 to get your answer in years).

At the risk of sounding like a math teacher, you can adjust your numbers a little bit by changing your variables: the amount of money you need to save, the amount you're saving each month, or the amount of time you have to save. Let's just lean into this math teacher thing and do a quick equation together:

---

28 PocketGuard and Wally are two alternatives to Mint that I haven't personally used, but have heard good things about. They offer similar features to Mint: PocketGuard helps analyze your spending patterns and looks for ways that you can save money, such as better monthly deals on phone bills and Internet service. Wally helps you set a budget, track your spending, and manage your payments (it even sends you reminders when your payments are due). All three services are completely free.

- Savings target: $30,000

- Monthly savings: $500

30,000 ÷ 500 = 60, which divided by 12 is 5.

So if I need to save up $30,000 and I'm able to set aside $500 each month, it will take me 60 months/5 years to save up for my trip. (And yes: those numbers are roughly what I used to save up for my own trip).

Now, if I want to leave sooner, I'll either need to increase the amount I'm saving each month, or decrease my savings target.

Decreasing your savings target means you'll either need to adjust your travel budget style or shorten the length of your trip (back to your spreadsheet! Grab the wine!), or commit to working during your trip — we've got a chapter dedicated to that very topic in Part Three.

On the other hand, to increase the amount you're saving each month you have just two options: you can either spend less, or earn more. (Boy, it sounds like a real piece of cake when I write it out like that, doesn't it?)

It's much easier to cut your spending if you've got lots of surprising variable expenses — money that you've been spending without realizing how much it adds up. You might reduce your food spending by eating out less and cooking more (cooking big batches of food on the weekends and meal planning will help!), make coffee at home instead of stopping at Starbucks, carpooling or taking transit to work a few days a week, or cutting back on late-night impulse buys on Amazon and Friday night trips to Target. If you have a lot of unnecessary variable costs, you're in a great position to start saving up money.

You'll need to tighten up your spending across the board to really make a dent: after all, cutting out that before-work $5 latte only saves you $1,300 per year, which will buy you roughly two round-trip treks to Machu Picchu or 1.5 weeks in the Galapagos (yes: all of my savings math is counted in South American travel experiences).

But on the other hand, foregoing your daily Starbucks can also pay for an entire month in Colombia for two people, which is *definitely* worth it. Whenever I'm tempted to buy something I don't really need, I like to remind myself that I can get a room in a hostel for under $10.

For me, building up my savings required a combination of cutting down on my both variable expenses and my fixed costs. I decided that paying for my Very Big Adventure was well worth the tradeoffs of living in a smaller apartment, cooking most of my meals, ordering soda water at bars,[29] and spending adventurous weekends camping and hiking instead of staying in pricier accommodations.

Lowering your Fixed Costs

While I was working on my own savings and getting used to sticking to a budget, I found that most of my expenses were coming from fixed costs like rent and utilities — and I had to make some difficult decisions. If you're in a similar position, that may mean shifting your lifestyle to live below your means.

Here are few ways to start chiseling away at your fixed costs:

- **Lowering your phone bill**

If you're paying off your phone, trade it in for a cheaper version. Switch to a lower-cost phone plan, or split a shared phone plan with friends or family.

If none of those options work, there's always the old tried and true method: call up your phone provider and (politely) threaten to cancel your service. They'll usually offer a "retention" discount to keep you as a customer. If they don't, cut ties with them and switch to a less expensive phone provider who values your business! (Feel free to put on your best "let me speak to your manager" impression at this point, but please don't ream out the poor customer service person who happened to answer your call — it's not their fault).

Over the years, I called up AT&T to politely ask for a discount on my phone and internet bills so often, their retention line was saved as a "Favorite" in my phone.

- **Cancelling cable**

If you're currently paying for cable TV, this one's easy. Drop that sucker out of your life — you'll be amazed how much mindless entertainment you can get from Hulu, Netflix, Amazon, Disney+, and/or HBOMax. Plus, this will be excellent practice for when you're traveling anyway!

---

29   Listen, y'all: even if you're just drinking soda water and secretly carrying a flask, *always* remember to tip your bartenders.

To make things even cheaper, opt to share your accounts with family and friends. Each member of my family pays for a streaming service, and the rest of us mooches just use their login. Plus, it makes it easier to know who's watching what so we can text them and ask if it's worth it. Aww, family bonding over TV — it's like a trip back in time to the good ol' days!

Need to make a bigger dent in your fixed costs? Here are two somewhat more extreme ways to whittle down your monthly expenses:

- **Reducing your housing costs**

When I met Jeremy, I had just downsized from a one-bedroom apartment to a tiny, 500-square-foot cottage in order to save $150 per month.[30] The cottage was barely more than a studio (and only a well-placed wall kept it from being classified as one). But it was charming and cozy, with an orange tree and a fig tree (which I immediately nicknamed Ella Figsgerald) growing front and a giant avocado tree in the lot behind. I could reach out my window and pick avocados: for a Kentucky girl, this was the height of California living.

But when Jeremy moved in with me, my cozy little treehouse cottage suddenly felt very cramped. There was barely enough space for me and my belongings, let alone Jeremy's boxes of artwork and film school textbooks. We both ended up getting rid of some of our belongings — and eventually got used to constantly squeezing past one another. And it turned out to be fantastic practice for long-term travel!

Reducing your monthly housing payment can be a major boost to your savings, especially if you're able to move your stuff on your own or with the help of friends. Check apartment listings in your area to look for cheaper options.[31] You're looking for smaller square footage, fewer bedrooms or bathrooms, and fewer amenities. Here in the Bay Area, things like a dishwasher or air conditioning are a major luxury that I've never once been able to snag in the decade I've lived here — but hey, washing all those dishes was excellent practice for cleaning up after myself in shared hostel kitchens![32]

---

30   It might not sound like a lot, but that $150 per month adds up to $1,800 per year, which is $9,000 over the course of five years! That move alone paid for a significant chunk of our trip.

31   I'm a big fan of PadMapper.com for browsing apartment listings.

32   In the summer, the cottage was often a sweltering 90°F indoors. We spent many evenings sitting outside under Ella Figsgerald, eating figs and waiting for it to cool off enough to go back inside.

If you can't find a cheaper place alone, consider roommates. You can round up a few friends to split the cost of a house with several bedrooms, or browse through Craigslist to see if anyone's seeking a roommate.

If you'd rather not move and you've got a little extra space to spare, getting a roommate will be an immediate boost to your savings — much easier if you have an extra bedroom, of course, but there are a few non-traditional living arrangements you might consider. (Jeremy once split a studio apartment in San Francisco with seven people. He had one corner of the room, separated by a hanging sheet. Comfortable? No. Great training for hostel dorms? Yes!)

Just be sure you do your due diligence with anyone you bring in to live with you: if you're renting, ensure that you're not breaking your lease by subletting (it's much better to add them to the lease so everything's on the level). If you own your home, conduct a background check and make sure to draw up a lease so you're legally protected in case anything happens.

Homeowners have a few more options. Refinancing your mortgage may be a good option to reduce your monthly payment or interest rate. You can also rent out your entire home to cover your mortgage, and then move into a lower-cost apartment. There's a decent chance you'll have to get a tenant to sublet your house while you're traveling anyway, so why not do it a little early and pocket the extra cash?

- **Lowering your car payment**

After Jeremy totalled my car, we were able to apply all of our car-related expenses to our travel savings. Living in the Bay Area made going car-free easy: there's comprehensive public transit, walkable neighborhoods, and shared car services, bike rentals, and scooters are available on every corner. We were able to complete most of our errands without needing a car, and when we did need one — for groceries or just weekend trips — we rented one.

Unfortunately, owning a car is a necessity for most people in the United States. The country is built around driving, and if you're not living in a major city like we were, it's downright impossible to go car-free.

That said: if you do live in or near an urban area with public transportation, consider getting rid of your car and getting a bike (electric, motor, or just a good old fashioned 10-speed). Going entirely car-free will save you from monthly car payments as well as insurance and gas expenses, plus you'll never have to worry about paying for surprise maintenance or accidents.

When you do need a car — which everyone does at some point — you can join a carshare service such as ZipCar or GetAround, or even just rent a car from a nearby rental company like Enterprise.

If going car-free isn't an option, do your best to reduce your car payments and downgrade to the cheapest car possible that will get you where you need to go (you'll only need it for a few years anyway). Cut back on driving as much as you possibly can, and carpool whenever possible. If you drive less, you may even be able to negotiate a lower-cost car insurance payment.

While it's definitely a major lifestyle shift, living below your means, sharing your housing, and reducing your reliance on driving will help you build up your savings much faster. Plus, it will help make the transition to long-term traveling much easier.

Debts & Loans

Fixed costs like debts and loans are a little tricker, and require careful strategizing. When you're paying down debts or student loans, you do have a few options for reducing your monthly payments. But it's important to keep in mind that the longer you take to pay off a loan, the more you're paying in total, thanks to accruing interest. Even though a lower payment monthly is nice for short term, it will end up taking you longer to pay it off and it will potentially add quite a bit more money to the total cost. So, embark on this option carefully: the choices you make now may be screwing over your future self![33]

If you're paying off debts or loans, spend a few months calling up your creditors and lenders to inquire about lowering your monthly payments and reducing your interest rate. They're usually more willing to negotiate with you if you've

---

33 This also holds true for the choice to save for a long-term trip instead of putting money away for retirement, investing your extra income each month, or saving for a down payment on a house. You may decide, like I did, that the adventure of a long trip is worth it — but do consider whether you'll be able to make up the savings you're spending after you return. Use an online retirement calculator to estimate the compound interest you might be missing out on by waiting to save for retirement — it adds up like crazy. It might be worth pushing your trip back by a few months if it means putting a small piece of your savings aside in a retirement account to grow while you travel!

got a good credit score and a history of making timely payments (and also if you ask nicely).

You may even consider refinancing or consolidating your debt to get a more manageable monthly payment — but don't accept a higher interest rate, if you can avoid it.

Credit card debt is one area that I wouldn't recommend this approach. Credit card loans are typically high interest, which adds up fast and becomes incredibly difficult to pay down — if you're paying the minimum amount each month, chances are you'll be paying it forever, since you're likely only really covering interest and not chipping away at the actual amount you owe (the principal). I strongly encourage you to pay off credit card debt before you start saving for your trip — throw all the extra money you've been able to muster up at that credit card debt and pay it off as quickly as you can.[34] (And then go treat yourself, because paying off credit card debt is a HUGE deal!)

If you've got cash on hand to throw at your debt, you might try offering a lump sum to pay off the rest of the loan — some creditors may be willing to cut you a deal if you're able to pay them on the spot. This is a great option if you've got some extra cash, but when you're saving up for a major expense like a long-term trip, you'll need to decide whether it's worth paying that debt down now or keep paying the minimum on it until you return.

If you need help with setting up a debt management plan, the National Foundation for Credit Counseling and the Financial Counseling Association of America are completely free resources that can help you set a realistic plan for tackling your debt, with recommended tools and methods to reduce your payments. The Suze Orman Debt Roll-Down approach is also a fantastic method for paying down debt, which recommends that you start with your highest interest rate first, and as you pay off balances, apply your old monthly payment to your other debts.[35]

Now let's talk about the elephant in the room for the unfortunate majority of United States citizens: student loan debt. When it comes to student loan pay-

---

34 To give you a leg up, you might consider transferring your balance to another credit card with 0% APR for a year. That gives you a whole year to pay down the principal without acquiring more interest, which can make a major dent. But be careful: those deals often come with a massive interest rate once your "free" year is over! Only try this method if your debt is definitely something you'll be able to pay off within a year.

35 More about this method, including a calculator to help measure the time it will take to eliminate your debt, check out suzeorman.com

ments, the whole "just call up your creditor and ask them nicely to make you a deal" thing flies out the window. Trust me: we've tried.

That said, you do have a couple of options to reduce your monthly payments. If you have federal loans, you can enter into a federal loan repayment plan[36], such as income-based repayment, which ties your monthly payment to your income level. Since you already plan to quit your job (or at the very least, take an income hit), you'll be able to reduce your payments down to nothing, or almost-nothing during your trip. Which is all well and good, but don't forget: you have to keep proving that you're not earning any money, or your loans will go into default — which is a major hassle. Sadly, I speak from experience — I'll tell you the tale of that disaster in Part Two.

Private loans are a little tricker, but you may have some options: call up your loan service provider to ask.

Another good option to consolidate and refinance your loans using a student loan refinancing service like SoFi. When you refinance, the company you work with will pay off all of your loans, and you'll owe them money instead. If your loans are all spread out across different companies, this can definitely make things easier, and you may also be able to lower your monthly payment or interest rate.

Crafty Ways to Earn Extra Money

Once you've chipped away at your expenses as much as you can, the next way to boost your monthly savings is to increase your income. Increasing your income is the hardest of all. It's never quite as easy as "just go get a better paying job," although … that would definitely help. I would love to help wave a magic wand for you and make this step easier, but the best I can do is to give you a lot of ideas!

- **Get another job or a side-hustle**

If you've got some extra time, you could take advantage of the gig economy or start a side hustle.

You might consider becoming a rideshare driver, delivering food, groceries or packages, or walking dogs on the weekends. You can become a website tester for UserFeel.

---

36 Take a look at the available federal loan repayment programs and contact your loan servicer to discuss your options.

You can also start working as a Mystery Shopper. You'll be low-key spying in order to ensure that a company's guidelines are being met, evaluating things like customer service, whether you're carded for buying alcohol, or in some cases, even setting up special displays in stores. You'll be able to select which gigs you pick up and where you go, so only choose things you feel comfortable with. Sometimes you'll have to pretend to be shopping for a big purchase, like a car or TV. I like to think of it like acting, not lying, and you might even have a few "lines" or a character to play.[37]

If you've got entire days off during the week that you'd be open to spending in a classroom with students, you can become a part-time substitute teacher (which will be hugely appreciated by the teachers you're helping out).[38]

Do you have a skill you can monetize? Sure you do! Get creative: you can make money doing everything from tarot readings to drawing pictures or writing silly songs on Fiverr; or freelance writing, translation, editing, or design work on Upwork. You can even get work as a Virtual Assistant doing administrative tasks for small business owners like leaving comments on Instagram, sharing pins on Pinterest, photo editing, or answering emails. As a blogger, I rely heavily on a team of Virtual Assistants to help me with a wide range of tasks! You can also find remote gigs on FlexJobs.com.

Since your work will be totally online, you'll also be able to continue your side hustle as you travel, and getting a few paid gigs under your belt before you leave will be a huge help.

- **Share your stuff**

These days, you can make money on just about everything. You can list your car on GetAround.com, for folks who need a ride for a few hours. We typically rent GetAround trucks or vans when we need to pick up Craigslist furniture finds or move.

---

37 There are many Mystery Shopping platforms, each with different clients and opportunities. Start with Market Force, Intelli-Shop, Sinclair Customer Metrics, and Best Mark. My two top tips from years of mystery shopping are to batch all of your mystery shops together so you don't have to drive as much, and complete and submit your survey paperwork directly after each shop (like, in the car before your next stop) so you don't forget any details.

38 The process for becoming a sub varies by state, but in California, it was surprisingly easy. You'll want to look up how it works in your state.

If you have an extra bedroom and you aren't thrilled at the idea of a roommate, consider renting out your space on Airbnb.

If you live somewhere a little more rural or you've got some land, you might be able to rent out a campsite in your backyard on Airbnb, HipCamp, or Tentrr. You can provide as little as an empty lot, or string a few lights, roll a few stumps in, and build a little firepit to make things cozier and land more visitors. (Just be sure to check your local laws first, to confirm you're allowed — and to get an idea of how difficult and expensive the process will be to acquire the right permits.)

You can also rent out just about everything else in your home: let people use your backyard, office, extra bedroom, home gym, pool, music room, kitchen, or anything else you can imagine on PeerSpace. This is a great option even if you don't own your home, although you'll need to confirm that you aren't breaking your lease.

- **Earn credit card points and miles**

This can be one of the most profitable ways to earn extra cash for your trip, but it can also be the riskiest. Before I dive in, please imagine the word DISCLAIMER flashing over your head in bright, neon lights: *do not* try to play the points and miles game if you sometimes need to carry a credit card balance! Credit cards can be a slippery slope into expensive, high-interest debt which can take years to dig yourself out of — and that's exactly what big banks and lenders count on when they offer free money in the hopes that you'll sign up for their cards. So if you're still working on paying off your credit card debt, please pass this section right on by (and come back in a few years! I'll be here).

Another caveat is that you'll need a fairly high credit score, in the high 600's or better. Below that, you'll have trouble qualifying for cards with the highest rewards. It's better to focus on building up your credit score, and then come on back when you're ready.[39]

If you're at a point where you won't need to carry a balance on your credit cards and your credit score is in a good place, you can start to experiment with credit

39 After years of working on Jeremy's credit score, we have a few tips. First, pull one of the three free credit reports you're entitled to each year from TransUnion, Equifax, or Experian (CreditKarma is also a helpful tool), and dispute every single negative claim — some might fall off and disappear, and some might be negotiable. Next, apply for a secured credit card with a low balance to start building back up your credit, set up autopay, and buy a pack of gum with it every so often. Those cards are designed for folks with no or low credit, and they're a great starting point for working on your credit score!

card churning. Essentially, you'll be signing up for and using credit cards specifically to earn points, miles, and sign-up bonuses. To make this worthwhile, you'll need to set everything up on autopay so you don't unintentionally pay any interest, and be very careful never to spend money you wouldn't have otherwise just to earn more points.

Sign-up bonuses are my personal favorite way to churn: they're often worth hundreds of dollars or the value of an international flight. In order to get the sign-up bonus, there will be a required minimum spend amount, often something like $3,000 in three months. I'm usually able to hit the sign-up bonus requirement just by doing all of my spending on a single credit card for the duration of the sign-up bonus period, and I also plan ahead to sign up for a new card when I know I have a big expense coming up — say, a pricey plane ticket, or holiday shopping. I space out new card sign-ups to avoid doubling up and missing out on a sign-up reward; I typically only open one new card at a time.

You'll need to do some research to figure out which credit cards make the most sense for you. I focused on cards that I could use for the trip: cash back rewards on categories I spent the most in (like restaurants, travel, and groceries), points that could be exchanged for travel, and miles for airlines that I was likely to fly during my trip.

The most useful cards I opened were general travel rewards cards, like a Chase Sapphire card; an American Express Blue Cash Preferred card, which pays 6% back on groceries; and specific airline cards to help me pay for plane tickets during my trip, like Avianca, American Airlines, United and LATAM. Airline miles are usually transferable between airline "partners," so for instance, your American Airlines miles can help you pay for an inexpensive short-haul flight during your trip on Japan Airlines, Fiji Airways, or SriLankan Airlines.

It can all be very confusing, so I recommend seeking out the advice of experts. My favorite resources are the Churning Subreddit, and The Points Guy blog, and NerdWallet.

I highly recommend starting a spreadsheet to keep track of everything (because, of course I do) so that you don't miss things like how much you need to spend on each card and by what date in order to hit the required minimum, or the date of your one-year card anniversary, which will incur a high annual fee.[40]

---

40 Although a few of my favorite cards do have annual fees which more than pay for themselves in rewards, when I sign up for a credit card just for the sign-up bonus, I typically don't want to pay an annual fee or keep the card open. In those cases, I either call the card issuer to ask nicely if they'll wave the annual fee, or I just cancel the card outright.

Personally, I opened about 20 cards over the course of five years, whose rewards paid for thousands of dollars worth of travel expenses before and during my trip. It took quite a bit of finagling, but the time I spent definitely paid for itself; and to my surprise, credit card churning even increased my credit score!

Travel Scholarships and Stipends

There are a few travel stipends and scholarships that can help you fund your trip:

- **Hostelling International USA** annually awards travel stipends of up to $2,000 to young Americans under 30. Check out whether you are eligible for a travel stipend and learn how to apply at hiusa.org/travel-scholarships

- If you are an aspiring travel photographer, filmmaker or writer, then check out **World Nomads' travel scholarships** for creatives. Scholarships include travel costs and the opportunity to work with and be mentored by a professional creative on a real-world project for a client. Past scholarship winners have created successful travel blogs, published photos in major publications, and gone on to work in film production. Get more on World Nomads' unique scholarship program at worldnomads.com/create/scholarships

- **International Volunteer HQ (IVHQ)** offers four Volunteer Abroad Scholarships every year that include a sponsored two-week volunteer program, a $1,000 travel voucher, and travel insurance. Learn more how to apply at volunteerhq.org/ivhq-scholarships/

- Gabby, the amazing travel blogger behind **PacksLight.com,** maintains a curated list of travel scholarships, fellowships, and other travel opportunities. Make it a habit to check her site regularly to jump on new opportunities: packslight.com/opportunities-dashboard/

Now that you've tightened up your figurative purse strings and put a plan in place to reduce your expenses and increase your income, you can start putting aside money into your Long-Term Travel Fund. I recommend setting up an automated system to deposit money regularly from your checking account into a savings account to keep yourself honest. I'm a big fan of SmartyPig, which lets you set up a savings account for each of your savings goals (and you can name it something like Long Term Travel Fund, which is weirdly super motivating!).

If you typically get paid in cash, create a physical place to deposit a set amount of your earnings each week or each month, and hold yourself accountable. Yes: I'm talking about a piggy bank. (For a slightly more grown-up version, I'm a big fan of a shoebox with a hole cut in the top).

Also, and this is especially important if you'll be saving up money for a very long time: don't forget to treat yourself! You're working hard to save money, and it's okay to enjoy the fruits of your labor from time to time.

What if Saving Isn't Enough?

It's not always realistic to pay for a long-term trip with savings. Do your best to save up enough for a round-trip flight and a month or so of expenses so that you have a cushion to fall back on, and make a plan to work during your trip. Set yourself an "oh sh*t" number: when your savings fall below that amount, it's time to stop moving for a while, hole up in one place, and work on building your cushion back up. We've got a chapter of options for working while you travel in Part Three.

Many options for working while you travel won't require specialized skills, but a couple are worth starting on early to get a head start, like remote work or freelancing. If you're hoping to earn money online as a contractor, Virtual Assistant, or blogger, you'll want to start growing your business as early as possible so you can start racking up clients or growing your readership ASAP — both of which take a lot of time. Another option that requires advance effort is to get a Teaching English as a Foreign Language (TEFL) certificate, which will help you find a job in a school or online, so that you can teach English as you travel. You'll find tips for exploring each of those opportunities in Part Three.

And now, you're ready. You've got a solid plan. A deadline (more or less). A timeline, at the very least. You've started! You're in this! It's going to take a while — maybe a few months or even a few years — but you can do it. I know you can! You've got this.

So, when you're ready to start planning your trip, booking things, and making itineraries, come on back and we can get started.

See you in a few years!

PART TWO: THE PLAN

Planning & Booking Your Trip

Oh my gosh! It's you! And wow — you look awesome. Are you doing something new with your hair? I love it.

Anyway, you have officially made it to Part Two. This section of the book takes place about a year before your trip. You're ready to nail down a date, book a one-way plane ticket and start filling out an actual itinerary, with real plans. Your trip is no longer just an imaginary possibility somewhere in the distant future: it's here. You're making it happen. And it's time to actually sit down and plan it. You're really doing this thing!

But along with that excitement comes a whole bunch of logistical hoops you'll have to jump through. Like, what do you do with your mail while you're gone? And what are you going to do with all your stuff? What about your cell phone plan? Do you need to visit your doctor?

So. Many. Logistics.

Luckily, I've already figured out everything you need to know so I can walk you through it. I even went above and beyond and made some catastrophic mistakes, so I can guide you through what not to do, too! You're welcome.

If you can get through all the logistical stuff without hyperventilating (and listen, feel free to skip each step and then come back again when you really need it — it's a LOT to take in at once!), we'll cover everything you need to know to prepare for your trip.

And then it's time to say goodbye. No, not to me! I still have so much to tell you! I'm not ready to leave you yet! But you will need to say goodbye to your job, your home, your family and friends, your favorite restaurant, and, you know … *gestures broadly at everything*.

Hey, deep breaths: we're going to tackle it together, one step at a time.

But wait — before we jump right into things, can we talk?

Specifically, I'd like to talk about planning versus spontaneity. As in, do you really need to plan out your whole itinerary before you leave? Or is it better to leave things open-ended and just figure things out as you go?

If you're the kind of person who thinks planning an itinerary is half the fun of taking a trip, you are my people. I savored this part of the process like it was a nice, hot bath, soaking in it until my skin got all wrinkly and only getting out when the water was unpleasantly cold. I dragged out the process of planning our two exciting months of travel over a whole, glorious year. I created a massive travel document (more on that bad boy soon) and filled in pages and pages of excruciating detail, including every single thing I might possibly need to know about my first two destinations.

Even by my standards, it was overwhelming — we're talking like, a solid 50 pages of detailed information about places to visit and things to do there, only a third of which was directly relevant to my trip.

To put it mildly, I had a little bit of trouble editing myself down.[41]

The actual itinerary I created was a lot like my travel document: cluttered and overwhelming. In just a month of traveling in Colombia, we managed to squeeze in eight separate destinations, moving at breakneck speed and traveling from one place to the next every 3-4 days on average. I was a woman on a mission: I only had a year to see as much of the world as I could, and I was going to make every last minute count!

But I also did something very unlike me: I attempted to give spontaneity a chance. I chose to leave everything from month three onwards open-ended, thinking that after we landed in Peru, I'd sort of just figure things out as I went along. People who traveled long-term seemed to be the type to play it by ear — at least in my limited knowledge of them, which was based entirely on stalking incredibly attractive nomadic couples on Instagram.

Why did I stop planning after the first two months? Maybe I figured that after traveling in my typical, frantic way — a style I'd developed out of necessity, born from having to fit packed itineraries into limited vacation time — I'd suddenly undergo a travel transformation and join the ranks of tanned, beautiful Instagrammers without a care in the world. By then, I'd probably just be able to figure things out as I went, allowing the universe to guide me via sunrise yoga and meaningful chance encounters with strangers, no longer shackled by the limitation of

41 She says, writing a full-length book that probably could have just been a chunky blog post …

being someone who thrives off of a good to-do list and has never made a single decision without first researching five other options.

Or maybe I just spent so much time agonizing over every single moment of the first eight weeks of my trip that I just ran out of time to plan the rest of it.[42] In any case, it was a terrible idea.

I did, at least, have a rough idea of my planned itinerary: I knew I wanted to start the trip off with six months of traipsing through South America, and then, I figured, I'd just go around Southeast Asia for a few months, and then do a casual thru-hike of the Appalachian Trail over the summer, which I would surely be physically prepared for after months of backpacking.[43]

By now, it should come as no surprise that almost none of that actually happened.

As the end of our well-researched and planned first two months of our trip approached, we found ourselves huddling in cafes and hostel lounges on our laptops, frantically researching the next places we wanted to visit and how to get there — instead of out exploring and enjoying the too-limited time we'd allotted ourselves in the places we still were.

So, to cut back on time spent indoors staring at a computer and planning our next move, we gave up on researching. We overcorrected, doing the bare minimum amount of planning — which boiled down to, essentially, showing up at a bus stop with the name of our next destination and nothing else — and reassuring ourselves that we'd just have to go with it. We were out of time.

For two months we wandered aimlessly around Peru by bus, deciding where to go based on places we'd seen mentioned on online forums or recommended by other travelers we met along the way. Without our usual research to guide us, we ended up spending hours staring out the window on long bus rides that would have been entirely unnecessary if we'd planned our route better, stayed in a series of crappy hostels in towns without much to offer tourists, and visited places we didn't know anything about on a haphazard itinerary that made absolutely no sense.

---

42 According to Jeremy, this is what actually happened.

43 Not only is backpacking nowhere near as physically demanding as I thought it would be, but it actually really threw a wrench into my newfound fitness regime. During my year-long trip, I lost quite a bit of hard-earned muscle and replaced it with happy travel weight. I returned home with a comfortable 40lbs of delicious Peruvian ceviche, French pastries, Belgian fries, and Argentinian wine, which I have carried with me as a souvenir ever since.

At one point, we visited a seaside surfing town because someone on reddit said it had great vibes and amazing ceviche (it did).[44] Days later, we hopped on a bus to head into the mountains because someone at a hostel showed us a photo from a hike which looked really cool.

But there are a few things that even spontaneous travelers should research in advance, and one of those things is altitude.

If I'd spent a little more time researching, I would have known that traveling from the coast directly to the high-elevation mountains is an awful idea, and I would have given us a few days to acclimate. Instead, I ended up with a nasty bout of altitude sickness which hit me the minute I stumbled off the bus. It felt like the worst hangover of my life combined with the flu: every tiny movement was agony. The world was spinning, even when I closed my eyes. It took all of my energy just to lie in bed and stare at the ceiling, gasping for air and trying not to throw up.[45]

Meanwhile, Jeremy struggled through a difficult — but beautiful — hike to Laguna 69[46], an alpine lake in Peru's snowy Cordillera Blancas mountain range at over 15,000 feet above sea level. That hike was the only thing we'd come to the town of Huaraz to do, and I missed out on it because of my own lack of preparation.

Honestly, our two months of ill-prepared wandering through Peru was a mess, culminating in the soul-crushing finale of our trip: Machu Picchu. The Inca Trail trek to Machu Picchu was, by necessity, one of the only things we'd booked long in advance for our time in Peru. But we hadn't accounted for continuing the physical training we'd been doing before our trip; although we'd done a few hikes here and there in Colombia and Ecuador — which had thoroughly kicked our butts[47] — we'd spent

---

44 The town is called Huanchaco. In addition to their excellent seafood, they're known for their traditional surfing boats, which are hand-woven from reeds. The *caballitos de totora* have been used by local fishermen for over 3,000 years.

45 A quick note on altitude sickness: it's often very mild, but it can actually be pretty serious, and even fatal. Drinking a lot of water and acclimating more slowly will help stave off altitude sickness, and if you have a more severe case, descending to a lower elevation will give you immediate relief. To play it safe, always build in a few days of acclimatization before any athletic procedures, like hiking. In my case, it took about two days until I was able to walk again (at which point I dragged myself to a nearby cafe and ordered a cup of some magical herbal tea made from coca leaves and muña, which completely cured the rest of my symptoms).

46 Nice.

47 At one point during our 4-day Quilotoa Loop hike in the Andes Mountains of Ecuador, we wandered so far off the trail that we ended up crawling up the side of a mountain on our hands and knees. It turns out that hiking in the mountains in South America is way, WAY harder than strolling through the redwoods in California.

a whole two months in Peru just bopping around on buses and eating ceviche. On Day One of the hike, we trailed several hours behind our group. The next morning, exhausted and defeated, we turned around and hiked back. It was an expensive failure that not only ruined the bucket list adventure that I'd dreamt of and trained for back home, but shook our confidence and our enthusiasm for traveling.

Our tentative itinerary had us heading to Patagonia to tackle the W, a five-day trek through Torres del Paine that is one of the most famous and scenic hikes in the world.

Instead, we accepted a generous offer from my family, and booked a plane ticket home. We were tired, miserable, disappointed, and all we wanted to do was spend a few days celebrating the holidays with our family, soaking up comfort and familiarity.

A few weeks at home was exactly what we needed to revive our excitement for traveling. We booked a cheap plane ticket to Europe and headed back out again.

We thought we'd learned our lesson: Jeremy and I are just not suited to play it by ear. But in Europe, we overcorrected and planned ourselves another challenging itinerary, moving from place to place every few days.

That breakneck speed lasted for about a month until we were thoroughly burnt out and found ourselves spending most of our time in coffee shops, hunched over our laptops trying to plan our next move. It took us nearly a full year to find the right balance.

Don't make the same mistakes as we did: do your best to anticipate your travel style in advance. If you're a planner, plan out enough of your trip to make you feel comfortable, and plan a little extra time in between each destination to allow for reworking your route, just in case. If you're spontaneous, don't shoehorn yourself into too many pre-planned activities. Travel is hard enough — don't make it even harder on yourself by setting unrealistic expectations!

Several years and hundreds of trips later, we've finally perfected the art of travel planning and found the balance between too-rigid itineraries and too little preparation. We've learned that although we both prefer to research destinations in advance and book a few things early, it's important to leave plenty of room in your itinerary for moving everything around once you arrive. We've also learned from trial and error (so many errors!) to always pay extra for the flexibility of changing your dates or canceling and getting a refund, in case you need to make last-minute adjustments.

A well-planned trip requires room for failure and flexibility: if you map out each detail of every single day, you'll feel even more stressed when your travel plans inevitably fall apart and your perfectly planned day — or week, or month — is ruined.

We found out the hard way that long-term travel requires moving at a much slower pace than you're used to, and requires spending at least a day or two each week (and a week or two each month) to do absolutely nothing. Travel is both mentally and physically exhausting: it's crucial to give yourself time to recover.

During these periods of rest, you'll want to stay in one spot long enough to get settled and develop a few comforting routines. The human brain, it turns out, thrives on routines — having "your" coffee shop and "your" grocery store is every bit as soul-restoring as sunrise yoga[48].

Now that we've learned to strike a balance between over and under planning, Jeremy and I really enjoy the travel planning process! Researching all the exciting things we're going to be doing on our trip only adds to our anticipation, and preparing for the worst eases our anxiety. Plus, we get to make spreadsheets and stuff, which gives us the warm fuzzies.

Speaking of which... remember that spreadsheet we made together back in Part One? I think about it all the time. Well, it's finally time for us to revisit it... together.

Creating Your Trip Roadmap

At last, it's finally time to get down to the good stuff: creating a detailed, organized document for your trip. Oh, excuse me, I'm drooling.

I hope you won't mind a deviation from our usual routine. Although I am a lifelong lover of spreadsheets, for this particular task I find that I actually prefer a nice, blank document. Into that document, I throw absolutely everything from random tidbits of advice that I've found online to screenshots and photos to embedded tables.[49]

To start with, you can go ahead and paste in your budget spreadsheet from Part

---

48 I have absolutely no data to back this claim up, and I'm not going to apologize for it.

49 The service I used to plan my trip is a Microsoft program called OneNote, but if you don't have access to that, plain old Google Docs works just fine.

One. Look at that! It looks amazing already. We are such good partners.

This document will eventually become your Trip Roadmap: a digital travel guide including absolutely everything you'll need during your trip, from your itinerary to greetings in the local language to maps and walking directions.

When it's all filled up (or you've just run out of time to put more stuff in it), you'll export it as a PDF and save it offline on all of your devices. That way, it's available online as well as accessible on your phone, e-reader, and computer, so that when you inevitably land in a new country where your phone doesn't work and there's no WiFi, you can still pull up the name of your accommodation and all of your booking information, which is helpful for hailing a taxi at the airport as well as for those demanding Customs officials who need the exact address of the place you'll be staying before you're allowed to cross the border.[50] It's also helpful for when Customs officials ask to see evidence that you plan to leave their country, including a plane ticket to somewhere else, or even a hotel you've booked in another country to confirm you'll be leaving overland. And no, they won't accept "the WiFi here is terrible and I can't pull up my email right now" as an excuse.

If creating a massive PDF that will become your lifeline while traveling feels overwhelming, here's how I like to begin. I create a "chapter" in my Trip Roadmap for the first country I'll be visiting, create a nice, satisfyingly blank table, and fill it up with the following:

- Entry/exit requirements — will I need to get a visa in advance?

- Language spoken, with a few basic phrases (hello, please, thank you, where is the bathroom, how do I find…?)

- Local currency (what's the exchange rate like? Is there an easy way to calculate back to my home currency so I know what things "really" cost?[51])

- Required medications and vaccines

- Address and contact details for the local U.S. Embassy (just in case)

50 Another helpful tool is an app called TripIt, which automatically compiles all of your booking information as it arrives in your email. It's a nice back-up plan to glance at on the go, but I find that it can get a little messy on longer trips.

51 Jeremy likes to find little tricks like this everywhere we go. The trick for Colombian Pesos was "divide by three and remove two zeros." Euros were "divided in two and add half." My trick, on the other hand, is to use an app called Globe Convert to avoid doing any math. I also track our cash expenses using an app called Trail Wallet.

After I've gotten the basics filled in, I move on to the fun stuff:

- What are the most famous local food and drinks in this country?

- What are the must-see attractions?

At this point, I start pasting in everything that sounds even mildly interesting: photos I find online, paragraphs from blog posts (with reference links included, so I can find them again)[52], suggestions buried in forum comments, restaurants that look interesting, pictures of cute hostel pets, and so on.

Once I've got several pages of a complete mess, filled with too many suggestions to feasibly account for in my itinerary, I start to pare everything down. I remove duplicates; I take out things that, on second glance, don't actually sound as interesting as they did at first. I'm left with a much more manageable list of things to do and places to see, which I can then start shaping into an actual itinerary.

This is where the challenge of logistics comes in. Mapping out a route isn't as easy as opening a map and seeing what looks close together.[53]

Instead, you'll want to figure out the most sensible way to arrange your destinations in a way that is doable by transit and minimizes travel time (and elevation changes). I like to start by researching itineraries online and trying to find a few that include most of the places on my pared-down list, and then add or remove from them as necessary. Usually, whoever created the itinerary has already done half the work of figuring out the most sensible route for me, or reworked their suggested itinerary based on their experiences.[54]

52 I actually didn't include links in our year-long honeymoon Trip Roadmap, which was a big mistake. Not only could I never revisit those helpful blogs for more tips, but when I eventually turned pieces of my planning document into blog posts, I neglected to credit the bloggers who'd originally made those suggestions. Years later, a fellow blogger called me out on one of my earlier posts: I'd given an extremely specific travel tip that she'd recognized instantly as hers. I was mortified and updated my post immediately, but it still haunts me to this day. If you're pulling tips from all over the web, throw in a link to your sources, too — whether you'll be publishing them online later or not.

53 We've included tools to help you plan and book your trip in the "Resources" section of the book, and we also have a detailed guide to trip planning published on Practical Wanderlust.

54 Although we have many published itineraries on PracticalWanderlust.com, almost none of them are exactly the same as the itinerary we actually did. There's always something that just wasn't worth it that, in hindsight, should have been swapped with something else, or a route we wished we'd taken instead.

One of the most challenging parts of itinerary planning — especially for a country you've never been to before, where you don't speak the language and aren't really sure what to look for — is the logistics of getting from place to place. In many places, it's impossible to book a ticket in advance or even know whether there's a way to get between places via transit.

For us, it was the bus system in South America. We spent months trawling online forums and searching for bus routes between places, and what we found only made us more confused. Most people would just mention taking a bus offhand, with no further details — leaving us with only more questions. Where was the bus station? How did you get to the bus station? What was the name of the route? How much did it cost? Do we need a ticket in advance? How long does the bus ride take? Will there be a series of full-volume horror movies playing on the bus, or should we bring our own entertainment?

Once we arrived, we quickly learned why the answers to those questions were difficult to find: some were simple to figure out, but some of them had no answers at all.

Finding the bus station was usually an easy task: all we had to do was hail the nearest taxi — and there was always a nearby taxi — and ask the driver to take us to the bus station.[55] Every taxi driver in the entire continent of South America, we found, knows exactly where the bus station is.

To figure out which bus ticket to buy, all you have to do is look for the name of the place you're trying to get to on a sign above a ticket counter. Failing that, find someone who works at the bus station and tell them where you're trying to go. You'll end up at the right ticket counter, although there's no guarantee that the bus you need leaves anytime soon — there's often about a 50/50 chance that you just missed the only bus leaving all day. Unfortunately, this is the only way to find out the bus schedule. It is not published online, and it changes too frequently for anyone to be able to help you plan in advance — even the all-knowing taxi drivers. Just assume the worst and hope for the best, and never count on being able to arrive on the day you'd really like to. If you really have to be somewhere in a timely manner, you'll want to figure things out when you arrive, or else take a trip to the bus station a few days before your target departure date.)

---

55 The exception is when you're going to a very small or not-so-touristy destination. Then, the "bus station" might just be a random corner or spot on the street where a shared van occasionally drives past, and your driver may have to ask other locals to figure out where exactly to drop you off. In those cases, there's a good chance you'll never really be sure if you're headed in the right direction until you've arrived at your destination. But hey, it's all part of the adventure, right?

Once you've got your ticket, waited anywhere from 2-8 hours, and asked everyone along the way that you are, in fact, boarding the correct bus, you'll finally be on the way to your next destination. This is where time estimates would come in handy: is this a quick two hour bus ride, or an all-day-long affair? In some places, finding out is half the fun!

In Colombia, for instance, a route may take 3 hours to drive, but the actual time you'll be on the bus will also include spending hours driving around town trying to pick up more passengers before actually leaving, stopping at the driver's favorite restaurant along the way for a leisurely lunch, and then spending several hours sitting in traffic on some random stretch of road in the middle of nowhere waiting on a team of unconcerned road workers.[56] Eight hours later, someone will let you know that you've made it to the place you were trying to go, and you'll stumble off the bus at your destination, full of delicious bus snacks. Transit days are an adventure in and of themselves.[57]

Back at home, safe and sound on your couch, you won't yet know what kinds of ridiculous overland transit adventures await you; do your best to plan out a route that makes sense, and let the rest go. I promise you'll figure it out when you get there.

Once you're neck-deep into mapping out your itinerary, it's time for you to take the most exciting step of the entire journey: you're finally ready to book your very first flight![58]

56 We'd initially had concerns about bathroom breaks or getting hungry on buses, but we needn't have worried: we found that buses stop frequently to let passengers take bathroom breaks or visit restaurants. We also discovered the joys of "bus snacks," when vendors selling home-made snacks hop onto the bus at a traffic stop or flag it down on the side of the road somewhere and walk up and down the aisles with inexpensive baskets of delicious sweet corn tamales, bags of coconut milk, or fresh fruit. Bus snacks, we learned, are even better than street food.

57 Border crossings are even more fun. One memorable crossing at La Balsa from Ecuador into Peru turned into a three-day affair involving a bus, a packed van, a rickshaw, and a "chicken truck." After three days of slowly making our way down through Ecuador's lush green hills into the rolling fields and deserts of Northern Peru, we found ourselves racing through a canyon on a perilous cliffside. This was the only time during our entire trip that I was legitimately afraid for my life — usually, I'm the only one concerned when a bus aggressively races other cars, swerves in and out of oncoming traffic, and leans terrifyingly into mountain turns; local passengers are typically completely nonplussed. So when the locals in our *collectivo* began pleading with our driver in Spanish to slow down, I knew we were screwed. When the woman seated next to me clasped her hands and started praying out loud, I was convinced this was the end. There was only one passenger in the van who was totally, blissfully chill: a rooster, seated next to me on his owner's lap, eyes closed in happiness as his owner aimlessly stroked his head with one finger. That rooster was vibin', and it gave me hope. I have done my best to channel that rooster ever since.

58 Unless you don't have a valid passport yet, in which case, skip ahead to that section and then come right back when you've got one!

I've never been very good at committing — there's always more research to be done, and more options to look into.[59] It took several months of pulling up one-way flights from San Francisco to Cartagena, Colombia, and chickening out again before finally, six months before our planned date of departure, I held my breath, sat on my hands, watched Jeremy hit "confirm," and let out a terrified shriek: it was real! We were going! Oh god, were we actually going?!?!

Jeremy spent the next 24 hours talking me out of cancelling the flight.

But booking that first flight meant we could finally start cementing our plans: shortly after, we booked our first hostel, then the next, then the next. With each booking, we took a screenshot of our confirmation and stuck it into our Trip Roadmap document, along with as many details as we could find on how to get to each spot — many hostels include helpful details online that you'll need to know, such as "tell the bus driver to drop you off on Kilometer Marker 28 and look for the large tree on the left; we're just a mile down the road on foot."

As you book and finalize your trip, include everything you've booked in your Trip Roadmap, plus as much information as you can find online: addresses, hours of operation, phone numbers, contact information, the nearest train station, screen-shots of your booking details, and so on. Not only will you inevitably need one of these crucially important pieces of information at some point during your trip, but it will also give peace of mind to everyone back home.

The final step is to share or send a copy of your Trip Roadmap to your loved ones at home, so that if you go MIA (and it's not because you're on a trek through the Himalayas or staying in a lodge in the Amazon or something awesome) they'll know who to contact to confirm that you're okay.

59 One notable exception would be my husband. All he had to do was show up to our first date in a black pleather jacket, jet-black jeans, white converse shoes, and a dark green plaid shirt. He was smoking a cigarette in this James Dean, starving art-school-student/barista sort of way, his Califor-nia-blonde hair and bright red beard glinting in the sunlight, and he gave me this great, big, friendly smile. I was *instantly* smitten. (And he quit smoking a month later without me even needing to ask!)

Ethical & Responsible Travel

When I was busy planning my year-long trip, falling in love with hostels and solving logistical problems, I didn't spend much time thinking about how my travels would affect the places I was visiting. After all, I was following along on well-trodden backpacker paths; surely I was just a drop in the bucket, one tiny part of a wave of tourists.

But during our trip, I started to notice things that didn't feel right. Like how many tours that were advertised to backpackers like me boasted of interacting directly with wild animals — letting monkeys sit on your shoulder, feeding wild sea turtles, taking a photo holding a parrot or riding an elephant. Those tours had all sounded like so much fun when I was looking them up online back at home; the animals seemed happy enough in the photos, and all I really wanted in life was to make friends with llamas and snuggle with sloths. Was it really harmless fun? Was interacting with those wild animals a deeply embedded part of local culture? Or did the wave of visitors, which I was now part of, create an entire industry that profits off of disrupting the habitats of those wild animals?

My impact on local culture and communities also wasn't something I spent much time mulling over in the planning phase of my trip. I was excited to meet locals, and I wanted my interactions with them to be "authentic" rather than a typical, canned tourist experience. I didn't stop to ask whether, by nature, "authentic" interactions between local communities and visitors are themselves a tourist experience — or whether "authenticity" through the lens of an outsider existed at all. It wasn't until I took a photo of a traditionally dressed Indigenous person in Peru and then was asked to pay for the photo I'd taken that I stopped to wonder: are locals actually standing around the square dressed up in traditional clothing because it's part of their culture and tradition, or because visitors like me want to see a spectacle of Indigenous people wearing costumes?

I didn't come up with many answers during my year-long trip, but it was the first time I started asking questions about ethical and sustainable travel: how does tourism impact local communities, environments, and cultures? Is that impact positive or negative? How can I ensure that when I travel, I am contributing positively?

In the years since my round-the-world trip, I've both joined the tourism industry and become a member of the media, complete with an audience and a platform that reaches millions of travelers each year. My role is not only to prepare those travelers to take life-changing adventures by giving them advice and tips, it's also to carefully consider the effect that travelers will have on the destinations they visit and provide education about their impact.[60] If someone visiting a destination has taken my advice in preparation for their trip, I feel a deep sense of responsibility for their actions as they travel. Understanding the impacts of tourism on local destinations is no longer just a personal curiosity; it's a critical part of my job.

Thankfully, there are a number of academic institutions dedicated to studying and answering these very questions. And so, let me briefly adjust my nerdiest pair of glasses and take a brief dive into the moral and ethical implications of travel. I know — things just got REALLY juicy.

The Impact of Travel

I've learned — and seen firsthand — that travel can be a powerful force for good: encountering different ways of living widens cultural perspectives (Maddux, W. W., Adam, H. and Galinsky, A. D. 2010) and encourages empathy and kindness. Travel has a wonderful tendency to make us better people.

Tourism can also be a vital source of economic growth and a valuable source of revenue for a community by increasing overall GDP, creating jobs, and providing opportunities for employment (Lemma, Alberto 2014).

It can even positively impact the environment by raising awareness of the value of the local environment and contributing to a desire for environmental protection, as well as directly financing conservation (Islam, Faijul. 2013). After all, if visitors are drawn to a destination's beautiful local environment, preserving that environment becomes a matter of economic importance.

---

60   This veers a little bit into "the ethics of travel blogging," but long story short, this is also why you'll never see us recommending visiting somewhere illegal, trespassing, or geotagging wilderness destinations. You will never see us stepping off a path or climbing over a barrier just to take a photo, or touching or interacting with a wild animal without an explanation of the nuances of that interaction. And if you happen to be along with us on a tour or press trip and break one of these cardinal rules, there's a good chance we'll call you out on it. When the world is watching — whether that's through a blog or on social media — it's your responsibility to act as a role model.

But tourism can just as easily bring negative consequences. Locals can be displaced to make room for tourism-related infrastructure, cultural heritage sites and native habitats can become degraded from overuse, and the carbon emissions from mass tourism are significant contributors to the warming of our planet (Lenzen, M., Sun, Y., Faturay, F., Ting, Y., Geschke, A. and Malik, A., 2018).

Mitigating your negative impact as a traveler while supporting the positive effects of travel can feel like a balancing act. The tipping point for when too much tourism shifts from being a net positive to a net negative is often described as "overtourism," an academic term that describes the phenomenon when too many tourists converge in one specific place to the point where it negatively impacts locals (Dodds, R. and Butler, R. 2019). This can lead to destabilizing economies, negative social impacts, and even civil unrest.

If you've crossed this tipping point, you won't just feel unwelcome as a visitor in these places, but you might encounter downright hostility; which makes sense, because your visit is adversely affecting the lives of locals.

Knowing where your presence will contribute to overtourism, and where your visit is more likely to have a net positive effect on the local economy, is incredibly tricky to do. But one thing that helps is to keep in mind that tourism has a life cycle.

At first, tourists to a destination are welcomed. As the number of visitors rises, the relationship becomes less euphoric and moves towards apathy. The third phase, as tourism reaches a saturation point, is irritation. The fourth phase is antagonism: residents actively push back against tourists and view them as the cause of local problems.

In other words, in places that are "up-and-coming" destinations, tourism is new and exciting and generally welcomed by local communities. But as time goes on and tourism grows, that sentiment shifts, and tourism is no longer seen as beneficial — even as locals in one major city may be protesting in the streets and demanding that tourists leave, just a few miles away there could be a smaller town that would love the opportunity to welcome tourists.

Looking at travel through this framework helps to explain why in Colombia we felt welcomed everywhere we went. Locals stopped us on the street to ask us how we were enjoying our stay, and encouraged us to share stories from our travels with friends back home so they would come visit too. Colombian locals, it seemed to us, were overjoyed to have tourists — which makes sense when you consider that Colombia has spent decades trying to shake off a characterization as a war-torn, dangerous country caught in the crosshairs of violent drug cartels. Decades later, Colombia is only just beginning to be universally recognized as a beautiful and safe place to visit — and that is an important part of reframing its identity. While Colombia is still thought of as a "dangerous" place to visit, tourists are likely to be welcomed with open arms.

By contrast, when we arrived in Cusco, Peru, where tourism comes on the back of a century of colonialist archaeological "discoveries," we felt significantly less welcomed. Tourism to Machu Picchu — with its complex legacy as both an icon of Incan heritage as well as an example of cultural commodification, cultural appropriation, and the romanticization of Indigenous culture (Ross, J. 2016) has reached a tipping point, and decades of a growing tourism industry have resulted in a worrying over-dependency on tourism. Worse, the financial benefits of tourism are leaking out of the local economy, as the money earned by tourism often does not recirculate locally, but is used instead to pay for imports required by tourists or pocketed by international corporations and foreign investors (Jönsson C. 2015). Decades of mass tourism had not only done little to resolve Peru's rampant poverty, but it had served to widen the inequality gap. No wonder local sentiment was somewhat less enthusiastic.

Without understanding the factors that led to the different experiences we had in these two countries, it was easy for us to draw a dangerously inaccurate conclusion during our trip: Colombians were inherently friendly and welcoming; Peruvians, not so much. Yikes. (Even bigger yikes: I published an ill-informed and whiny article complaining about Peru on my travel blog; it's long since been deleted, but I still feel ashamed of it to this day).

Thankfully, I now know better than to fall into the trap of making harmful generalizations, and I hope that you will too. If you catch yourself experiencing something similar during your trip, I encourage you to think critically about the way your presence may be perceived by local communities (and where those communities may fall in the tourism cycle), as well as the cultural and historical context that frames your visit. By doing so, you'll be improving your worldview, increasing your empathy, and being a more responsible traveler.

Above all, always remember that when you travel, you are a guest in someone else's home — and your presence has a real impact on local cultures, economies, and environments. Traveling responsibly means taking steps to enhance the beneficial impacts of travel, while working to mitigate its negative impacts. By personally committing to travel responsibly, you'll be an agent of positive change.

	Responsible Tourism	Irresponsible & Overtourism
Social	Increases cultural understanding between travelers and local communities Raises awareness of global issues that other communities are facing Improved infrastructure results in improved standard of living Encourages the preservation of traditional customs and fosters civic pride	Decreases quality of life in local communities Leads to the erosion of traditional cultures and values
Economic	Creates jobs and new business opportunities, especially in rural communities	Bypasses local business owners and supports multinational companies, resulting in decreased financial support for the local community Can increase local property prices and living expenses, outpricing locals from their own community
Environmental	Helps promote and fund the conservation of wildlife and natural resources through ecotourism and tourism revenue from parks and preserves Creates alternative sources of employment for those previously employed in industries with a large carbon footprint (such as deforestation)	Increased pollution through litter, increased waste and transportation emissions Threatens overuse of natural resources Exploits local environments and wildlife, causing long-term and sometimes irreversible damage

My goal is for you to keep some of these considerations in the back of your mind as you plan your trip and embark on your adventure. At the same time, remember that you are only one person and the responsibility of the entire tourism industry is not on your shoulders. Make the best decisions you can, try not to be a dick, and keep an open mind to learn more as you go.

That said, I do have a few actionable steps you can take as you plan your trip! Here are a few ways you can travel more responsibly:

- **Destinations**

When planning your itinerary, aim to include smaller or lesser known destinations in order to balance the time spent in (and impact on) more popular places.

It's easier to have a net positive impact when visiting places that are actively seeking and encouraging tourism. When visiting places experiencing overtourism, it will be harder to mitigate your negative impact.

Researching local sentiment regarding tourists will also help you determine whether your impact is more likely to be negative or positive. Traveling during the tourism off-season is also a good way to avoid contributing to overtourism when visiting popular destinations — plus, it's cheaper!

You can also choose to financially support destinations that are committed to encouraging and enforcing responsible and sustainable travel behaviors. The non-profit Global Sustainable Tourism Council maintains a list of certified sustainable destinations, and GreenDestinations.org hosts an annual awards ceremony for the top 100 sustainable destinations of the year[61]. They're both excellent places to start compiling ideas of sustainable destinations to add to your itinerary!

- **Lodging**

Accommodation will likely be your largest expense while traveling, which also means that the money you spend on accommodation also has the biggest potential economic impact.

Make staying with locals or in locally-owned businesses a priority, whether that be in a locally-owned hostel or guesthouse, an eco-lodge run by a local Indigenous community, a community homestay, or renting a private Airbnb room in a home

---

61 You can find the Global Sustainable Tourism Council Top 100 destinations on their website.

owned and lived in by a local resident.[62] Not only will you ensure that your dollars are supporting the local community, rather than giant multinational hotel chains, but your travel experience will benefit as well; local hosts can show you the hidden gems of the city and recommend where the best restaurants and hole-in-the-wall places are.

You can also direct your efforts to financially support accommodation options that focus on reducing their environmental impact, such as eco-lodges or eco-hostels, or hotels that focus on sustainability. You can search for green accommodation using BookDifferent.com or EcoHotels.com.

- **Transport**

Flights are, unfortunately, a significant source of carbon emissions which contribute to global warming. However, there are some ways to mitigate your impact. In fact, you may already be helping without realizing it. Low-cost budget airlines are typically more environmentally friendly and are often pioneers in sustainable aviation and biofuel development[63]. They're not necessarily doing it out of the goodness of their hearts — fuel efficiency means better profit margins — but still, it's a win-win.

Whenever you fly, you should consider offsetting your carbon footprint. Purchasing a carbon offset for a 10-hour flight costs around $15-$30 and goes towards funding a sustainable project, like one that captures carbon (such as planting trees) or reduces the release of more carbon emissions (such as a renewable energy project in a rural community).

Some flight booking platforms will offer you the option to offset when booking your ticket, but you can also calculate your carbon emissions and buy an offset from a third party such as Cool Effect or Sustainable Travel.

Once you arrive at your intended destination, try to reduce your carbon footprint by

---

62 A quick note on Airbnb: depending on the destination, Airbnb can be either a fantastic way for a local resident to earn extra cash, or a disruption to the local housing supply and economy which contributes to gentrification and displacement. In other places, it may be completely illegal. Before you book an Airbnb, do some research to evaluate local sentiment. I typically start by Googling "Airbnb controversy [destination]," which usually pulls up a few local news articles about protests, pushback or legal battles if any exist. When in doubt, stick with a private room in an occupied home, as that ensures your money is going to a local resident and not disrupting the housing supply.

63 Budget-friendly Norwegian Airlines is one of the pioneers of sustainable aviation — and one of my all-time favorite airlines. Read more about their commitment to responsible tourism here: norwegian.com/us/about/experience-us/responsible-travel/

traveling overland and using public ground transportation whenever possible. It's not only more environmentally friendly, but it will stretch your travel budget further.

- **Reducing Waste**

As you travel, make an effort to reduce waste wherever you go to minimize your travel footprint.

An easy place to start is with water: in many places without drinkable tap water, you'll need to buy a never-ending supply of plastic water bottles to stay hydrated (and most of those countries don't have recycling infrastructure). To reduce your plastic bottle waste, bring a sturdy reusable water bottle and a water sterilization solution such as a SteriPen, a small, rechargeable device that kills bacteria with UV light. You'll also save money — during our trip, the SteriPen paid for itself after a month of daily use![64]

Likewise, bring a few sustainable solutions with you to help reduce waste, like a long-lasting shampoo bar rather than a heavy plastic bottle,[65] a small container for restaurant leftovers, a reusable bag for shopping (doesn't have to be fancy; a balled-up plastic bag does the trick), or a washable cloth to use as a handkerchief or napkin.

I've found that it's easier to reduce waste on the road when everything you own must fit into your backpack and everything you have ends up being multi-use. Our food tupperware was a critical piece of our travel kitchen and our travel towel did triple duty as a cleaning rag and napkin. By the time we returned home again, we'd gotten so used to minimizing waste that we started transitioning towards a zero-waste household. For example, we haven't purchased paper towels since we got back from our trip!

- **Indigenous Tourism**

---

64 Another favorite water purification device that I use frequently is a LifeStraw Water Bottle. It lets me drink water from the tap (or a dirty puddle on the ground, if I'm really desperate) but it has no ability to purify water for cleaning, which can be a downside for long-term travelers who like to raw fresh fruits and veggies.

65 Shampoo and conditioner bars are fantastically travel-friendly! They never spill or leak, no plastic waste, and they last for ages. My favorites are made by LUSH. Just don't forget a container to store them in — an old plastic tub works just fine, and LUSH also sells reusable aluminum containers.

When visiting an area with Indigenous communities[66], you may want to seek out opportunities for Indigenous tourism, which can be an excellent way to learn about and support marginalized communities. But before doing so, it's important to carefully consider who your visit will actually benefit: you, or the Indigenous community? Reflect on your intentions so as not to tokenize Indigenous peoples; "primitivist" tourism is damaging, even with the best of intentions.

Likewise, Indigenous peoples should not be a selling point or commodity. While an Indigenous-owned community or cultural center is a fantastic and responsible resource for learning about and supporting the community, be wary of attractions that advertise or cover Indigenous history or culture but are not created by or in partnership with the local community, because "Indigenous people may or may not have much agency in how that interaction transpires and how much profit they directly derive." (MacCarthy, M., 2020). An easy-to-remember rule of thumb to follow is "nothing about us, without us."

That said, in other cases, tourism may be embraced by Indigenous communities as an opportunity for economic development and cultural expression. Book Indigenous-owned and run tour companies whenever you can, especially when you're looking to experience and learn about those Indigenous communities.

On the flip side, don't just barge in. Entering an Indigenous community without a guided tour or an invitation can be seen as an invasion of privacy, denying their dignity and respect, and reducing a community to objects of the "tourist gaze." Instead, book a guided tour to ensure that you are financially supporting the community and giving them full agency[67]. Also keep your eyes open for Indigenous-owned businesses, artisan markets, or tour companies to support during your travels!

- **Ethical Animal Tourism**

There are many ways animal lovers can responsibly enjoy wildlife, while ensuring the humane treatment of animals is the top priority.

As a rule of thumb, always avoid directly interacting with wild animals in their natural habitats. All wild animals should be observed from a distance, and every

66 Native-Land.ca has an interactive map that you can use to find out which Indigenous communities live in the areas where you are traveling.

67 To find a vetted and responsible tour or homestay created and led by Indigenous communities, you can book multi-day tours through an organization like TreadRight or VisitNatives.

care should be taken not to disrupt their natural habitat. That includes never feeding, touching, petting, or capturing wild animals, as this can harm wildlife, create unsafe dependencies and attitudes towards humans, and in some cases even result in an animal's death.

There are many attractions that promise a closer experience with captive animals. Many of those tours or attractions use words like "sanctuary" or "rescue," or claim to give back to conservation efforts. And while some may be telling the truth, it's smart to be skeptical; too often, those terms are no more than marketing buzzwords. It can be hard to tell, but it helps to see if they partner with any reputable wildlife conservation organizations or if they are accredited by professional associations.

To determine whether an attraction is treating animals ethically, consider whether what is being done is for the benefit of the animals, or whether the animals are being made to do things outside of their natural behavior for the benefit of visitors.[68] Steer clear of any organization that advertises animals doing shows, tricks, rides or any behavior that is unnatural for that animal. Ask yourself, "Would this animal be doing this in the wild?"

Another red flag is when an attraction advertises a lot of physical touching as part of the experience, such as petting a dolphin, holding a tied-up alligator, or riding an elephant — that can be physically painful as well as incredibly stressful for the animal. Controlling the animal in any way so that visitors can take a photo with them is also a huge red flag, as that kind of unusual behavior typically involves cruel training techniques or drugs.

To avoid these kinds of unethical animal attractions, do your due diligence before patronizing a tour or attraction that involves animals. Browse through the attraction's website and read multiple online reviews to look for:

- Photos taken with animals

- Evidence of visitors touching, holding, or feeding animals

---

68 An extra layer of nuance comes into play when animal captivity is part of the traditions or cultures of certain Indigenous communities, such as elephants in captivity in Nepal which are used by local Indigenous communities to safely travel through the jungle or to grow food, or reindeer herding in the Sámi Indigenous communities of Northern Europe. Personally, I do my best to weigh these experiences carefully in their greater cultural context rather than passing judgement on them through the lens of my cultural expectations.

- Advertising experiences with baby animals (this may indicate breeding, and young animals should never be interacting with crowds or separated from their mothers)

Ultimately, if you've done your research, you can only do so much. On several occasions, we found ourselves on tours we originally thought were ethical, only for our tour guide to start tossing food to wild animals to bring them closer, or picking up animals to show visitors. If this happens, don't beat yourself up about it — but don't participate, either. Speak up if you feel comfortable doing so, or post a review online afterwards letting other travelers know this experience is not ethically or responsibly treating animals. Tourist demand has a huge impact on the way these tours are conducted, and a negative comment or negative press online can drive real change — but at the same time, please don't let your guilt keep you up at night. We all make mistakes, and it's how we learn!

If you're interested in learning more about responsible travel, I'd encourage you to spend some time diving into Impact Travel Alliance, a global community and nonprofit whose goal is to improve the world through travel. They are focused on education, advocacy and community-building around sustainable tourism, and are a wonderful resource of thoughtful and informative articles as well as community events organized by chapters of travelers worldwide.

Crossing Your I's and Dotting Your T's

O nce your itinerary has taken shape, you've booked a few things, and you're approaching your departure date, it's time to tackle a whole new set of logistics: all the stuff you have to take care of before you leave for your trip.

Those last few months will be a scrambled blur of to-do lists, last-minute freak-outs, and forcing yourself to take care of mundane tasks involving paperwork and other incredibly unexciting things.

But even though it's one of the least exciting and enjoyable parts of long-term travel, neglecting all the odds and ends you're leaving behind means giving yourself a giant mess to deal with while you travel (which distracts you from actually enjoying yourself), or worse, an even bigger mess to deal with when you come home again. Coming home from a trip is already hard enough without leaving yourself logistical nightmares to puzzle through!

But even with the best of intentions, it's difficult to know where to start. In this section, we'll cover all the things you'll need to take care of before you leave, along with crucial mistakes to avoid.

Get a Passport

Before you can even book your first flight, you'll need to get a passport. This process takes about ten weeks, so allow yourself a few months to ensure you're not scrambling last minute (or you'll end up paying a hefty rush delivery fee).

If you already have a passport, you'll need to make sure that it will be valid for the entire time you are planning on being away, PLUS six months. Many countries will not admit you if your passport will expire within six months. Is it a needlessly specific rule? Yes. Could you end up stuck in a foreign country if you don't follow the rule? Also yes. If you're cutting it close, play it safe and renew your passport.

If you are applying for a passport for the first time, you will need to schedule an in-person appointment at a passport acceptance facility[69], like a post office, public library or AAA office. You can find a detailed description of the passport application and renewal processes on the U.S. State Department's website. The most important thing to know is that you'll be taking pictures which you won't have a chance to update for another ten years, so run a comb through your hair and make it count.

Not only is your passport a ticket into a foreign country, but it has a fun second job: collecting border entry and exit stamps! I love collecting those little stamps — it's like a tiny scrapbook of travel memories. Except unlike a regular scrapbook, if I lose it, I'm screwed!

Apply for Entry Visas

Although most of the countries we visited granted us tourist visas at customs when we crossed the border, certain countries do require visitors to apply (and pay) for tourist visas in advance, which depends on everything from the country on your Passport to your intended length of stay. Don't forget this step, or you'll be turned away at the border! When creating your Trip Roadmap, I recommend indicating which of those visas you'll need to apply for to make this step easier — U.S. citizens can find visa information by country on the Travel.state.gov website.[70]

Buy Travel Insurance

I am a walking disaster. I am clumsy, forgetful, scatterbrained, and generally prone to mishaps. But up until a few years ago, I had never purchased travel insurance in my life. I'd never even heard of it. But after filing multiple insurance claims during our year-long honeymoon, we now refuse to travel without it.

---

69   Check out our Resources section for more details about where and how to apply.

70   While you're at it, you might as well sign up for the Smart Travelers Enrollment Program! The program will let the local U.S. Embassy know about your visit. You'll receive important information from the Embassy about safety conditions in your destination country, as well as enable the Embassy to contact you in the event of a natural disaster, civil unrest, or even a family emergency.

"But Lia," you might be thinking, "you're clearly just cursed with terrible traveler's luck. Surely a normal person can make it an entire year without needing travel insurance, right?"

Well, before you jump to that conclusion, let's take a trip into my anxious brain, which is forever working on fun and exciting worst-case scenarios. Let's imagine that you're off on the trip of your life, having an amazing time somewhere far-away, tropical, and stunning. You're being completely safe and taking all the right precautions: you're not going out alone at night, you're only drinking bottled water, you said no to the guy on the street who offered you "cheap headache medicine," and so on and so forth.

But then, something beyond your control happens: despite all of those precautions, you twist your ankle, you get food poisoning, your travel companion runs a scooter into a tree in a monkey forest in Bali... you know, things that could happen to anybody, probably (okay, fine — I might be slightly more accident-prone than the typical traveler).

Without travel insurance, those scenarios look a little like this: you try to figure out how to get yourself to a doctor, but you aren't really sure where to find one. Thankfully, your incident happened somewhere that you actually have internet or phone service (wow, that was incredibly lucky).

You find yourself Googling "doctor" and "clinic" in the local language, but everything on Google Maps and TripAdvisor looks like it might be closed... or for animals only, maybe?

Then you realize you're not even sure if your health insurance covers a doctor in a foreign country. You struggle through crappy WiFi trying to log into your health-care provider's website (what the heck is your password again?!). It would be easier to just call their helpline, but it's 3am back home and you really need help, like, now.

You know what? Screw it. You hop in a random taxi and ask your driver to take you to the nearest doctor (aren't you glad you wasted an hour Googling the local word for doctor??). You're taken to somewhere that wasn't even on Google Maps and you just have to trust that this taxi driver knows more about local healthcare providers than an algorithm and a 10-year-old forum discussion on TripAdvisor, Reddit, or the Rick Steves website (oh my gosh, how much time did you waste searching for local doctors instead of getting help!?!).[71]

---

71 For anyone currently playing out this nightmare scenario and wondering what to do, Travel Insurance providers will help you find the nearest clinic and get there safely.

Let's also imagine another complication: say you're diagnosed with an ear infection, but your flight leaves tomorrow. You'll have to extend your stay until the medication clears it up, which means you'll be paying for the additional hotel nights, the rescheduling fee for your flights, AND all of your treatment and medication — including a painful shot in the butt.

Or maybe there's a freak blizzard which cancels your flight, costing you your hotel fee AND the cost of booking a hotel to stay in until the snow clears up, plus whatever tours or activities you had booked (incidentally, this is also the story of our recent trip to Canada).

Or maybe your phone gets snatched out of your hand, or your luggage goes missing.

Or maybe it's not even something that happens to you: maybe something happens to somebody back home, and you need to hop on a plane right away. Like when my beloved 95-year-old grandfather was unexpectedly put into hospice care, so we canceled several months of our trip in order to fly home and care for him... only to find out he was faking his own imminent death. (It's a bizarre but true story, which we tell with great relish on our podcast — Jeremy does a great Grandpa Bob impression — but long story short, that crafty old man spent six months on bed rest eating junk food and making people wait on him hand and foot before being kicked off of hospice, and as of this writing he is 97 years young and in fantastic health). You're on the hook for last-minute flights, plus non-refundable or already paid-for hotels, tours and transportation fees.

In case you couldn't tell, all of the above has happened to us on various trips over the years. Our travel insurance policies almost always end up paying for themselves, making them well worth both our peace of mind and the cost of the policy!

And honestly, we've been lucky. None of our (many) incidents and mishaps thus far have been life-threatening. We've never needed to be airlifted to a hospital, sent back home for intensive care, or any of the other more serious things that travel insurance covers.

When it comes down to it, if you can afford to travel, you can't afford NOT to buy travel insurance. Considering the fact that you may or may not be able to find a health insurance plan to cover you while you're away, your travel insurance also may become your primary healthcare coverage.[72]

---

72 U.S. healthcare plans vary by state and, it seems, by year. If you're currently covered by your employer, a COBRA plan can be a good option; if not, public healthcare is sometimes available, and also sometimes incredibly expensive. The year we left, there was no penalty for not having health insurance (some states weren't offering public healthcare at all) so we relied on travel insurance to cover us in the event of a health emergency, and considered COBRA a backup plan that we thankfully didn't end up needing.

There are a number of travel insurance providers out there, and while coverage varies, here's a fairly standard list of what most (decent) policies should cover.

- **Medical and Dental Coverage:** This is one of the biggest benefits of travel insurance. If you get sick or injured while traveling, travel insurance will cover you to get the care you need — and help you find health care providers wherever you are in the world. A good policy typically includes just about everything: hospitals, doctors, medication, and even evacuation or an air-lift if you injure yourself somewhere remote or can't get yourself to the hospital.

- **Trip Cancellation or Interruption:** If you need to cancel your trip for a covered reason, or cut your trip short, you'll be covered for all non-refundable expenses. But be sure to familiarize yourself with what's covered: things like sudden illness or a death in the family are covered, but things like losing your nerve, getting talked into staying by your boss, or backing out of your trip at the last minute because shit got real are not. That said, if you're still on the fence about your trip, some providers do offer "cancel for any reason" or "cancel for work" policies.

- **Theft and Lost Items:** If your belongings get stolen or lost while traveling, most travel insurance policies will help you replace them up to a certain amount. This typically doesn't cover expensive gear, so if you're toting around a bunch of expensive camera stuff or technical equipment, you'll want to buy a separate policy to cover them.

- **Lost, Damaged or Delayed Baggage:** This policy typically covers the cost of replacing lost or damaged luggage, as well as all the stuff in your bags. There's usually a fairly restrictive limit, though, so I recommend carrying valuables or electronics in your carry-on just to be safe.

- **Weather-Related Delays:** If you've ever experienced a canceled or delayed flight due to weather, you probably already found out that most airlines won't help you out (which is my least favorite airline policy, second only to ridiculous baggage size restrictions). But with travel insurance, you'll typically be covered for everything from a place to stay to missed reservations to rescheduling fees.

- **Unexpected Company Bankruptcies:** This is certainly less likely than a lot of the other issues on this list, but it does happen. If you've booked a tour, flight, cruise, and so on and the company you paid suddenly goes under, you could be left high and dry — unless you have travel insurance, of course.

- **Death**: It's not exactly fun to think about, but travel insurance will help get you — or, er, whatever's left of you — back home to your family to make arrangements.

There are some limits on what travel insurance won't cover, like your own poor decision making (including experimenting with things that aren't strictly legal) or nervousness about issues that haven't actually happened yet. You'll also want to get specific insurance to cover any expensive gear, jewelry, or electronics you'll be bringing with you (or better yet, if you don't really need it, just leave it at home).

There's also usually a pre-existing condition clause, so if you have health conditions, you'll want to read carefully through the fine print on your policy to determine whether you'll be covered or not. But before you write this off thinking you don't have any pre-existing conditions, think again! Have you been treated within the past two years for literally anything that might rear its ugly head again in a way that could affect your trip? If so, you might actually have a pre-existing condition you didn't even think of as a pre-existing condition. If you have a recurring or even occasional condition that may affect your trip, be sure to research this clause before booking.

Many travel insurance providers also refuse to cover medical issues resulting from unusually risky "adventure travel" activities. Which, sure, that seems fair. Why should, say, an extreme snowboarder or habitual skydiver get the same kind of coverage as a traveler like, say, my mom, who once tripped over a rock in Hawaii and broke her little toe? (And yes, that WOULD be where I inherited my clumsy gene.)

Unfortunately, it gets a little tricky in the small print. Certain travel insurance providers have a conservative approach to what's considered "extreme." For instance, one well-known travel insurance provider that shall remain un-recommended won't cover any snorkeling-related injuries.

I don't know about you, but I'm a generally terrified and anxious person, and I consider snorkeling to be a relaxing, enjoyable, low-risk activity. I would never have thought to double-check snorkelling. If you're even a mildly adventurous traveler, you'll want to double check this policy before booking. World Nomads, one of the most popular travel insurance providers — and the one we chose for our year-long trip — is designed for adventurous travelers and is a popular choice among backpackers specifically for its wide-ranging adventure travel coverage.

Travel insurance also isn't designed to replace standard medical care, including preventative care — most people just aren't traveling long enough to really need it. But there are exceptions, such as the annual travel insurance policy from Safety-Wing, which was designed specifically for digital nomads and long-term travelers. If SafetyWing had existed when we took our trip, we probably would have gone with them for our travel insurance coverage![73]

When you're evaluating travel insurance providers, I recommend looking for the following:

- **Must cover the basics.** At a bare minimum, any halfway decent travel insurance policy should cover unexpected medical expenses while traveling, lost and stolen luggage, trip cancellation and interruption, and emergency evacuation or repatriation. If that's not all included in a policy, I wouldn't book it.

- **Clear, transparent information about what is and isn't covered.** Surprises: great for keeping a marriage exciting, terrible for travel insurance. The last thing I want is to find out that a once-in-a-lifetime experience isn't covered — after I already booked it. I'm seeking clear, easy answers to the question "what's covered?" and I don't want to have to look hard to find it.

- **Easy-to-find pricing information available online.** I don't want to have to call and talk to someone to get a quote. I hate talking to people on the phone. I don't want someone to "sell" me on their services. Just put the whole thing online so I can evaluate it in the comfort of my own home, quietly and anti-socially.

- **Reviews and positive experiences from other travelers.** I don't even book a hostel or visit a restaurant if there aren't enough positive reviews,

---

73 Another huge plus for SafetyWing: they're one of the very few travel insurance providers we've found that covers pandemics, including COVID-19.

much less a travel insurance policy! If a quick Google search or Facebook post finds more negative feedback about a travel insurance provider than positive, I'm out. That said, angry customers are typically more vocal than delighted ones, so I do try to balance out my research and keep that in mind.

- **Coverage for your specific needs**. This might include travel companion coverage for your partner or your children, home country coverage (some travel insurance only covers you if you're abroad, or a certain distance from home), and specific destination or country limitations.

The two travel insurance providers I recommended, World Nomads and Safety-Wing, meet all of the above criteria and are a fantastic fit for us as adventurous, frequent travelers (who often find themselves in a pickle). They're also both excellent options for backpacker travel insurance.

With all of that said, if you do want to roll the dice on your long-term trip — which I highly, HIGHLY discourage doing — there are ways to help yourself if you do get sick while traveling. You can contact the local Embassy for a list of local doctors and medical facilities, or search a list of English-speaking foreign doctors in the International Association for Medical Assistance to Travelers for the price of a voluntary donation (the organization is a non-profit).

However, you'll be stuck footing the bill for taking your chances. And in my experience, travel insurance on a long-term trip is well worth the extra expense.

Visit Your Doctor

When I marched into my doctor's office and informed her, with grandiose importance, that I was soon leaving for a Very Big Adventure, she was like, "Super cool. But what do you need, exactly?"

I had no idea. She was a doctor; I was a 24-year-old wearing a paper robe whose professional life involved selecting Hello Kitty T-shirts for small children. I'd always assumed doctors just knew everything. They didn't usually ask me what I wanted, like I was ordering from a menu.

I didn't realize that medical recommendations for destinations are available for travelers to reference online. If I had pulled together a list of the recommended vaccines and medications based on the countries I was considering visiting in advance, I could have saved a whole lot of sitting around in my doctor's office in one of those miserable, freezing cold paper robes while we Googled travel vaccines together (or, even better, I could have gone to a travel clinic, which specializes in travel vaccines and medications).[74]

Here is what I know now: you'll need to be up-to-date on all routine vaccines before heading off on your trip. These include your childhood vaccines as well as fun grown-up vaccines, like a tetanus booster and the annual flu shot. Check with your doctor to see what routine vaccines you may be due for depending on your age and vaccine history.[75] Some common vaccines, such as Hepatitis B, require several weeks or multiple shots to become active, so plan ahead!

Of course, I didn't, so I was missing my final round of shots when I left. I lived to tell the tale, but I'm not going to pretend it didn't keep me up at night worrying. To keep you healthy and worry-free, you'll find a Vaccine Checklist in the References section at the end of the book to review with your doctor.

Depending on where you're going and what activities you have in mind, non-routine vaccines may be required or recommended. And you could be prevented from entering certain countries without proof of your vaccination history, such as an International Certificate of Vaccination or Prophylaxis for yellow fever.[76]

In addition to vaccines, you'll need to be aware when traveling to destinations where you'll be at risk for mosquito-borne illnesses like malaria, dengue and Zika. If you are traveling to high-risk areas for malaria (you'll find a map on the CDC website) you'll want to bring enough anti-malarial pills with you to cover your entire trip. There are several different options for anti-malarial drugs, all of which are prescription only. Each has different rules to follow and varying pros and cons, so to make things easy for you (and your doctor), we've organized them into a tidy table, which you'll find in the References section.

---

74   You can find a travel clinic using the International Society of Travel Medicine's Online Clinic Directory.

75   An up-to-date list of routine vaccines can be found on the Center for Disease Control website.

76   Yellow fever is an important one for a lot of destinations, but the yellow fever vaccine is not frequently stocked at most clinics. Book an appointment well in advance and let them know what you need so they can order the vaccine.

Unfortunately, no antimalarial drug is 100% effective, so you will need to combine taking antimalarial medications with personal protective measures. The best ways to prevent these diseases are to use an effective insect repellent[77], wear long pants and long sleeves, and use an insecticide-treated mosquito net when not sleeping in a mosquito-free setting.

If you're a coast-dweller like me, you'll likely need to ask for an altitude sickness medication as well. There are two drugs that can help alleviate the symptoms of altitude sickness and help your body acclimate to high altitudes (acetazolamide/ Diamox and dexamethasone/Decadron/DexPak). Make sure you understand how to take them properly, as you may need to begin before you plan to ascend to a higher altitude.

If you take any other pills, over-the-counter or otherwise, you'll want to bring as much of it as you can along with you, and keep it in your carry-on luggage, sealed in its original container with the original label and prescription to prove to customs officials that none of the contents have been tampered with and you have medical permission to carry such drugs.

Unfortunately, many medications have limits to the number of doses that can be handed out on request. If you can't get enough of a certain medication to cover your entire trip, ask your doctor to provide extra prescriptions with both the U.S. name for the medication and its generic name (pharmacists overseas may not recognize U.S. drug names).

However, many pharmacies will only accept prescriptions written by one of their country's doctors, so you'll need to visit a local clinic or doctor to show them the prescription you've brought with you and ask for the same or an equivalent medication. To avoid scrambling, work medication top-ups into your itinerary, so you'll be in a city or somewhere that you can easily find options for local clinics. And don't forget to save the receipt for your travel insurance provider — although you may find that many medications are significantly cheaper abroad than they are in the States!

Even if you're only bringing over-the-counter medications with you, you'll want to do a quick check to see what's banned in your destination countries (for example, Vicks and Sudafed are banned in Japan and Adderall is heavily restricted in Europe). Don't try to get clever and ship medication from abroad, either: it's su-

---

77   I have a lot of opinions on this, which we'll discuss in the Packing chapter.

per illegal and can result in huge fines or even jail. Also, do not share medication while abroad — sharing Adderall in Europe, for instance, can get you arrested!

If your required medications are banned, check whether a letter from your doctor will allow you to enter the country with your medication (if you can't find information online, check with the local embassy). The letter from your doctor (on letterhead) should include:

- Medicine name (including its generic name)

- Statement that the medicine is not a narcotic and that you (full name) is carrying X amount of the medicine (boxes, grams, etc.) to last X number of months/weeks.

- Statement that the medicine is necessary for your condition (name the condition), and that you cannot go without it during your travels abroad

Other important things to discuss with your doctor could include any physical limitations that you may need to account for in your travels, getting a signed piece of paper that says you're fit to travel, and reviewing any tests or check-ups coming due that you may need to reschedule for either before or after your trip. Get a full physical, schedule your annual check-up, get your teeth cleaned, and give yourself the cleanest bill of health that you can; depending on your insurance policy or travel situation, you may have to go without most basic preventative care for the duration of your trip.

Collect Important Documents

I honestly don't know if I would have bothered with this step if my parents hadn't been such nags about it. My document filing system consists of a box labeled "important documents." Whenever something official-looking comes in the mail, I just toss it in there and hope for the best.

But my parents were both insistent and passive-aggressive at the same time, in a way that only parents are capable of. They kept sending me articles with titles like "Why You Need a Living Will" and "Travelers' Remains Found on Beach: If Only They'd Remembered to Send their Parents a Copy of their Travel Insurance Policy Before Leaving."

It was an effective strategy.

And so, even though we never bothered to fill out a prenup, Jeremy and I did spend a romantic evening together creating Living Wills and coming up with cutesy ideas for burial ceremonies (we'd like to have our ashes mixed together and then planted with a baby redwood tree).[78]

We also filled out Power of Attorney forms, so that in the event that both of us were attacked by a rabid llama and incapacitated, someone we trusted would be able to make medical and financial decisions on our behalf.

We then shipped off the whole packet of doomsday papers to the members of our family who we'd entrusted with carrying out our rabid-llama-attack-and-subsequent-death wishes, who I'm sure filed them away in their very own Important Documents boxes, never to be looked at again.

As annoying as my parents were about the morbid paperwork I needed to fill out in preparation for my own demise, they were right: you'll be far away from home and doing potentially risky things. It's a good idea to set up a plan for what you'd like to happen in the event of an emergency, and give that plan to the people you trust to carry it out.

While you don't need a lawyer to draw up the paperwork — the free options you'll find by Googling "Living Will Template" or "Power of Attorney Forms" will do just fine — you will need to find a notary to make things official. Start with your bank, most provide free notary public services to their customers. AAA also offers reasonably priced notary services — chances are you'll be visiting AAA anyway to get your passport photos or an International Driving Permit,[79] so you might as well make a day of it.

---

78 A Living Will is only one type of "Advance Directive" document. An advance directive encompasses a legally binding set of orders concerning your wishes surrounding future medical care. The document will come into play in the case of severe medical situations in which you're not able to communicate your wishes or make decisions, and should explain your preferences regarding specific medical treatments, resuscitation efforts and life-sustaining efforts. If you have strong opinions about what you'd like to happen to you in those circumstances, you'll want to fill out and file these documents before you leave. We've included suggestions for free websites you can use to create your own Living Will and Power of Attorney forms in the "Resources" section of this book.

79 Some countries require you to have an International Driving Permit in order to rent or drive a car, so if you're planning a road trip, do your research in advance to see whether you'll need one. They're easy to obtain at your nearest AAA and fairly inexpensive.

There are a few more documents to pull together before you leave, but don't worry, you won't need to schlep around a bunch of papers. Although there are a few you'll want to have on you at all times, most of your important documents can be scanned and uploaded somewhere secure.

Important Documentation to Bring With You[80]

Although you'll need to have your physical passport with you on your person most of the time while you travel, it's also a good idea to make a hard copy of your passport and keep it separately from your physical passport in case the original gets lost or stolen. Without a passport, you could be stuck at a border and even denied entry into your home country, but having a physical and digital copy of your passport will help you make a police report if needed and file for a replacement. (Important side note: If your passport is lost or stolen overseas, contact the nearest U.S. embassy or consulate ASAP. Passports that are reported missing are immediately deactivated, so someone else can't use your passport illegally.)

In addition to a physical copy of your passport, there are a few health-related documents you may need. Certain countries require travelers to get specific vaccines, and a very small number also require travelers to show a vaccination certificate before they are allowed to enter the country. The most common of these is a Yellow Fever card, which should be given to you when you get your Yellow Fever vaccination.[81] Always check the CDC website for the most up-to-date information on required vaccines.

Finally, if you have a pre-existing condition, include a signed note from your doctor stating you are fit to travel. This will come in handy if you end up needing to use your travel insurance, as some popular insurance providers have clauses affecting pre-existing conditions. Because I have a heart condition and a pacemaker, I asked my cardiologist for a signed note stating that I was perfectly healthy with no suggested travel limitations, which they were happy to sign.

Important Documentation to Scan and Keep Digitally

Most of the important documents that you'll be scanning and keeping digitally will only be needed if something terrible happens to you, which of course, it probably won't — but do it anyway, just in case.

---

80 You'll find an Important Documents Checklist in the References section at the end of this book.

81 Yellow Fever is found in some places in South America and sub-Saharan Africa. The CDC website has lots of info.

Hang on though — don't just start scanning and uploading pictures of your birth certificate to Facebook! It's very important to take precautions that will keep your personal information safe and avoid identity theft.

Personally, I recommend using Dropbox: it's free and easy to use, very secure, and you can protect your files with a password.

I already mentioned your passport, which you'll want to keep a scanned copy of. You'll also want to make a digital copy of your birth certificate, marriage license if applicable, social security card, and driver's license.

Upload a copy of your traveler's insurance documents in there too, as well as anything else that you might need in the event of a health crisis or theft (passwords to log into your bank account? Details your credit card company might need to send a replacement card?). And of course, be sure to include a copy of your travel itinerary document.

Once all your digital documents are compiled neatly in one secure online location, share the link and password with a select few trusted loved ones — and let them know that they'll probably never need it.

Prepare Your Cell Phone

The summer we left for our trip came to be known by a significant portion of nerds as the summer of Pokemon Go. All over the world, humankind was out exploring cities, cell phones in hand, battling invisible monsters together and singing Kumbaya.

Or at least that's how it felt to us whenever we checked Facebook.

I have never had such bad FOMO in my entire life. I wanted to play Pokemon Go so bad! It felt like a cruel joke that I was flying around the world but wouldn't be able to reap the arbitrary benefits of capturing Pokemon that were specific to certain parts of the world. At one point, we sat outside on a street corner in the Galapagos Islands, attempting to load the game fruitlessly on terrible free WiFi so we could capture a single virtual critter.

By the time we returned from our trip, the world had moved on. We're still playing the game four years later, but I have nothing but regret when I think about what could have been. I could have had, like, SO many cool Pokemon.

And to think, all of that misery and pain could have been avoided if we'd just sprung for a plan with data!

Sure, sure, Pokemon Go isn't exactly the main benefit of having the internet at your fingertips wherever you are, but you never know what will take the world by storm while you're offline! You wouldn't want to miss out on like, a hilarious viral meme, right?! (I've definitely outed myself as a complete nerd, haven't I?)

All jokes aside, it was somewhat jarring to miss out on what everyone else was talking about because we weren't idly scrolling reddit, Facebook and Instagram each day like we usually do. We missed a whole year of American pop culture, not to mention that we were traveling during a presidential election year — and if that's not the time to stay glued to the news cycle, then I don't know when is.

The good news is that if none of that matters to you, chances are you can save a lot of money on your phone plan by just switching your phone to airplane mode and using free WiFi that's available pretty much everywhere.

You'll also need to either downgrade your plan, cancel it entirely, or put it on hold. Putting your phone plan on hold will typically cost a small monthly fee, but you won't lose access to your old phone number and you'll be able to resume service easily once you return home. Call your service provider to ask for the specifics. And don't forget to let your loved ones know that your phone will be offline!

For those of us who do want to stay connected, your choices will depend heavily on whether you have a locked or unlocked phone.[82]

- **Option One: Unlock your phone and buy prepaid local SIM cards as you travel.**

Most phone providers will unlock your phone for you upon request as long as the phone has already been fully paid for — you just need to call customer service and ask.

If you have the ability to unlock your phone, then you'll be able to purchase inexpensive prepaid SIM cards in each new country as you travel. You'll simply

---

82 If you can't unlock your phone, before you commit to using an old flip phone you found at the thrift store, make sure to check whether it will work in your destination countries. At the risk of sounding like I'm making up gibberish technical terms, due to technical variations, some phones — especially older Sprint and Verizon phones — may not support something called "quad-band GSM," which is what you may need while abroad. Read through the user manual (or, because nobody saves those, just Google it) or call your phone provider's customer support to ask.

remove your existing cell company's SIM card (and put it somewhere extremely safe where you won't lose it), then pop in a prepaid SIM card purchased from a local company once you arrive in your destination. Like magic, you'll have full access to your phone again — and a shiny new international number.

Using prepaid SIM cards is by far the cheapest option for using your phone abroad. Most prepaid SIM cards will cost somewhere in the ballpark of $20 for a month, which includes enough credit for calls, texts, and 3G or 4G data — although sometimes there will be limits on certain activities like browsing the internet or texting.

Once you run out of credit, you can top up your prepaid plan by recharging via the company's website, their app, or using a code purchased at a local shop or market.

But this is where things can get a little tricky. Depending on where you are in the world, there's a big variability in how and where you can get a SIM card. Depending on the country, it can take anywhere from a few minutes to several days to receive a local SIM card. In Australia and Nepal, for example, you can purchase and activate a prepaid SIM card at a local mobile company within ten minutes. However, in Germany, it can take up to a week to verify your identification documents. And in South America, purchasing a SIM card or topping up your plan with credit at a store, gas station, or roadside cart is extremely easy, but activation may take an hour or two, during which time there's a good chance you'll have no idea what's going on, especially if your Spanish classes didn't cover techno-jargon.

Long story short, purchasing a local prepaid SIM card may only be worth it if you are staying abroad in a country or region for a longer period of time — it's not worth the hassle for a short stay, but well worth it if you'll be bopping around the country for several weeks.

- **Option Two: Unlock your phone and buy a global SIM card.**

The middle option, in terms of pricing, is a global SIM card, which can be used worldwide and allows you to switch between a U.S. number and foreign numbers. Incoming text and calls are usually free, regardless of where you or they are on the globe.

You can choose from a variety of prepaid plans, including pay-as-you-go or pay per gigabyte of data used. This option is easier than purchasing SIM cards in each country you visit, especially if you'll be visiting a lot of countries, and it's significantly cheaper than buying an international roaming plan with your current cell phone carrier.

Before you commit, you'll just need to make sure you'll have coverage wherever you're going. Global SIM card providers worth taking a look at include World-SIM, OneSimCard, Telestial, and Google Fi.

- **Option Three: Keep your phone provider and pay for an international roaming package.**

If you're unable to get your phone unlocked, you still have a couple of options. The easiest, but by far most expensive solution is to purchase an international roaming package for the duration of your trip from your current provider.

First and most importantly, you have to actually call your phone provider and change your plan — your plan won't automatically change when you show up in another country and start using your phone! If you skip this step, you'll get charged thousands of dollars for every millisecond you spend idly scrolling on Instagram or Snapchatting your grandma. I can't stress this enough — it is an incredibly expensive step to skip.

Your phone provider will probably have an option for an international monthly plan or pay-as-you-go daily rates, which are definitely overpriced, but sort of reasonable if you'll only be using your phone for emergencies.

If you're the kind of person who doesn't spend any time on their phone, like my mom — bless her Luddite heart — go ahead and use a pay-as-you-go plan. Just make sure you turn your phone to airplane mode and only turn on your data when you really need it. Most of the time, you'll be able to take advantage of free or paid WiFi, which can be found across the world, everywhere from hostels to cafes to train stations. In addition to enabling your Instagram addiction, WiFi will also let you use messaging services like WhatsApp to message and call your friends and family back home, and you can pay for Google Voice or Skype credits to make and receive calls.

But frankly, I don't recommend this method for any trip longer than a few weeks. Instead, try to get an unlocked phone! You can purchase a cheap one from a store, a friend, or Craigslist — these days, most people probably have an old phone lying around that will work just fine with a local or global SIM card.

No matter which option you choose, it helps to keep an old, unlocked phone stashed in your bag for emergencies. This habit has saved us several times! A lot can happen to a phone on a long trip: your phone can get lost, stolen, damaged or smashed to pieces. Bringing along a just-in-case unlocked phone (especially a crappy one from several years ago that nobody will be tempted to steal) that you can stick a local SIM card into is a great backup plan — and it will keep you from missing out on really good Pokemon.

Request an Absentee Ballot

Yes you can — and should — vote during your trip! U.S. citizens can sign up to receive an absentee ballot, which can be sent electronically, printed out, and mailed.[83]

Our trip happened to coincide with a presidential election, so a month before election day an absentee ballot landed in my inbox. All I had to do was print it out and mail it in.

Of course, "printing it out and mailing it in" is much easier said than done. I was in the middle of Peru without a clue how to find a printer, and I didn't know the Spanish word for "post office."

It took a lot of asking around to find a local print shop, which charged us for each page we printed. I'm not going to lie: we balked at the $15 print fee. That's like, three days worth of lunches — or a night in a private room! Was our civic duty worth the expense?

By the time we arrived at the post office after another round of wandering aimlessly and asking locals where we could mail a package, we were patting ourselves on the back. The simple act of voting had taken us a full day of confused navigation. We were practically heroes.

But our sails were quickly deflated. We hadn't brought our passports with us to the post office. (Why did we need our passports? Why did we always need our passports?).

---

83 If you're a citizen of another country, make sure to research your own country's election laws well before your trip to give yourself plenty of time to request a ballot.

We'd have to take a taxi back to our hostel to get our passports and then come all the way back — expensive, and a hassle. The clerk was unimpressed, rules were rules. "But you could pay for postage now and find somewhere to drop off your package," she suggested.

That sounded easier, at least. She rang us up, and our stomachs dropped. In order to get our ballots mailed in time for the election, postage was ridiculously expensive.[84]

We very nearly didn't vote in that election, but civic duty won out over laziness. All told, it took us two full days of trying to print out our ballots and navigate the Peruvian postal system, but by golly, we did it. We EARNED those little "I Voted" stickers![85]

I wish I had some advice to help you here, but this will just have to be your very own adventure. Best of luck, and remember: you're doing your democratic duty!

Get a Fee-Free Bank Account and Credit Card

You'll need to figure out how you'll access money during your trip in advance of your departure, or you could be in for an expensive lesson. Many bank accounts and credit cards charge "foreign transaction fees," which means that every time you use or withdraw money while abroad, you're paying an extra 1%–3% for every dollar you spend. Add that to fees for withdrawing cash from ATMs — and sometimes extra fees for international ATMs — and over the course of a long trip, that adds up to hundreds or even thousands of dollars that you could have spent on travel!

Check with your bank to see if they charge foreign transaction fees, and if they do, you'll want to get a more travel-friendly checking account and credit card. My personal choice is Charles Schwab, who offers a foreign transaction fee-free checking account (and even pays a small interest on your balance!) and a debit

---

84 I wish I could remember exactly how much it was — I want to say something like $100, but I could just be inflating it in my memory. Whatever it was, I've been stewing over it for years now.

85 You don't actually get stickers if you vote absentee — sorry! I know, I was bummed too. I love those little stickers!

card that refunds all ATM fees. Capital One 360 is another option that waives foreign transaction fees, although you'll still be on the hook for ATMs. For credit cards, both Capital One and Chase offer several cards with no foreign transaction fees — and you'll rack up rewards for spending money on travel, too.[86]

If you focused on building up your credit score in Part One, you should have no trouble opening a bank account with Charles Schwab and getting approved for a travel rewards credit card. But if your credit score leaves something to be desired, it will be very difficult to avoid fees.

Traveler's checks are, unfortunately, a relic of the past that cannot always be easily cashed. Exchanging money before you arrive in your destination country also typically costs more than exchanging upon arrival, and although you can order currency from your bank before your trip, carrying around a bunch of cash is not a good idea for traveling safely.

The best option in this case is a travel-friendly, multi-currency debit card from Transferwise, our favorite online solution for sending and receiving international currencies. Otherwise, your best bet is to minimize digital transactions and use cash as often as possible.[87]

Whichever option you choose, make sure you let your bank and credit cards know that you'll be traveling before your trip. Otherwise, your globe-hopping purchase habits could be flagged as fraudulent and your bank may freeze your cards! (Better hope you sprung for a phone plan that allows international calls...) Thankfully, this is easy to avoid: many banks offer an easy, online way to set up a travel alert, but if not, just contact your bank and credit cards before you leave to let them know.

---

86 At the time of publication, my personal favorite foreign-transaction-fee-free credit cards are the Chase Sapphire cards and the Capital One Venture Rewards card (and its annual-fee-free counterpart, the Capital One Venture One). The Chase Sapphire line offers more protections for travelers, including primary car rental insurance and some coverage for trip interruption or cancellation, but the annual fees are higher.

87 One option that seems appealing on the surface is a prepaid Travel Currency card, but on further research it seems that those, too, have high fees.

Putting Everything On Hold

You may imagine that taking a long-term trip means giving yourself permission to skip away from household management tasks for a while. You can't pay a bill you didn't receive, right? Problems you don't know about might as well not exist! All that stuff you're not taking with you on your trip? It's not important! Just wave a magic wand and send it all to the dump, or storage, or whatever — who cares?

I can say with absolute certainty that in the future, you will very much care.

The act of putting your life on pause is not just about clearing away the obstacles preventing you from skipping your way across the globe on a Very Big Adventure. Much more importantly, it's about laying the foundation for you to come home to a life that is at least mostly not in shambles, which allows you to pick up more or less where you left off without having to start completely from scratch again. The more attention you pay to this step, the easier the process of returning home will be.

Of course, I say that only after years of hindsight and months of opening up boxes we'd hastily stuffed with no real thought before our trip only to find bits of trash, expired pantry items, and odds and ends I couldn't even remember owning, much less packing up.

Our biggest oversight by far was in neglecting to pay enough attention to our mail and to Jeremy's student loans. We set each up with a system that we thought we could just forget about during our travels — only to come back to an expensive nightmare that took us years to fix.

Our mail, we'd thought, was an easy solution: my dad had a P.O. Box he checked regularly, and offered to look after our mail for us, which we happily accepted. My dad is an excellent nag: if there was anything important that we needed dealing with, he'd let us know, repeatedly. We set up mail forwarding to send everything from our old address to his P.O. Box, and checked that item off our To-Do list. Done!

Next up, we tackled the looming misery of student loans. Jeremy was already on an income-based repayment plan, so all we had to do was call up his student loan provider to let them know that he wasn't earning any money and just like that, payments magically fell to zero. Easy!

But as anyone who's ever suffered through the headache of student loans knows, it's never that easy. What we didn't realize is that we'd need to keep confirming with the student loan provider that Jeremy was still, in fact, earning nothing. They'd let him off the hook as long as he stayed in contact and jumped through all their paperwork hoops.

But we weren't very good at staying in contact. We were off having fabulous adventures with llamas in South America.

At some point, an extremely important piece of mail was sent that carried in its sealed envelope the fate of all of Jeremy's student loans. If we missed this one incredibly crucial piece of mail, his precious zero-dollar student loan payments were doomed.

We missed it.[88]

The letter may or may not have ever arrived. Maybe it was addressed to a version of our names that we didn't set up to forward to my dad's P.O. Box. Maybe the post office just didn't catch it. Maybe it fell out of a box on a truck somewhere. Maybe it slipped between the seats in my dad's car. Maybe I prefer to continue to believe that the hand of fate guided that envelope instead of thinking that my dad, for the first time in his life, missed a crucially important opportunity to nag me into doing something I needed to do.

In any case, as we happily skipped our way through the snowy streets of Copenhagen drinking Glühwein and finally learning the meaning of Christmas, Jeremy's student loan payments happily skipped their way from zero right back to what they were before we left.

We didn't realize what had happened until we returned. Six months of missed student loan payments. Six months of angry words like "default" and "delinquent."

Jeremy's credit score, which he'd worked so hard to pull up to a number that was more disappointing than shocking, tumbled off a cliff. Again.

---

88   And nobody ever told us what its all-important contents contained, either. I can only assume it was a contract that needed to be signed in tears or blood, stating that Jeremy was, indeed, still jobless and thus could not be squeezed or garnished for interest payments.

It took us about a year and a half after we returned to recover. We ended up consolidating most of Jeremy's loans, which removed several of the delinquent accounts. And in the years after we returned, we continued living below our means in order to pay off several of the smaller private loans, which had unreasonably high interest rates.[89] It was a mess. But several years later, Jeremy's credit score is nearly perfect (which he never misses an opportunity to gloat about).

Do your future self a huge favor: get your ducks in a row before you leave, so that you can make the transition to regular life a little bit less difficult. Trust me: it's going to be challenging enough without leaving yourself a welcome-home gift of messy paperwork and several boxes of trash!

Your Mail

To make mail management easier, before you leave, opt into receiving mail electronically as much as possible. Choose the "paperless" option from all of your banks and credit card accounts, cancel any magazine or newspaper subscriptions, and remove yourself from spam mail lists by registering at the Data & Marketing Association's consumer website. For just $2, you'll be junk mail free for ten years! Now, that's a nice gift to leave for yourself on your return home.

For the rest of it, online mail services can help you receive and manage your mail while you're traveling. These services receive your mail for you and send you scanned images of the envelopes. You'll be able to tell them what to do with each piece of mail: open and scan, forward, shred, recycle, or even cash checks.

Although this is a great option, most online mail services are a bit on the pricey side and won't hold the physical mail items for more than 45 days (although they can forward you mail at an additional fee). Some charge per piece of mail, and others have monthly plans. There are a variety of services out there, including Traveling Mailbox, Earth Class Mail, and US Global Mail.

If money is tight, the cheapest option for managing your mail while you're away is to ask a trusted family member or friend. I know: this did not end well for us.

---

89 I'll skip getting on my soapbox here and pointing out that it should be criminal to lock anyone, much less a very young and inexperienced adult, into a 14% interest rate to pay for a for-profit art school that is constantly at risk of losing its accreditation because it may or may not be a scam. But rest assured, none of Jeremy's 12th grade students graduate without being well and fully informed.

But listen, other than that one horrifically important piece of mail we missed, it went just fine!

Before you leave, go over what you'd like them to do with certain kinds of mail, such as scan and email you a copy, throw it away, or file it for when you return. You should also provide your 'mail manager' with a written authorization stating that they have permission to pick up mail for you (use both of your full legal names), along with your signature and a copy of your ID. This written authorization can be used by your mail manager to pick up any packages or redeliveries at the post office as needed.

If they feel comfortable, you can redirect your mail to their address by setting up a temporary one-year change of address with the USPS, which can be done cheaply and easily online.[90]

Another option is to set up a local P.O. Box (a great idea if you have a small business or are freelancing and need a U.S.-based address while abroad). You can link your P.O. Box with an online USPS account to see and manage deliveries from afar. If your mail manager will be collecting mail from your P.O. Box, you'll need to submit some paperwork to add them as an "associated individual."[91]

Bills and Loans

You put in so much work saving up for this trip! Now, it's time to make sure all your U.S.-based bills are paid and taken care of while you are gone.

- **Set up a loan payment strategy**

If you have a car, personal loan, or house payment that you will still need to pay during your travels, you'll want to set up automated payments so you can think about it as little as possible.

If you have multiple loans, it's worth talking to a qualified financial counselor to find out whether credit consolidation — combining all your debt into one monthly payment — could help lower your monthly payments and/or overall

---

90 You can set up your change-of-address on the USPS website.

91 Give yourself plenty of time to apply for a P.O. Box as there may be a waiting list! For step-by-step instructions on how to open a P.O. Box and other basic FAQs, check out the USPS FAQ page on their website.

interest rate (and also make it easier to manage your finances). However, there can be fees associated with credit consolidation, such as balance transfer fees, closing costs and annual fees, so make sure to consider both the pros and cons. The National Foundation for Credit Counseling and the Financial Counseling Association of America can direct you to free resources and information on whether credit consolidation would be a good option.

Check with your loan provider whether there is an option to defer your loans while you are away. While private loan deferment is limited, some public loans — such as federal student loans — may qualify for deferment or income-driven repayment plans.

Speaking of which: if you are one of the forty-four million Americans with student loan debt, it's important to have a plan of how to keep your student loans current. Unpaid student loans will affect your credit score, continue to accrue interest, and can even result in legal action like your wages being garnished.

Before you leave, put a payment plan in place — and keep up-to-date with it so that you don't make the same mistake we did. Setting up a monthly automatic payment plan for your student loans may actually qualify you for a small reduction in your interest rate! Make sure your contact details are (and stay!) up-to-date in your Federal Student Aid record, and log in regularly just to confirm everything is as it should be.

Most loans are eligible for one of the four income-driven repayment plans.[92] You can also explore whether you qualify for deferment. Deferment options are rare among private student loan providers, but if you have federal student loans, you may qualify[93].

Remember that your interest will likely continue to accrue if you defer payment or go onto an income-driven repayment plan, increasing the amount that you will need to eventually pay back.

• **Cancel all unnecessary services and auto-renewals**

---

92 Information on income-based repayment plans for Student Loans can be found at studentaid.gov

93 Information on Student Loan Deferment can be found at at studentaid.gov

Go through your bank statements from the past year — or, if you started tracking your budget digitally way back in Part One, just log into your budget tracking app — and make a list of all your recurring and automatic small and large bills. Go through the entire list to pause or cancel everything that you won't need while abroad, like:

- Memberships: Costco, Sam's Club, local clubs, Amazon Prime

- Subscription services: boxes of cute bow-ties, magazines, online services or education

- Entertainment: Hulu, Netflix, Amazon, Prime Video, Disney+, how are there so many?!

- Donations: Patreon, annual automatic contributions to nonprofits

- Gym and fitness classes

- Cell phone plans: many service providers allow you to temporarily suspend your mobile plan while you're abroad — but usually for a monthly fee. When you suspend your line, you won't receive any calls or text messages but will be able to reactivate and use the same line once you're back. The Prepare Your Cell Phone section has more information and options to consider when thinking about mobile use abroad.

If you've been playing the credit card points game, call up the cards with a pricey annual fee and either cancel them, or ask nicely if you can have your annual fee waived.

Your Stuff

Before you even think about packing up all your stuff and finding somewhere to keep it until you get back, you need to get started on getting rid of as much of it as you can. Seriously: start NOW. The more stuff you have to store, the more expensive it will be, and the more stuff you'll have to come home to!

We assumed that after we came back home again, we'd be delighted to reunite with our belongings. We loved our stuff! It was "our" stuff — all the things we'd acquired together over the years. Precious mementos from our life, like that chair we picked up off the street and reupholstered together, or the star-shaped stress ball that we used as a Christmas ornament every year, or the taped-together glasses that Jeremy was wearing on the day we met, or the Ikea couch with three broken legs where we ate dinner each night. (We did, at least, finally convince ourselves to part with the broken couch.) We loved all that stuff at the time, so we figured we'd miss it and be happy to return to it after our trip. Also, we didn't want to give ourselves the expensive task of buying new furniture or clothing to replace all of our old stuff; we were planning to spend all of our savings on travel, after all.

What we didn't realize is that spending a whole year without our stuff would make us way less attached to stuff in general. The act of packing up our belongings and saying goodbye to them was so cathartic that unpacking them again later was actually jarring. Did we really save a broken, duct-taped pair of glasses?[94] And a random old stress ball with a bent paperclip in it?[95] And a jar lid with no matching jar?[96]

We weren't excited to see any of that crap again; we just felt weighed down by all of our belongings. Again. Also, we didn't feel like the same people who had packed up those boxes all those many years ago (it was only a year, but travel time is weird — we'll explain later). We felt like different people, in a different phase of our lives, suddenly saddled with the burden of a bunch of old stuff we'd already mentally said goodbye to.

I wish I could go back to the week we packed everything up and smack that stupid stress ball out of my hand. Its memory — along with the random bits of trash we used as Christmas ornaments until we bought real Christmas ornaments the year after we returned from our trip, finally ready for adulthood — was enough. Instead of being delighted to reunite with every weird bit of crap I'd said goodbye to, I was just saddled with the burden of getting rid of it — again.

So, think of your trip as a serendipitous opportunity to completely declutter your life. Go through your home and pack up only the things that you really want to keep, and get rid of the rest!

In the process, you might even be able to scrounge up a few extra dollars: set up a yard sale or sell your stuff on Facebook Marketplace, Nextdoor, Letgo, Craigslist,

---

94 Yes.

95 Also yes.

96 This is possibly the one that makes me the most angry.

or eBay. These days, there are apps for selling all kinds of stuff, from clothing on Poshmark to old LEGOs and DVDs on Decluttr. We spent a weekend before we left hosting a yard sale and managed to drum up an extra few hundred dollars to add to our trip budget!

That said, photographing and listing your stuff and hosting a yard sale takes a ton of time, which you may not have if you're also working through the rest of your logistical task list and tying up other loose ends. In our neighborhood, anything you don't want can just be left out on the curb to be picked up by interested pass-ers-by. There's also a fantastic organization called BuyNothing[97] with local groups hosted on Facebook spread out all across the world. You can both get rid of your unwanted stuff with relative ease, and maybe pick up some sweet new travel gear from your neighbors. We've scored some amazing stuff on BuyNothing over the years, and it's a great way to get to know your local community, too!

You can also donate items to local charities, many of which offer pick-up services. Don't donate items that are broken, completely worn out, gross, or hazardous; volunteers then have to spend precious time sorting through all the junk! Some great charities that offer pickup services include PickUp Please, Habitat for Humanity ReStore, or GreenDrop. You can also search for local charity donation pickup services online.

Once you've rid yourself of as much as you possibly can, it's time to pack everything you'll be keeping up and put it somewhere. The less stuff you have to move and store, the easier this task will be.

By now, you can probably guess this was not an easy step for us. Even though we'd been living in a tiny, 500-square-foot apartment with nothing more than a few secondhand pieces of cheap Ikea furniture to our name, we managed to spend several thousands of dollars moving it all across the country to my mom's house in Kentucky for storage.

We'd initially wanted to keep it nearby, but once we priced things out we found that shipping all of our belongings across the country to keep it at my mom's house for free actually cost the same as paying for a storage unit next door in Berkeley. The San Francisco Bay Area cost of living strikes again!

---

97 You can find your local BuyNothing group online. I love ours — not only is it fantastic for getting rid of unwanted clutter, but it's a gold mine for free furniture when you return, too!

But there were also other factors that we were taking into consideration: we might need to access our stuff on the road, especially since we were still under the misconception that we would be thru-hiking the Appalachian Trail in a few months' time. We set aside boxes of camping and hiking gear for ourselves, so that we could swap out our grungy backpacker stuff with grungy thru-hiker stuff. If we'd left our belongings in California, we would have also needed to pay for a place to stay — nobody we know in the Bay Area has a spare room for guests, especially guests with backpacks full of grimy backpacker gear. Storing our stuff at my mom's in Kentucky was a safe bet, since we have enough friends and family with extra space that we could easily hole up there for as long as we needed — which we took advantage of twice during our trip.

We also weren't entirely sure yet where we would be settling back down again after our trip. We might return to the Bay Area and pick our lives up exactly where we'd left them, but we might also be flat broke and unable to find jobs, which would quickly wipe the Bay Area off our list of possibilities.

We were also considering settling down somewhere else. Maybe in Louisville, where my family lives, or perhaps somewhere totally new to us. As we prepared to leave everything behind and quit our jobs, Jeremy was already feeling the ache to return to teaching. So, he decided to apply to grad school during our trip and let the results of his application determine where we might end up living upon our return. His top choice was a Masters of Education program at New York University. Kentucky, located directly between California and New York, seemed like a pretty safe bet.

And so we packed up several boxes of trash and stuff we definitely didn't need and paid for a very expensive moving service to ship it all the way across the country to Kentucky.[98]

If you don't have an inexpensive option to store your stuff nearby — like in someone's spare room — and you need to ship your stuff across the country like I did, compare rates of long-distance movers on a platform like Unpakt or Move. Shipping a small apartment worth of stuff from New York to Los Angeles, for instance, could cost from $2,800 to over $5,000. Look for moving companies that give

---

98   On a recent visit home, we realized we never actually got back all of the stuff we'd stored at my mom's house: there are still several carefully labelled boxes tucked in the back of her storage closet. I have long since forgotten what might be inside, and I'm not at all looking forward to finally unpacking them.

quotes and charge by weight rather than by total cubic feet, as total cubic feet is easier to game by scammy movers.

Another option is to rent a storage unit. You'll have the choice between non climate-controlled storage units — where your belongings will be subject to fluctuating outdoor temperatures — and climate-controlled storage units. Most stuff will be fine in a basic non climate-controlled storage unit; however, if you have a lot of climate-sensitive belongings (like artwork, a nice wine collection, an instrument, records, or some types of wooden furniture and electronics), you may want to consider a climate-controlled storage unit.

Another great option is to use a service like Neighbor, which allows people to rent out their garage, driveway, shed, attic, spare bedroom, personal parking lot, or any other storage space they've got lying around unused. It's usually cheaper than a storage unit, and you might even be able to find somewhere climate-controlled, too.

Regardless of what you choose: the less stuff you have, the less you'll spend.

Your Car

After the great car-totalling disaster of 2014, we opted to go car-free, which saved us the hassle of having to store or sell our car. If you've got a vehicle to account for, you might consider loaning it to a trusted friend or family member to drive (and cover your car payments) while you're away.

If you'll be storing your stuff with a loved one, you could load up your car with all the stuff you're storing and drop it off wherever you'll be keeping your belongings, thus forcing yourself to pare down your belongings to a minimum and saving money on moving costs all in one convenient step![99]

Just make sure whoever's looking after your car also doesn't mind being responsible for its well-being: cars should be driven on a regular basis to keep the axles

---

99 Shoot, we already booked your departure ticket together in the last chapter and here you are road tripping across the country to drop your car off. I sure hope you factored that into your plans before you booked that ticket!

greased, or whatever.[100] If you want to return to a car in decent condition, ask them to keep it relatively clean and free of debris — not parked under a tree that drops fruit, for instance — and make sure there's nothing living inside, having their own Very Big Adventure and feasting on your car's internal organs.

If you aren't sure whether your car babysitter will be driving your car regularly, or you're using a long-term car storage solution like Neighbor, there are a few steps to take care of before you say goodbye:[101]

- Inflate your tires fully (unless you can store it on a jack stand) to prevent gravity from taking a toll

- Fill your gas tank to nearly full

- Add fuel stabilizer to help prevent corrosion in the fuel lines and engine

- Change your oil and oil filter

- Top up your antifreeze

- Remove your battery and keep it somewhere climate-controlled

- Cover your car to protect it from the elements

You'll also need to consider what to do with your car insurance policy. Before you cancel it outright, consider suspending or reducing your coverage instead.[102] Suspending your coverage means you won't have a coverage lapse, which can affect your future insurance rates. But it also means that the vehicle won't be covered if anyone wants to drive it while you're gone, and it also won't be insured for any non driving problems like fire, animal damage, vandalism, damage from falling objects, or theft.

If suspending your coverage won't work for you, or local laws dictate that you must have some form of insurance for your vehicle whether you're driving it or not,

100 I have no idea how cars work and have totalled four of them — without a single collision with another driver. But according to Google, you have to drive cars regularly because it wakes up the transmission, brakes, suspension, power steering, air conditioning, fluids, seals and gaskets. That sounds completely made-up to me, but there you have it.

101 I learned more about cars researching this section than I've learned about them ever in my entire life.

102 If you're still paying a loan on your vehicle, you'll likely be required to continue paying for car insurance in order to protect your lender.

contact your insurance provider to ask about reducing your coverage while you're away. Depending on the plan, you may be able to cover just the bare minimum, which for many states is typically just liability insurance, (although some states also require uninsured/underinsured motorist coverage, personal injury protection and/or medical payments coverage). It's also smart to include comprehensive insurance, in case your car is damaged while being stored. Comprehensive insurance will pay to replace your car if it's stolen, and it also covers non driving problems.

But honestly? It might just be easier to sell the thing. And hey: if you can, keep the savings so you're able to buy a new car when you return!

Your Home

If you're a renter, this is one of the easiest steps: you just need to let your landlord know you're moving out. Try to time your trip so that you don't break your lease, which is super expensive. And give yourself a few days before you leave to clean up the apartment so you can get your security deposit back! That's it. Now, you can skip away, free as a bird, to the next chapter. Bye!

Homeowners: now that we're alone, let's talk. If you own your own home and can't afford to pay the mortgage on an empty place, you'll want to look into getting a tenant. But first, check with your lender first to confirm that it's legal to rent out your house to tenants; some mortgage companies will require you to switch to a different type of mortgage. If they find out you are renting your house without permission they can technically repossess it for breach of contract!

If you're in the clear with your lender, your next step is to shop around for a highly rated property manager.[103] Becoming a landlord is definitely a big responsibility, but with the help of a good property management company you should be able to relax knowing that your tenants will be well taken care of (and hope your home is too). You can, of course, manage your tenants from afar, but even after the hassle of listing your home and finding tenants, you'll need to be on call 24/7. It's essentially a part (or even full) time job. If you can swing it financially, a property manager is well worth the expense.

Although a year-long contract will give you better financial security and stability,

[103] You can use the National Association of Residential Property Manager website to find local property managers in your area.

depending on your location, you might also consider setting your home up as a short-term rental on Airbnb or Vrbo. There are property management services that manage short-term rentals too, like Vacasa and TurnKey. They'll handle everything: managing bookings, cleaning the apartment, conducting inspections, and providing 24/7 customer support for renters.

In either case, you'll likely need to upgrade your home insurance policy — check with your provider to make sure you'll be covered.

Speaking of which: leaving your home unoccupied for long periods of time can be risky (or at least, is viewed by home insurance providers as risky). If you plan to leave your home unoccupied while you are away, you'll likely need to take out a different type of home insurance. Most standard policies only cover your unoccupied home for up to 60 days, but you can purchase unoccupied home insurance to cover the remaining time. Annoyingly, unoccupied home insurance usually costs around 50% more than your normal home insurance, but covers less.

You'll also want to take some extra steps to prepare your while you're away:

- Turn off the water heater and gas (unless you live somewhere seasonal, in which case you'll want to leave your thermostat set above freezing)

- Turn off your water at the main valve and then drain the remaining water in the pipes by opening all the faucets

- Lock all windows and doors

- Stop all mail and newspapers being delivered to your house (refer to the Mail section for more information on how to manage your mail while you are gone)

- Empty the refrigerator and all trash

- Unplug the fridge and leave the doors open to prevent mold

To reduce the risk of theft and vandalism, let a trusted neighbour know that you are leaving and ask them to keep watch on the house, or ask a friend to stop by every once in a while as well to check on everything. If you're concerned about theft or squatters, you can also give the impression of still being at home by setting up smart plugs to periodically turn lights or music on and off, and ensure that someone takes care of landscaping. If you really want to go all out, you can install security cameras and even leave GPS tiles on valuable household items, so you can track them if they end up getting stolen.

You might also consider letting a house sitter mind your home and belongings — and water your plants! We'll cover house sitting in Part Three.

What to Pack ... and What to Leave at Home

Some people leave packing until the last minute, but I — you probably guessed — spent months planning, researching, test-packing, and weighing every item for our trip. You're probably also not shocked to hear that there were spreadsheets and diagrams (or maybe you are, in which case, let me assure you: there are always spreadsheets).

Each item had to earn its place in my pack. I did copious research before everything I bought (or added to our wedding registry, which was filled with romantic gifts like insect repellant and water purification devices). And on my master packing spreadsheet, I carefully recorded the weight of each item, measured on a little cooking scale in our kitchen.

My goal was to be as ultra-light as possible, a term I'd picked up from the hiking and backpacking community. I was still under the impression that I'd spend the second half of our year-long trip thru-hiking the Appalachian trail, so I wanted my pack to be as light as possible; my goal was to keep it under 20lbs without water and food.

Trying to shave precious ounces, I sawed off the ends of our toothbrushes, snipped tags out of our clothing, and sawed off the extra straps on our backpacks. (Jeremy's backpack straps are now permanently frayed and too short, and it irritates him to no end.)

I also needed every item of clothing in my pack to justify its existence. It needed to coordinate with multiple other items, not be prone to wrinkles, and be lightweight and quick-drying, and I wanted as many high-performance textiles as possible. I was finally putting my fashion design degree to work![104]

I packed and re-packed my bag over and over again, evaluating my brand-new packing cubes to see what they would fit, and taking my fully-packed bag with me

---

104 I think I use my fashion design degree more as a travel blogger than I ever used it during the five years I worked in the corporate fashion world, but it's mainly to patch holes, repair ripped seams, and write long blog posts about the technical properties of merino wool. I can also identify textiles by touch, which is kind of a nifty super-power, I guess.

on walks through our neighborhood. After each test, I'd go home, mull over my spreadsheet, whittle the ends of our toothbrushes, and worry about my knees.[105]

By the time we left for our trip, I thought I'd cracked it. Every single item in both of our bags was researched, re-researched, tested, weighed, packed, unpacked, rolled, unrolled, and thoroughly vetted. I'd achieved packing perfection.

Or so I thought.

What Not to Pack

Even with all my research about what to pack for long-term travel, what I really needed to know is what NOT to pack. Because the worst part about packing for long-term travel is that whatever you bring, you're stuck with it until you either toss it or shell out the money to mail it home.

Which is why, three months into our trip, we again made a pilgrimage to the Peruvian post office with a box full of crap we really didn't want to schlep around with us, but couldn't quite bear to throw in the trash. For $100, we were able to mail home treasured items like a scarf I found in a hostel lost & found that we used to wrap up a tiny kitten we found on the street, an alpaca sweater[106] we bought at an artisanal market in Ecuador, and an apron with a ceviche recipe on it. (To be fair, a few things we mailed home were intended to be gifts for loved ones, which we didn't have any space for since we were planning to stuff our backpacks with bottles of wine from Argentina.)

The impromptu package home left us more room to continue lugging around the rest of the stuff we'd brought. Like, for instance, two giant, chunky "universal" travel adapters which we never used once: all the plugs in Colombia and Ecuador are standard U.S. plugs, and the ones in Peru were special outlets that fit both European and US plugs. Both Chile and Argentina mysteriously required Australian plugs which our "universal" adapters mysteriously didn't have. And in Europe?

---

105 If you're worried about the impact of a heavy backpack on your knees, just bring a suitcase! It's mildly inconvenient to carry a suitcase down cobblestone roads or dusty unpaved paths or up stairs, but it's also mildly inconvenient to schlep around a heavy backpack. Travel is full of inconveniences! I personally do prefer a backpack to a suitcase, but if you don't, a suitcase will do just fine.

106 It was actually made from cheap acrylic yarn. Fun fact: real alpaca is cool to the touch — and not dirt cheap.

The darn things were too big to use — they kept falling out of the outlets thanks to their own weight.

It turns out all we needed was a tiny little $1 adapter that can be found literally everywhere, from the front desk at our hostel to convenience stores on every corner. No matter where we went, it was easier and cheaper to buy a travel adapter once we arrived.

We lugged those stupid universal travel adapters around for months before finally leaving them behind in a hostel somewhere in Europe for some poor schmuck to get excited over.[107]

I also regretted bringing along powdery, glittery eyeshadow and bronzer. Yes, I brought makeup on a year-long backpacking trip. A year, I thought, is a long time to go without looking your best, and I've always loved wearing and applying makeup — I was even a freelance makeup artist as a side-hustle in college. Makeup was an essential I couldn't live without!

But within a week, my precious makeup broke all over my backpack into a million pieces of powdery irritation.

I shouldn't have been surprised. When my backpack wasn't being tossed into the trunk of a car, shoved underneath a bus, dragged on the ground behind a rickshaw, or crushed beneath the weight of 1000 other backpacks in a hostel storage room, it's been banged around by me, the clumsiest person in the world.

But backpacks are made to withstand this kind of pressure. My delicate travel-sized eyeshadow and bronzer? Not so much. Lesson learned: I should have left my powder makeup at home, and brought hardy, cream-based makeup instead.[108]

---

107   Hostel lost & founds are treasure troves of things that other travelers have intentionally dumped along their travels. Need some new clothes? Check the lost & found! Looking for a Lonely Planet guide to the region? There's definitely one in the lost & found! The only thing you'll never find is a lock — those are always in high demand.

108   After a year without makeup, it's like my body physically rejects it: no sooner have I completed the perfect winged eyeliner than my eyes start watering and my nose starts running. These days, the most I can get away with is an extremely bold lipstick, which has become my trademark look only because it serves as an excellent distraction from my constantly watering eyes and runny nose. That said, I have found a few products over the years that hold up to the demands of travel, and have written a blog post all about the best makeup for backpacking practicalwanderlust.com/the-ultimate-guide-to-beauty-and-makeup-for-travel

Another one of my genius travel packing ideas was to bring incredibly old smartphones instead of our shiny new ones, which I was afraid would get stolen — not realizing that at this point, nearly everyone else in the entire world also has a smartphone, and by the time we left for our trip, ours were about a year away from being either shiny or new.

For a full year, each of us had to rely entirely on a smartphone that was so old, they were practically museum pieces. In terms of the tech world, we'd become my mom.

Although the phones served the purposes of being easily unlocked and outfitted with foreign SIM cards from each country just fine, there were some major downsides.

For starters, mine had the battery power of an old sock. I'd charge it all night long, only for it to stay on for ten minutes, and then die again with a puttery, exhausted sigh. I might as well have not brought a phone at all.

Meanwhile, Jeremy didn't want to shell out for a protective cover for his crappy old phone, so of course on the very first week of our honeymoon, he dropped the thing on concrete and shattered the screen. We spent a full day looking for a cell phone kiosk that sold really old protective phone screens just so he'd stop getting glass shards in his fingers.

We also neglected to realize that cell phones double as our cameras; most of the photos from our first few months were so blurry, it was hard to tell what we were doing or where we were. We had to rely on using another camera instead — which was much more expensive than the phones we couldn't use at all.

And while it was some small relief knowing that nobody would ever want to steal our jank old phones — and we have some peace of mind knowing that if they DID steal them, it would kind of just be a relief at this point — we would have been fine bringing our newer, spiffier phones (with protective casing, of course).

In addition to stressing out over our cell phones, I spent a lot of sleepless nights before our trip worrying about theft, kidnapping, and various other anxiety-inducing worse case scenarios. I'd find myself down Google rabbit holes filled with stories about people getting their bags stolen off buses from right under their noses.

And so I bought us a super-heavy steel cable and lock. The idea was to tie our bags together and then to some sort of secure object, like a pole, to keep them from getting stolen.

This is a great idea in theory, except that our bags were almost never sitting around or near a pole. They're either on our backs, sitting at our feet, or locked away in a luggage compartment underneath a bus.

So, since the cable lock was just unnecessary weight, we mailed it home.

One week later, at a bus station in Ica, Peru, one of our bags was snatched from right underneath our noses. Jeremy had set our daybag — filled, as it always was, with our most valuable electronics[109] — next to us on the seat, and then turned to say something to me. In the second his eyes left our bag, it was snatched up and vanished into a sea of people.

Somehow, Jeremy reacted quickly enough to spot the thief, who had hidden our bag in the middle of several shopping bags and was hurrying towards the doors of the bus station. Without a word, Jeremy took off after him. My heroic husband sprinted through the streets of Ica, probably yelling "STOP THIEF!" They say not to chase thieves, but safety be damned![110] This was a bag worth DOZENS of dollars.

When my brave husband finally caught up to the thief, he gave him a gentle tap on the shoulder and said "Ummm, excuse me sir?" Bless his heart, he doesn't have an impolite bone in his entire body.

But suddenly, he felt a return tap on the shoulder. Plot twist! The scoundrel had a partner! Ever the people pleaser, Jeremy turned around and threw out a harsh "I'm sorry; I'm a little busy," and turned back just in time to catch a glimpse of

---

109 When traveling, we prefer to keep all of our electronics together in one bag, which we keep on us at all times (except in this one instance, of course). If you do the same, make sure not to keep your passports in that bag, too! We always keep our passports on us tucked into a money belt, along with credit cards and cash — plus backup cards hidden away in our bags. That way, even if a bag does get stolen, you'll still have your passports and access to your money, which are the most important things you'll need.

110 I'm half joking, but seriously, never run after a thief. It's super dangerous! If your stuff is valuable enough to risk your life for, you should really just leave it at home. The contents of that bag included a crappy point-and-shoot camera, an old Kindle e-reader, and a cheap Chromebook laptop. NONE of it was irreplaceable, and we were extremely lucky that we wanted our bag back more than the thief did.

our bag dropped behind a trash can as the thief jumped into a crowd and took off into the midday sun.

It was a genius move actually; had Jeremy not (very politely) brushed off the second guy, he would have made the rookie mistake of going after the first. But ne'er-do-wells take heed! Never mess with a traveler who physically can't stand upsetting someone… or your whole dastardly plan will be foiled.

We never took our eyes off that damn daybag ever again.

When you're figuring out what to bring with you, it helps to do some research and look for advice from travelers who have recently visited the destinations you'll be visiting; you can post on a travel-related subreddit or in a Facebook group asking for advice. But as a general rule of thumb, most generic products will be available to buy when you need them; you only really need to worry about bringing specific things with you.

What We Wish We Packed

We didn't just pack things that we didn't end up needing — we also neglected to pack some things we really should have.

For starters: an extra computer. In order to save weight, we brought just one teeny, tiny, travel-friendly Chromebook, thinking we'd switch off using the internet while the other one read or journaled or meditated or carved blocks of soap into tiny llamas or whatever things we assumed we would suddenly develop an interest in while traveling.

In reality, one of us hogged the laptop while the other looked helplessly at their to-do list, feeling unproductive. If I was working on the blog, Jeremy couldn't research our next destination or plan out our next move. And while he was busy booking hostels and not logging into his Student Loan dashboard, I was angrily trying to get my decades-old phone to work so I could interact with followers on our brand new Instagram account.

This lasted for about four months, when we finally caved and picked up an inexpensive computer in Lima, Peru. The brand on the box just said, "WOO." Most of the keys were mislabeled. The operating program was in Spanish. And it wouldn't turn on unless it was plugged in. But we were desperate, and it did the job. Jeremy loved his WOO, and being able to use his own browser — if nothing else — meant I had precious more time to obsess over my tiny baby blog. The WOO may very well have been the reason why our blog took off so much in its first year!

Another thing we neglected to bring with us was a full-sized towel. Instead, I brought this ultralight, dinky, 12×18 inch microfiber travel "towel" (more like a large washcloth, really). It didn't even cover one of my thighs at a time, much less the middle section of my body. It was about as warm and cozy as wearing one sleeve (not a shirt or sweater with one sleeve. Just one sleeve). I couldn't sit on it at the beach, unless I only wanted half of my butt to be protected from the sand.

As far as towels go, it was completely worthless.

Why did I bring a washcloth with me instead of an actual travel towel? Eight ounces. I wanted to save eight ounces of weight. Apparently eight ounces was worth it to never be able to dry myself off and spend an outrageous amount of money on renting towels from hostels.

Every single time I used that stupid towel, I was filled with rage: at myself, at the world, and at whoever made such a useless, idiotic piece of fabric.

And so, one day, we marched to the market and bought a towel. A regular towel; not a quick-drying microfiber travel towel, but a massive, giant, fluffy towel. It was green and it had sloths on it, and it was wonderful. I resisted the urge to burn the washcloth and mailed it home instead.[111]

By the end of our trip, we were carrying two full-sized, fluffy bath towels, a pair of slippers, and a small bathrobe. I refuse to allow myself to suffer the injustice of a too-small towel ever again.[112]

I also found myself wishing I'd brought more shampoo and conditioner. Backpacking wreaked havoc on my hair. From being dunked in saltwater and dried via boat ride to my daily "screw it, messy bun" routine to being constantly washed in chemical-laden water, it was tested to the max and it failed those tests.

---

111 I still have it. Every time I look at it, it makes me angry. I should have left it behind in a hostel somewhere.

112 This is also one of my favorite Fat Girl travel tips: my fellow fatties, always bring your own towel! Towels at hostels NEVER fit me, and the temple that is my body does not deserve to be insulted. I now always pack myself a luxuriously full-sized towel.

I'd packed two small travel-sized bottles of conditioner thinking I could buy some while I travelled. But the conditioner selection was deeply lacking and a zillion times pricier than back home. Conditioner may have been the one thing — other than peanut butter[113] — that was more expensive to buy outside of the USA.

When we flew home for Thanksgiving, I stocked up on full-sized bottles of my favorite shampoo and conditioner, and carried them in my backpack for the next eight months. The girl who sawed off the ends of her toothbrushes and decided that a tiny towel was worth saving eight ounces of weight was officially long gone.

My hair wasn't the only thing suffering during the trip. My clothing, which I'd spent so long agonizing over, was incredibly functional — and not at all cute. I may be practical to a freakish extreme, but I'm also stylish: I worked in the fashion industry before we left to go traveling, after all.

As we made our way across South America, I saw so many other travelers wearing cute little tops, sundresses, patterned shorts, linen rompers, and floppy hats — all so impractical, but so cute.

Meanwhile, my quick-dry performance hiking clothes matched my husband's. Yes: most of the clothing we bought literally matched. Shoes and all!

I underestimated how much I would miss being able to dress up a little bit: I'd brought with me exactly two cute dresses, one pair of jeans, and a million variations of safari-green, high-performance technical clothing.

During our trip to see family for the holidays, I unleashed my pent-up fashion frustration at the outlet malls near my sister's house in New Jersey, and spent the next few months feeling like myself again, all bundled up for winter in Europe — bright red lipstick, runny nose, and all!

---

113 I lived on cheap PB&J as a broke college student, so on the first day we arrived in Colombia, we headed straight to the grocery store to pick up a loaf of bread, a squeezable bag of jam, and a jar of peanut butter. But when we rang up our purchases, I was shocked: it cost nearly $20 for one tiny jar! I hoped it was a fluke, but no: peanut butter, it seems, is a luxury item in South America. I ate that peanut butter spoonful by luxurious spoonful until it was gone, and then I used the empty bottle for storage just to get my money's worth.

What to Actually Pack

Although we made many mistakes, most of the gear we brought with us (particularly on that first leg of the trip in South America) performed excellently. While I no longer weigh every item and obsess over a few ounces here and there, over the years since our trip, my packing persnicketiness has only become even more demanding. The gear and clothing I bring along on my trips now has stood the test of time, including five subsequent trips to South America, a jaunt through the Norwegian Arctic, and backpacking trips through Nepal, Panama, and Indonesia.

And other than high-quality hair products, we never found ourselves desperately needing anything. We found that, whenever we needed something, we could always find a market/mercado, corner store, or supermarket selling some version of it.

Besides, trying to hunt down specific items is an adventure of its own. There's no better feeling than spending hours wandering around trying to find a Band-Aid, only to finally spot them being sold individually in a tiny store tucked into a hidden alley. (Although perhaps a Band-Aid isn't the best example; Jeremy had just surfed his way into a pile of rocks in Trujillo, Peru, and was actually bleeding pretty badly.)[114]

Remember that your needs may vary depending on where you're visiting and the kinds of climates you'll experience. Do some research to figure out what the weather might be like during the time of year you'll be in each place, and don't make assumptions. Just within South America alone, each individual city and country we visited had completely different climates, from the cold mountain air in the high Andes to the relentless heat of Cartagena. We were surprised by how much colder most of the places we visited in South America actually were, and found ourselves stocking up on alpaca sweaters at artisanal markets and wishing we'd brought more warm layers.

I also spent a lot of time in advance worrying about fitting in and trying to dress "like a local." That was a waste of time: everywhere we went, we stood out as visitors — and the giant backpacks, daybags, and kitchen bag we lugged around with us didn't help.

---

114 Jeremy is almost completely blind without his glasses, which means that every time he does something water-related like surfing, snorkelling, scuba-diving, or swimming, he almost always gets injured. It's as adorable as it is worrisome.

When we left South America to head to snowy Europe — which we hadn't planned for in advance — we had to leave behind all of our warmer-weather clothing and stock up on wool base layers and warm down jackets. We wouldn't have been able to pack for both in one bag, but flying home for the holidays gave us the opportunity to swap out our gear.

We've included a detailed, itemized packing list in the Reference section of this book, which is a good starting point that you can customize by climate or your own personal preferences. In this section, we'll cover the gear that proved to be indispensable during our long-term trip (and subsequent years of travel).[115]

The Essentials

Although climate plays a big role in the clothing you'll pack with you, there are many non-weather-specific items that find their way into my bag for every single trip I take — such as the aforementioned travel towel.

I always bring along a teeny-tiny travel clothesline, because you never know when you'll have a wet bathing suit that needs hanging or some good old sink laundry to dry (which is how we get away with only ever bringing seven pairs of underwear along on every trip). Don't hang it up in your bathroom, where it's humid and damp — put it somewhere with natural, drying sunlight and plenty of air, like near a window or, better yet, outside in the sun!

Travelling long-term means rips, tears, holes, and popped buttons are entirely inevitable. I brought a small lightweight sewing kit and made regular repairs on everything from our clothing to our packing cubes and daybags!

Insulated reusable water bottles are not only environmentally friendly, but they have a major advantage over cheap, clear plastic water bottles: they actually keep your water COLD even in miserably hot destinations!

The bug repellant you bring with you can make or break your trip; nothing is more irritating than being eaten alive by tiny, flying insects carrying diseases. So when we found out that there was a bug repellent that adheres only to fabrics, leaves no smell or residue on clothes, and doesn't harm human skin, we bought

---

115 For specific recommendations for all of my beloved, tried-and-tested travel gear and clothing, I've got detailed guides on our blog: practicalwanderlust.com/tag/what-to-pack

a few bottles and spent a day outside spraying down all of our clothing, paying special attention to hems, cuffs, and socks. It was well worth the effort: we barely got bitten by any bugs during our entire five months of backpacking in South America! Permethrin spray lasts for up to six machine washes, but since we weren't washing our clothes very often (ssh, don't judge) and rarely using washing machines, it seems to have lasted longer for us. It worked like a charm: even in mosquito-ridden areas we had way fewer bites than our fellow travelers.

Applying Permethrin to your clothing will give it insect-repelling abilities, but for your actual skin, you'll need something else. Many travelers wear DEET-based bug sprays, but my skin hates it. I prefer a Picaridin-based bug repellent lotion: it's not greasy, I don't have to hold my nose and cover my mouth when I apply it to avoid inhaling gross chemicals, and it works for me.

Stuff to Put Stuff In

We schlepped our stuff around all year in rugged, 40L hiking backpacks. Built with a sturdy internal frame, the backpacks are designed to withstand the elements, and some even come with a rain cover, too — although in my experience, an artfully ripped trash bag works in a pinch.[116]

Before you commit to being a literal backpacker, I strongly recommend shopping around for the perfect bag — every backpack fits slightly differently, and a pack that fits someone else perfectly may not work for you. To tell if a bag fits you properly, you'll need to get help from someone who knows their way around a backpack to adjust the many straps.

Load up the backpack with about 30lbs of weight, and stand and walk around with it for a while. The weight of the bag should be evenly distributed between your shoulders and hips, and you'll want to pay special attention to your armpits, chest, and boobs to feel for any discomfort — it will only get worse on the road.

Much like dating, it's best to just pass on any bag that doesn't feel right and hold out until you find The One! The perfect bag will feel like an extension of yourself.

116 Let me clarify here, because I definitely made this mistake. Don't schlep a trash bag around in case of rain because you're too cheap to spring for a real rain cover, which is what I did. Invest in a real rain cover, like Jeremy did, because your belongings are important enough to spend a few bucks to keep dry; and then only use a trash bag "in a pinch" if something terrible has happened to your actual rain cover.

You may need to build up some calf or shoulder strength, but honestly, just carrying a fully packed bag around is an excellent workout in itself.

If backpacks aren't your bag, suitcases work just fine. But opt for something rugged; you'll be dragging it along bumpy cobblestone roads, unpaved paths, and up stairwells, not to mention tossing it into the bottom of every bus and plane you take during your trip.

In addition to our backpacks, we also brought two lightweight bags which folded down into nothing: a small backpack to use as a daypack, and a duffel bag that we used to carry around our food supplies, including groceries and snacks. We used them every single day, but grew to wish we'd opted for something more rugged: both of those cheap, lightweight bags needed almost constant repairs.

During the trip — and on every trip afterwards — I kept my clothing organized in a set of lightweight packing cubes. To make the most of them, roll, don't fold, your clothing!

We also brought along little inexpensive drawstring bags to use for laundry, to separate our shoes (and all the dirt and gross stuff caked on them), and a waterproof bag, which served both as a dry bag during water sports and a wet bag when we needed to pack up wet bathing suits or not-quite-dry sink-washed underwear.

Hiking and Outdoor Adventure Essentials

One of the biggest questions we pondered was how much outdoor gear to bring with us. We knew that we'd need to fly home to prepare properly to thru-hike the Appalachian Trail, but we weren't sure whether we might also want to bring along some camping gear with us to South America, like our hammocks or lightweight cookware. Ultimately, we decided to leave it all at home, and that was very much the right call. Even on the multi-day hikes we did, that gear would have been totally unnecessary: on guided treks like the Inca Trail, gear is always provided; and even on the challenging Quilotoa Loop in Ecuador, we never found ourselves needing to sleep outside. Had we stuck to our original plan of hiking the W-Trail in Patagonia, we would have been able to rent the gear we needed in town, too. But hiking gear was something we got plenty of use out of, and it doubled as our adventure sports gear, too.

Back at home in California, I can wear leggings to hike — but I can't butt-slide and knee-hit properly in them, like I needed to on the challenging hikes we were planning during our trip. After searching high and low, I finally found quick-drying hiking pants that are up to the task of handling mud, rain, gravel, sand, and jungle, with a lot of butt-sliding and knee-hitting — AND that were comfortable enough to actually hike in. This single pair of pants covers every kind of athletic activity. I've worn them not only hiking, but also parasailing, horseback-riding, and waterfall rappelling (albeit disastrously) and white-water rafting. They also double as snow pants with a warm base layer underneath!

Although it took up a fair amount of space, I also brought my trusty hiking hydration pack with us on the trip (shoved into the bladder section of my backpack) and I'm so glad I did! I brought it on every single hike and on long city exploration days using it as my daypack, complete with 100oz of purified water.

I also brought along a pair of lightweight, foldable trekking poles, which Jeremy found hilariously superfluous. Sure, trekking poles aren't really necessary on short, easy hikes (and yes, vigorously strolling along with my trekking poles visibly aged me by several decades). However, three days into climbing the rugged High Andes on the Quilotoa Loop in Ecuador (both by foot and, at one point when we were very lost, on our hands and knees) Jeremy's knees began to give out. Meanwhile, mine were fine, thanks to my trusty trekking poles. He limped along in stubborn silence for eight hours before finally collapsing in agony. I handed him my trekking poles and we hitchhiked the final leg of the route. And, as a great testament to my maturity and the wifely love I have for my darling husband, I did not say "I told you so."[117]

We opted to bring lightweight trail running shoes with us instead of heavy hiking boots, along with waterproof socks to whip out in the event we needed to hike through deep mud or ford a stream (this happened exactly once; but when it did, we were very glad we'd bothered to bring the waterproof socks with us).

First-Aid and Health

One of the most important things we brought along for our health was a device to purify our drinking water. On my first trip to Colombia, I made the mistake

117   ... until he was feeling better, and then I said it repeatedly and with great relish for the rest of our lives.

of sipping exactly one small cup of tap water a single time; I felt like I was going to die for the next three days straight. It was miserable, and I will never make that mistake again. Our handy little water purifier uses a UV light to kill living bacteria and viruses in even the most untrustworthy tap water. And although it was a pricey piece of gear, bringing it along meant we didn't have to buy multiple bottles of purified water per day — which is both expensive and environmentally unfriendly.

But even when I haven't chugged a cup full of bacteria, I do have an easily upset stomach. My body doesn't like dairy, gluten, corn, anything processed, or anything delicious. But it's really difficult to control what's in your food while traveling, and often the only thing available is something my stomach doesn't like.

So, I brought a bottle of stomach enzymes. They contain the things my stomach seems to lack to help it break down the elements in various foods and digest them. Since taking stomach enzymes, I've greatly reduced instances of heartburn or indigestion, and seen a huge increase in my health from the more readily available nutrients that my stomach is now able to unpack and utilize! These are a lifesaver for me while traveling.[118]

I also brought along several anti-nausea remedies for my poor sensitive stomach. I'm the kind of person who gets nauseous literally just thinking about a windy road or bumpy boat ride, and I feel like Dramamine gives me a superhuman ability to do things other than stare at the window on transit days. Dramamine was my lifeline on many, many long bus rides (always windy, always through mountains, always speeding) as well as boat rides, trains, rickshaws, and every other form of transportation we took during our trip. If they sold Dramamine in gallon jugs at Costco, I'd buy several cases.

I also brought along plenty of over-the-counter anti-diarrheal remedies. You can never have too many, and you will absolutely need them. I don't want to go into details. Just trust me.

Apple cider vinegar is another of my favorite first-aid essentials. I know, it's kind of random — but it's so useful! It's antibacterial and antifungal, a fantastically effective sunburn remedy, provides immediate relief for heartburn, and helps heal wet-bathing-suit rashes. It's also a gentle clarifying wash for hair, great for strip-

---

118 South America also has fantastic stomach-soothing local remedies, like Coca tea and muña, which I also relied on to help ease my poor stomach.

ping away salt or hard water buildup. We kept ours in a little travel-size spray bottle and used it regularly.

Toiletries

Whether you're sharing a bathroom with a hostel full of strangers, or you opted for the ensuite, whatever you bring with you on your trip may be all you're able to get. So if you have specific bath needs — like my shampoo and conditioner — bring plenty of those with you, weight be damned!

You may also decide that it's important to you to look and feel your best, and choose to bring along makeup or toiletry items to meet that need. Even though my makeup broke all over my backpack and I eventually gave up on it, I did like having the option to occasionally whip myself into a facsimile of my glamorous former self; it was so nice to be able to take a brief break from feeling like a grungy backpacker. Jeremy and I stopped once a month or so to get a manicure or a facial, and I even used a tiny, lightweight hair straightener to tame my frizzy hair from time to time.[119]

Regardless of your personal care preferences, your skin does take a beating when you travel, so take special care to moisturize like crazy. My skin is dry, sensitive, and acne-prone, so I moisturize it every evening with lightweight oil. We carried along olive oil for cooking, and I used that to moisturize my hands and hair, too.

Sun protection is also important for everyone, especially those prone to burning, like me. I do my best to keep my skin covered from the sun — a swim shirt is an excellent investment in your skin. I also bring along two types of sun protection: mineral sunscreen, which is better for the environment and protects your skin with a physical zinc oxide barrier rather than chemicals that soak into your skin and can end up in your bloodstream; and reef-safe sunscreen, which is designed to biodegrade and not harm ocean life.

We also brought along our favorite all-natural deodorant and lip balm, a few small bars of soap (you can never have enough soap on the road, I find), a razor to share between the two of us and, of course, our sawed-off toothbrushes.

---

119 These days, I've embraced my hair's natural texture and prefer to wear it curly, which is about a zillion times more work and requires me to carry around a small closet filled with hair tools, gels and serums. But it's well worth it: my curls make me feel absolutely amazing!

Ladies, I also highly recommend picking up a menstrual cup and getting used to using it. Pads and tampons can be hard to come by and expensive, not to mention they're wasteful and not terribly vag-friendly. But cup life is fantastic! I'll never go back. There's no leakage, it's lightweight and travel-friendly, stays in all day long, and cleaning and maintenance is easy (just wash with regular soap and water, or you can boil or spritz with vinegar if you need a lil' extra cleanliness). If you're considering making the switch, do it!

We keep all of our toiletries organized into a hanging waterproof toiletry case that we can bring us into the bathroom and hang right on the closest hook or shower door.

Kitchen Essentials

Although you'll probably enjoy local food for many of your meals, cooking your own meals from time to time will not only help you save money but can also be a nice, comforting routine. We cooked most of our dinners each night in hostel kitchens, and cooked nearly every meal whenever we rented Airbnbs or booked house sitting gigs.

Hostel kitchens and Airbnbs usually have a few things for cooking like salt, oil, and a spatula or two, but one thing they never seem to have is a variety of spices. And making a good home-cooked meal requires spices. So, we brought our favorites from home in little Ziploc baggies. When we need to cook a meal, we've got a variety of flavors to choose from, which makes building a meal from available local ingredients a lot easier!

You'll also want to bring along a little container to put leftovers in — leaving a plate of half-eaten food in a shared fridge is, unfortunately, an invitation.

Safety Essentials

Safety while traveling abroad is a huge concern, and for good reason: tourists are like a walking bullseye. While backpacking in South America, just being a Gringo wearing a backpack can make you a target.

As any hostel-hopper knows, you always need to have a lock! But in addition to locking up your valuables in the hostel locker, you also want to have locks on your day bags and on your bag when you're in transit. These little locks are more of a deterrent than anything: obviously any dedicated thief can just cut open our canvas backpacks if they really want to. But most casual thieves are looking for an easy mark: a pocket to slip their hands into quickly, a bag left unlocked on a bus, etc.

We lock every zipper on all of our bags with lightweight little locks and, aside from the bus station incident, we never had anything stolen.

During our trip, I finally learned to embrace my true self. And it turns out that in my heart of hearts, deep down in the very depths of my soul, I really, really hate purses. Purses are terrible! They're easily snatched and stolen, I'm forever leaving them behind somewhere, they render one of my arms useless, they make my shoulders ache, they're constantly getting tangled up in my coat sleeves and undoing buttons on my shirt — they are just a truly horrible invention and I hate them with every fiber of my being.[120]

A travel-friendly alternative to wearing a purse is to wear a money belt. Unfortunately, a money belt is totally useless for a huge amount of women's clothing, like dresses. Who designed these things?[121]

My solution is to wear a Bra Pocket. It's a little card-sized envelope made from silk that snaps onto my bra and hangs out inconspicuously between the girls, ready the moment I need to take out a card. Nothing got lost or stolen, I never have to worry about leaving it behind, and it's so comfortable that I often sleep in it. The only, very minor downside is that all of my cash ends up slightly damp — but then again, so did the cash in Jeremy's money belt. Frankly, I'd rather have sweaty boob cash than stolen cash.

I've also developed a deep appreciation of clothing that has useful-sized pockets, and in my quest for finding those mythical pieces of clothing, I stumbled upon the world's best pair of travel jeans. Made by a small, U.S.-based company called Aviator USA, these jeans are everything I've ever dreamt of: they're stretchy, they're cozy and soft (I've even worn them on planes!), and best of all, they have

---

120 I like to imagine that purses were invented by a group of mustache-twiddling, finger-tenting men sitting around a clubroom in front of a big sign reading "The Patriarchy," smoking fancy cigars and sipping fancy Scotch and brainstorming ways to keep women from achieving equality.

121 I know who: it was those cigar-smoking, Scotch-drinking assholes. "Money belts" probably came right after "Hey, let's never put any useful-sized pockets in women's clothing," which I'm sure received a round of hearty applause. Dicks.

SIX wonderfully enormous pockets, including two hidden zippered pockets — each large enough for a phone or passport to stay firmly tucked away, safe from pickpockets. I have about a million pairs and I wear them constantly.[122]

Electronic Gear

There was once a time when a traveler could take off for a world-wide adventure completely unplugged, free from the demands of posting on social media or keeping up with funny memes. They'd write home every once in a while to let everyone know they were okay and had taken up acoustic guitar and meditation, and on occasion they'd show up unannounced on Christmas Eve, covered in backpacker grime and hungry for a home-cooked meal.

Those were simpler times.

These days, long-term travel only has to be as unplugged as you'd like it to be. You can easily keep up with your friends on Facebook, start a WhatsApp group with your family to let them know what you're up to each day, watch new releases on Netflix, and even earn a living all through the magic of worldwide WiFi and a couple of devices.

Your electronic gear will depend on your preferences and needs, and they may adapt over time. Although we began our trip with a single cheap laptop, we ended it with two cheap laptops, which we upgraded to high-performance Macbooks the minute we could afford to.[123]

If you won't be working on the road and you have little need for a computer beyond casual browsing, a cheap little computer will do the trick — and, since it's inexpensive, you won't really worry yourself much about theft.[124]

---

122 My personal favorites are the Aviator USA Comfort Skinny in Jet Black. They're *heavenly*. I'll never go back to regular jeans!

123 I speak from experience when I say: sure, you can start a travel blog on a Chromebook! But don't. You can't run actual programs, so things like video and photo editing, file management, and graphic design become nearly impossible. Also, without WiFi, all you have is a useless pile of metal, which is less than ideal when you'd actually like to take advantage of a few hours of quiet airplane time or a rustic unplugged lodge to write or work or make digital art.

124 I once had my Chromebook laptop stolen (in the USA). The thief was so disappointed with it, they brought it back to where they'd taken it the next day. That thing is a piece of crap with a broken screen and would cost me $100 to replace, but we've been through a lot together; I gave it a joyous little hug when we were reunited.

Most travelers also likely won't need to bring extra cameras with them — if you bring a decent phone, that will do just fine. If you tend to do crazy things on your travels like go waterfall rappelling or white water rafting or snowboarding or snorkeling and you want to document your adventurousness for your loved ones back home, a small, waterproof action camera does the trick. We used to have a GoPro, but then Jeremy lost it on a mountain somewhere, so now we have a cheap knock-off GoPro instead.

As beginner bloggers, we also brought along a digital point and shoot, which did the bare minimum. But a few months later, our little blog had grown — and blurry photos weren't cutting it anymore. We levelled up with a mirrorless DSLR camera and a tripod and never looked back.[125]

One piece of electronic gear I encourage everyone to bring along is a digital e-reader. It's like bringing an entire library with you! Even though you'll often find lovingly dog-eared paperbacks in hostel lounges across the world,[126] an e-reader will keep your mind constantly occupied. They're also fantastic travel tools and double as tablets: you can use apps, download movies and audiobooks, and of course, pull up your massive Trip Roadmap.

Clothing

Choosing the clothing for our year-long trip was the biggest packing challenge of all. I had high standards for my clothing, and a pack stuffed with high-performance, high-tech gear to match.

But the item of clothing I ended up wearing the most during my trip was a pair of plain, ordinary jeans. Looking like a backpacking Gringo every single day got really old, really fast. Bring your favorite pair of jeans with you (although, be

---

125 That's not true. I look back all the time to the brief, wonderful period in my life where I didn't have to worry about taking good photos of everything. These days, I spend most of my trips cursing the day I decided to become a travel blogger while accidentally bumping my heavy, expensive camera and massive, expensive zoom lens into various cement walls, poles, and at least once, just straight-up dropping it on the ground. (Thank goodness for insurance.)

126 In my wildest dreams, I would one day like to arrive at a hostel and find a copy of this book there, complete with scribbles in the margins and coffee stains. It would top the current highlight of my professional life, which was being recognized by a blog reader at my favorite eco-hostel in tiny Minca, Colombia. There was no WiFi at the hostel, but he'd downloaded pages from our blog to reference during his trip. My heart!

warned: they'll probably end up with a few well-worn holes).

I was also grateful that I'd packed myself two dresses. Wearing them, along with a pair of comfortable bike shorts with roomy pockets, made me feel blissfully normal.

Otherwise, all of my clothing tended to fall into the "backpacker wear" camp. I wish I'd brought along more comfy t-shirts, a few cuter tops, and pants that weren't designed for either hiking or sleeping.

I was, at least, pleased with the textiles I'd chosen. I'd mostly stuck with natural textiles like breezy cotton, bamboo and linen, and I'd also brought along several items made from soft, stretchy merino wool. Performance merino wool is something of a miracle travel fabric: it keeps you cool when it's hot out and warm when it's cold out; when it gets wet, it stays warm while it dries. It naturally resists the growth of fungus and bacteria, so it never gets smelly — crucial for re-wearing clothes to save on laundry costs. It's even flame retardant — what more could you ask for?[127]

Most of my favorite travel clothing we brought with us was wool, from our cold-weather clothing to our hiking gear. I even had wool underwear, which doubled as a wool swimsuit. (Why didn't I bring a real swimsuit along with me? 12 measly ounces, that's why.)

One of Jeremy's favorite clothing items was a pair of quick-drying shorts made from the same material as his hiking pants. They also doubled as his swimsuit, which was somewhat more conventional than me, running around the Galapagos in a soaking wet black wool sports bra that definitely didn't pass as a bikini top.

I came to deeply appreciate my lounge pants, which doubled as my pajamas. There is nothing in the world that compares to the warm, cozy embrace of a nice pair of lounge pants.[128]

Lightweight, packable down jackets also proved themselves to be indispensable.

---

127   Hemp is a textile with similar properties, plus the additional benefits of being vegan and environmentally friendly: it actually cleans up the soil as it grows, and it requires little water! But because it's not quite as popular, it's a little harder to find than merino wool clothing.

128   I know what you're thinking: there is one thing that compares, and it's the feeling of removing your bra after a long day. But I removed my last underwire bra five years ago. (And I'll never go back.)

They're incredibly warm and insulating and pack into teeny tiny, lightweight little balls to stuff into your backpack until you need them. Our down jackets were a lifesafer in chilly Cusco and Bogota, and doubled as our main outerwear in Europe over the winter.

You'll also want to bring along a lightweight umbrella and a rain jacket. We even brought along matching rain pants, which I think we wore once.[129]

For shoes, we stuck to lightweight, flexible pairs that were easy to stuff into our little drawstring shoe bag. During my pre-trip training, I'd incurred a foot injury and found that the only shoes that didn't cause me to re-injure myself were wide-toed, lightweight, flexible barefoot shoes.[130] I brought along a pair of barefoot ballet flats that fit in the palm of my hand and a pair of flexible, velcro leather sandals that doubled as water shoes. When we flew home to switch over all of our warm-weather clothing for cold-weather clothing, I brought along just one single pair of shoes: leather, barefoot winter boots with a soft sherpa lining and a thermal insole. Five years later, they're still my favorite pair of winter boots.[131]

Essentials for Working on the Road

I spent about 20-30 hours a week during our trip holed up in hostels and coffee shops, hunched over my tiny little laptop plugging away at my growing travel blog. I figured aching shoulders and necks and stiff wrists were all part of the Digital Nomad dream. It's a small price to pay for being able to work from anywhere in the world, right?

Well, no. Your health is NOT a fair price to pay just so you can work remotely. And although these days I have a home base with a little desk and everything, I still find myself working on the road probably about four months out of the year — to this day, I still do my best work on planes and trains. I've since invested in three necessary pieces of gear that make it possible for me to bring an ergonomic

---

129 They felt a bit like wearing a sweaty trash-bag wrapped around either leg.

130 At one point, I got sucked deep into a barefoot-shoe research hole, devoured an excellent book called "Born to Run," and started hiking without any shoes at all. I spent a full year preparing for our trip hiking completely barefoot. Looking back, I honestly don't remember what it was like to be so cool.

131 My wonderful winter boots are made by VivoBarefoot, but they aren't always in stock. If you see a pair, snag them!

little workspace with me everywhere I go: an ergonomic mouse, an ergonomic keyboard, and a fold-up portable laptop stand.

In addition to protecting your health and your body, please don't forget to protect your information too and invest in a VPN service. As a digital nomad, chances are you'll be doing a lot of logging into stuff that you probably don't want to be hacked, like your website, your bank, or your Paypal account. With a VPN, your information stays secure and safe, even when you're desperately tethering to that random open connection in the airport.

Packing Checklist

Stuff to Put Stuff In	
☐ Backpack (or suitcase)	☐ Laundry/wet bag
☐ Daybag	☐ Shoe bag
☐ Packing cubes	☐ Toiletry bag

First-Aid Kit	
☐ Dramamine/motion sickness	☐ Band-Aids
☐ Imodium/anti-diarrheals	☐ Alcohol pads
☐ Emergen-C/immune support	☐ Hand sanitizer
☐ Tylenol/pain relievers	☐ Anti-malarial medication
☐ Melatonin/sleep aids	☐ Altitude sickness medication
☐ Allergy meds	☐ Prescription medications, as needed
☐ Moleskin blister pads	

Toiletries	
☐ Shampoo & Conditioner	☐ Tweezers
☐ Moisturizer (face & body)	☐ Folding scissors
☐ Chapstick	☐ Beauty & hair necessities
☐ Deodorant	☐ Toothbrush & toothpaste
☐ Baby wipes (for face, etc)	☐ Menstrual cup/supplies
☐ Bar of soap (& carrying case)	☐ Travel towel (full-sized)
☐ Sewing kit	☐ Travel laundry wash

General Essentials	
☐ Water bottle	☐ Travel clothesline
☐ Water purification tool	☐ Sunglasses
☐ Smartphone (unlocked)	☐ Mineral sunscreen
☐ Bug repellant	☐ Lightweight umbrella
☐ Money belt/bra pocket	☐ Camera
☐ Locks for bags	☐ Passport
☐ Sink stopper	☐ Driver's license

Hostel Necessities	
☐ Small flashlight	☐ Spices (for cooking)
☐ Laptop	☐ Tupperware (for leftovers)
☐ Plug adapters	☐ Lightweight slippers
☐ Outlet splitter	☐ Lightweight robe/large travel towel
☐ Phone chargers	☐ Ear plugs
☐ Kindle, books, cards, etc.	☐ Sleeping mask
☐ Locks for lockers	

Digital Nomad Necessities	
☐ Computer	☐ Laptop stand
☐ Ergonomic mouse	☐ VPN
☐ Ergonomic keyboard	☐ Mobile router or portable WiFi
☐ Portable charger	

Clothing (For Her)	Clothing (For Him)
☐ 7 pairs of underwear	☐ 7 pairs of underwear
☐ 5-7 pairs of socks	☐ 7 pairs of socks
☐ 1 swimsuit	☐ 1 swimsuit
☐ 1 pair jeans	☐ 1 pair jeans
☐ 1 pair shorts	☐ 1 pair shorts
☐ 1 pair hiking pants	☐ 1 pair hiking pants
☐ 1 pair lounge pants	☐ 1 pair lounge pant
☐ 1-3 cozy dresses or skirts	☐ 3-5 T-shirts
☐ 3-5 T-shirts & tank tops	☐ 2-3 long-sleeve tops
☐ 1-3 long-sleeve tops	☐ 1 sweatshirt or sweater
☐ 1 cardigan	☐ 1 hiking outfit
☐ 1 hoodie/sweatshirt	☐ 1 lightweight jacket
☐ 1 lightweight jacket	☐ 1 lightweight rain jacket
☐ 1 lightweight rain jacket	☐ 1 packable down jacket
☐ 1 packable down jacket	☐ 1 pair sandals
☐ 1 pair sandals	☐ 1 pair hiking shoes
☐ 1 pair hiking shoes	☐ 1 pair everyday shoes
☐ 1 pair everyday shoes	☐ 1 warm hat
☐ 1 warm hat	☐ 1 pair gloves
☐ 1 pair gloves	☐ 1 scarf
☐ 1 scarf (or sarong)	

This is the Hardest Part

When I announced my decision to quit my job and travel for a year, the reactions I received from friends and family — and acquaintances, and even random strangers — were surprisingly mixed. Many of my closest friends and family were supportive, happy, and excited for me to achieve my dream of traveling for a year. They were going to miss me and they wished they could come along too, but they were happy for me. Those were the easiest conversations, even if they were usually filled with tears and hugs. They were the people I messaged during my trip with photos and stories; they wanted to hear about everything I was seeing, experiencing, and doing.[132]

But most of my conversations did not go that way. Many of the people I assumed would be supportive were skeptical or doubtful; still others were passive-aggressive or even downright rude.

I quickly realized that not everyone was supportive or accepting of my decision to travel long term. And it turns out that my experience was actually fairly common — many people experience similar pushback.

There's no easy way to navigate those conversations and the relationships they represent, but I hope you will take some comfort in knowing you are not alone.

Difficult Conversations

It took me a while to put my finger on why quitting my job and taking a sabbatical year off rubbed so many people the wrong way. I don't think it's just that people who take time off to travel are bad at picking friends or generally have unsupportive families; the issue, I think, is deeply rooted in our culture itself.

Back in Part One, we explored the reasons why long-term travel is a radical act; how many other cultures view travel as an important rite of passage, while here

---

132 Those wonderful, dear friends and family members not only supported me both during and after my travels — they were also the first readers of my blog, laughed along at the first episodes of my podcast, and have continued to support me every step of the way. They'll probably be the first to read this book too! When you find those relationships, cherish them and nurture them. Even just one loving, healthy, supportive relationship like that can sustain you for an entire lifetime.

in the USA travel is seen as rejecting the core tenets of society and its narrow definitions of "success."

Keeping that in mind helps to frame why it can be so difficult for some otherwise supportive and well-intentioned loved ones to understand or support you: to them, quitting your job to travel means rejecting "success," and of course, they want you to be successful. Successful people are happy; success is the goal. Why wouldn't you want success?

For those loved ones, it can help to explain that the narrow definition of "success" as defined by job title, material comfort, or financial security doesn't align with your idea of happiness. You might ask them to try reframing your success as having the freedom to pursue your dreams and of achieving a challenging goal. But even if they don't come around, don't let it get to you. Only one definition of "success" matters: yours. And that's if achieving success really matters to you at all — it's also totally okay if it doesn't. That may be very difficult for other people to understand, but it's not your responsibility to process their feelings for them.

In my experience, even parents who are understanding of your dream of long-term travel may never be fully reassured. For them, an even bigger fear than your success is your safety. My dad, despite having spent months van-lifing across Europe and backpacking through Southeast Asia during college, was horrified when I decided to follow in his footsteps. I couldn't understand why: after all, it's so much easier to backpack now than it was back then! Granted, I also inherited my anxiety directly from his gene pool.[133]

It helped to reassure him that we'd be able to stay in constant contact; he'd be able to message me as often as he liked on Facebook messenger or WhatsApp, and I promised to keep him up to date on all of our adventures. Also, he had a complete, 50-page, indexed itinerary with contact details for every single accommodation we planned to stay at (and I made sure to indicate which days we were likely to be "off the grid"). The Trip Roadmap is cleverly designed not only to help you on your travels, but also to reassure anxious parents everywhere.

---

133 My inner spreadsheet goddess was inherited from my mother, who planned every family vacation with a stack of library books by her side. My need to solve every problem in the best and most efficient way was inherited from my father, whose perfectionism has propelled him throughout his career in the business world. In me, their best and worst qualities combined to create an anxious problem-solver who is incapable of doing basic tasks and cannot make a single decision without hours of research, and I think that's really the beauty of having children.

As for my mother, decades of accepting her own mother's reckless adventures had prepared her well for my departure. For years, my grandmother Katy skipped out on birthdays and Christmases because she was off mushroom foraging in Russia or walking in the footsteps of James Joyce in Ireland or eating her way across Iran. When Katy started dating again at age 90 my mother received a frantic call: my grandmother was taking her new boyfriend on "joyrides," hurtling through the Kentucky countryside in her Subaru station wagon. I like to think that my gene pool is a solid 85% Katy.

But while some of the pushback we received was at least well-intentioned, other reactions to our decision were not.

A few people cracked jokes about our finances, assuming we must be wealthy; still others pointed out our privilege, which made us feel guilty for seeking happiness. I wish I had an easy rebuttal for those people, but wealth and privilege are incredibly difficult and complex things to tackle. In some ways, it was a valid point: we are privileged, not only financially but by having a U.S. passport that opens the door to most countries in the world for us. Travel is, after all, a luxury, regardless of whether you're staying in expensive resorts or in hostels. But that doesn't mean we're any less deserving of the chance to enjoy it. Feeling ashamed of one's privilege also isn't a productive starting point for progress or change.[134]

Still other friends were passive-aggressive, offering support while at the same time making backhanded comments. For them, I think it was challenging to reconcile their excitement for our happiness, and the dissatisfaction they felt in their own lives. But I could understand how they were feeling: I felt the same way sitting behind my desk feeling miserable and unsatisfied, looking at beautiful people having fabulous adventures on Instagram and feeling as inspired and motivated by them as I felt resentful and jealous of their success. Why them, and not me? It wasn't that I didn't want them to be happy, it was just difficult to feel happy for them when I felt so unhappy.

We found that as we travelled, we had to strike a careful balance with those supportive-but-kinda-not-really friends. Talk up your adventures too much and they'll resent you further; share the truth about any of the downsides or chal-

---

134 If you are feeling guilty, then I encourage you to re-read the Ethical & Responsible Travel Chapter and the studies that were linked in the footnotes, as well as the books about responsible chapter included in the Resources section at the end of this book. Travel is inherently a political act, but by traveling responsibly, you can strive to have a positive impact on the people and places you visit.

lenges of long-term travel and they'll tell you you're ungrateful. They say things like "must be nice," when you tell them about an exciting adventure; or "yeah, but you're traveling, so it can't be that bad" when you're honest about feeling overwhelmed, homesick, scared, or tired.

It's hard to be honest with those friends about having either really good days or really bad days, and we found it exhausting trying to find a perfect balance. With those friends, it usually felt safer to stick to just the facts about what we were doing, and to ask them to catch us up on their lives instead.

Ultimately, our trip illuminated a lot of toxic relationships. Some of them were built on mutual suffering — "misery-loves-company" friends. When we were no longer miserable, they didn't want to hear about it. Feeling guilty about being happy isn't healthy; relationships with people who don't want you to be happy aren't healthy, either.

One of the most challenging relationships we struggled to navigate was with a close family member of Jeremy's, who took every opportunity to cut us down a peg. "Not that you'd care," they'd begin an angry text message or late-night voice mail, "but things back home aren't easy. Now that you're off traveling the world, I guess that doesn't matter to you anymore."

That particular relationship haunted us before, during and long after our trip.

The best advice I can give for navigating the minefield of reactions to your decision is this: prepare yourself for backlash. Steel yourself against it. Do the best you can to salvage the relationships that really matter to you; consider whether the more toxic relationships are really serving you.

And please, consider speaking to a professional therapist, who can help give you the tools to have these difficult conversations and process your reactions to them. You can even see a therapist virtually during your trip using an app like BetterHelp.

Quitting Your Job

Although the conversations with your family and friends will be challenging emotionally, the conversation you'll have with your boss can be one of the most challenging of all. For me, it was also the conversation I was most afraid of.

I'm not sure why, honestly. After the soul-crushing years I'd spent at my first job out of college, I'd landed a new job that was a much better fit. I liked my new boss, I liked my new coworkers, and I even liked my new company.

A few weeks into my new job, I connected with one of the directors in my office. She'd climbed the ranks in the company quickly thanks to her tenacity and unapologetic intelligence. She knew how to do everyone's job, and everyone else knew it, too. If anyone had a question or an idea, they'd ask her for advice first. Her very presence demanded respect, even though she was one of the youngest in the office, and one of the few women. I thought she was amazing.

Within months of beginning my new job, I asked if I could change departments and work directly for her. She accepted, and created a position for me — leaving the person who'd originally hired me high and dry as I vacated a role I'd barely even begun. It was a risky move, but I was thrilled.

My job changed completely. I was given new responsibilities and new challenges to solve. The solutions I developed and implemented made my coworkers' lives easier; I was finally helping people! My role even involved travel, and I flew across the country and even internationally on the company dime, racking up travel points and miles.

It was, all things considered, a sweet gig. I had a boss whom I liked and respected, a role with plenty of autonomy, a great company culture and friendly coworkers, and the emotional fulfillment of helping others. I even had cool perks: travel, a free on-site gym, office dogs, and even daily afternoon snacks made by the chefs at the on-campus cafeteria.

Was I really going to leave all of it behind just to chase after a crazy dream?

Even though I knew before my first day at work that I planned to leave within the next few years, I kept my plans secret from my boss and my new co-workers, except for a few who had become close personal friends. The secret hung over my head as my new boss and I talked about my future and the projects we'd tackle together in the coming months and years. She was ambitious, and I was too. Even after our little two-person department grew to four, it felt like we were in it together.

I was torn. I wanted to be honest with her; we had a great relationship, and I'd confided to her about everything from the challenges I'd faced at work to my new relationship with Jeremy. But I was afraid if I told her I was planning to leave, it would damage her trust in me. Maybe she'd stop giving me new responsibilities and start to take projects off of my plate. Or worse, maybe she'd resent me — she had, after all, stuck out her neck to create a position for me. I deeply admired her, and now I was choosing not to follow in her footsteps on a path she'd paved for me. I felt guilty and ungrateful.

And so, I put off having that difficult conversation. It never felt like the right time. I held onto my secret until just two months before my planned departure date.

And then, shaking with anxiety, I finally walked into her office and told her everything.

I was so terrified she'd be angry with me, or worse, disappointed. But her reaction was nothing like what I'd braced myself for. She was… excited. She was happy for me! It was going better than I'd even dared to hope for. She wanted to know all about my route, all the travel planning I'd been doing so secretly.

And then she asked me how long I'd been planning my trip. I told her the truth; I'd been dreaming about it for years, and I'd booked my first plane ticket six months ago. "Why didn't you tell me until now?" she asked, confused — and possibly a little annoyed.

In all of the times I mentally imagined this conversation, this had never come up. We now had just two months to prepare for my absence. With more advance notice, I could have trained my replacement, documented all of the projects I was working on to leave behind for a smoother hand-off, and skipped away knowing everything would be handled in my absence.

Instead, I spent those last two months scrambling to do all of that on top of my actual job (and planning my wedding) — and then offered to work remotely during my trip to handle the loose ends I hadn't been able to tie up. It was hard to make a clean break; I was still emotionally invested in the projects I'd been involved with, and I wanted to make sure everything was going well, even though I was no longer personally responsible for it.

Although I'd spend years dreaming of the day I'd finally quit, when it came down to it, I was truly sad to leave.

There's no easy or perfect way to quit your job. It will always be terrifying and a little messy. But you might be surprised: bosses, after all, are just people. A good boss views their role as one of mentorship; they want you to succeed.

When I left my job, I did so on good terms with my boss, which left the door open for the possibility of returning after I came back. And to this day, we have stayed in touch. She continues to support me, and I am forever grateful for the mentorship and opportunity she offered me.[135]

If you don't have a good relationship with your boss, the best way to let them know you're leaving is to do so while expressing deep gratitude for having had the opportunity to work with them. After all, whether you want to come back to your job or you'd really rather not, leaving a door cracked behind you as you leave may mean the difference between paying your rent after you come home again, or moving back in with your parents.

The absolute worst thing you could possibly do is to pull a theatrical stunt where you march up to your boss in front of everyone in the office to quit your job in a flurry of insults. Sure, we've all dreamt of telling a crappy boss how we really feel about them, but these things tend to have a way of coming back around to bite you firmly in the butt. Don't burn any bridges: you'll only set your future self up for doors slamming in your face later on!

The logistics of quitting will likely come down to your work culture and the relationship you have with your boss. Since my boss and I were close, having a personal one-on-one conversation rather than delivering my news in an email or printed letter was important to maintain that relationship (although I did still need to write an actual resignation letter, per HR).

If you don't work closely with your supervisor or you don't think they're in any danger of shedding a tear as you leave, you can write and deliver them your official resignation at the same time as announcing your decision to leave. Make sure it is professional, courteous, and includes words like "deeply thankful" and "opportunity," and attributes your decision to leave to nothing more than the desire to take a career sabbatical and travel.

For Jeremy, there was no long-awaited announcement or fanfare. He talked openly about his travel plans with his coworkers and team, and when it came time for his annual contract renewal discussion, it was more of a confirmation that he was definitely still planning on leaving during the next school year. The question of

---

135 Today, both she and I are CEOs and founders of our own companies. I strive to channel her mentorship when it comes to managing my own growing team and, now that I'm on the other side of the table, I know how exciting it feels to watch your team grow and thrive and chase unapologetically after their own dreams!

whether he might be able to return had mostly to do with whether the teaching position he was vacating would still be open. If that sounds like your situation, consider yourself lucky: this step will be easy!

Saying Goodbye

After the dust has settled and everyone has more or less accepted that you'll be getting on a plane and leaving for a while, it's time to say your goodbyes. To the people you love, it's just a temporary blip; after all, you'll still be available by phone, social media, and video call.

For me, the hardest part of saying goodbye was that it meant closing a chapter of my life. Usually when a life chapter ends and a new one begins, it's a subtle shift — a turn of the page you can only identify by looking back a few years later. But in this case, it was jarring. I was hyper-aware that everything was changing. Everything I'd grown accustomed to, all the things about my life that were comfortingly familiar, would be vanishing the moment I left. There was no way to know whether I would ever experience any of it again.

I started to feel weirdly nostalgic months before our departure date. My heart ached as I walked through my beloved neighborhood with its trailing eucalyptus and fragrant lemon trees, catching glimpses of the Oakland skyline, Alcatraz, and the Golden Gate Bridge in the distance. Each trip to our favorite restaurant was an agonizing goodbye — would this be the last time we sank into the sweet embrace of our favorite fish taco or steaming bowl of ramen?[136]

I even felt nostalgia for things I'd once hated, like my commute to work. My daily commute was an hour and a half each way (or a full two if anything inconvenient happened, which it usually did) and involved a 10-minute walk to the train station, an hour on a crowded subway (including a transfer), and another 15 minutes on the work shuttle from the train station (except for one day when I attempted to bike the final three miles, which added a solid, sweaty hour to my commute and was entirely not worth it).

Now, I found myself wistfully gazing out the window, admiring the golden mountains on one side of the train and birds bathing in the coastal wetlands on the other.

---

136 In hindsight, the answer was very much no. We moved back to our exact same neighborhood after our trip, and continued to live there, eating at the very same restaurants, for another five years.

With my escape imminent and my secret out in the open, I even found a new appreciation for what I'd once considered the monotony of office life. I indulged in long conversations with coworkers over stale coffee in the break room, revelled in the satisfaction of beginning a message "per my prior email," and lovingly documented my projects at work into organized lists of business processes. I savored my lunchtime workouts at the empty on-campus gym, and even cheerfully stayed after 5pm to finish things up.

When my last day of work arrived, I sadly peeled off the postcards I'd stuck on the walls of my cubicle and carefully wrapped up a photo of my grandmother, grinning at the camera on a hike through the Canadian Rockies in her 70s. I'd kept them on my desk as an ever-present reminder of my travel goals; now that I was finally leaving, to my surprise, I'd already begun to miss my job.

At the same time, our wedding loomed. And as much as we'd neglected to plan it in favor of focusing on the honeymoon, it came together wonderfully. Our family and friends flew out to California to spend a week sightseeing around San Francisco[137] and roughing it at our bachelor and bachelorette parties (Jeremy's at a yurt in Big Sur, mine in a rustic cabin in Big Basin).

The wedding itself was perfect. At the entrance of a redwood grove tucked in the Berkeley Hills, Jeremy's little sister handed out our wedding program, which we'd filled with drinking games, a list of inappropriate wedding hashtags submitted at our engagement party, and made-up biographies about each member of our wedding party. I walked down the aisle barefoot, grounded and fully present, feeling the soft moss between my toes and the ferns brushing past my dress. We said our vows[138] as sunbeams danced through the redwoods above us and our closest family and friends passed around our rings, imbuing them with well wishes and blessings before passing them back to us to place on one another's hands.

And as the sun set behind the hills and twinkling lights illuminated a garden landscape of cacti and succulents, our friends filled out Mad Libs wedding speeches that we'd written and placed on each table — and then read them fully in char-

---

137 As part of the out-of-towner gift baskets I created for them, I included a self-guided walking tour of San Francisco that we designed, turn by turn, to meander through our favorite neighborhoods. We printed it out onto a little brochure, and our guests loved it so much we eventually turned it into what would become one of the most popular posts on our blog!

138 I vowed to always acknowledge, if not laugh at, Jeremy's stupid jokes, which I have upheld to this day. Jeremy, however, vowed to rub my feet every night, which he has NOT upheld. I'll be calling divorce lawyers as soon as I finish writing this book.

acter after a few genuinely beautiful, heartfelt speeches — before we stole the spotlight at our karaoke wedding reception, performing three ridiculous song-and-dance numbers.[139]

It was the wedding of our dreams, and it was the perfect send-off to what would surely be the perfect honeymoon.

After the wedding, our family and friends left one by one. And then it was just us: me and Jeremy, in our tiny little apartment, packing up our life together.

Well, not quite. We did have some company in those last few days: a cranky neighborhood cat named Jasper. He was an old black cat with one missing tooth who'd shown up at our door one day and just let himself in like he lived there. He lived in a house down the street (along with two more cats, a dog, and a goat), but he had a neighborhood house picked out for each of his needs; we were his cuddle house. For years, I'd come home to find him sitting in our driveway waiting for me, and lately, he'd even started staying overnight, drooling peacefully at the end of our bed.

In that final week, Jasper came over each day and kept us company as we packed. On the day the moving truck arrived, our little apartment emptied of any evidence we'd ever lived there at all, I held Jasper in my arms, buried my face in the soft, patchy fur between his ears, and cried. Saying goodbye to Jasper was the hardest goodbye of all.

As the moving truck drove away with our former life inside, I gave Jasper one last pet and gently placed him on the ground. We shouldered our heavy backpacks, walked to the train station one last time, boarded our plane, and watched out the window as California grew smaller and smaller, our hands clasped tightly together across the seat divider.

The adventure of our lives had begun at last.

---

139 Jeremy and I are both major hams. We discovered a mutual love for karaoke early on in our relationship, and spent almost every weekend singing our hearts out at our favorite karaoke bar in San Francisco (it's called Butter and it's white-trash themed and ridiculous). Our first karaoke performance as a married couple was "(I've Had) The Time of My Life," and we even made a half-hearted attempt to learn the choreography from Dirty Dancing. Yes — even the lift. Jeremy managed to hold me a whole foot above the ground for nearly ten seconds!

PART THREE: THE TRIP

The Year-Long Honeymoon

Our plane touched down in Cartagena, Colombia at noon the next day. We climbed the stairs down from our plane, blinking in the bright Caribbean sun, and immediately sweating: it was about 100 degrees, and we were still wearing the down jackets we'd donned back home in chilly San Francisco.

We navigated through customs and baggage claim in a daze, barely remembering to stop at an ATM to pick up cash before we exited the airport.

I'd done some advance research to figure out how to get to our hostel, and I knew there was a bus a short walk away. But we were hot, tired, and overwhelmed, and it was so much easier to just flag down one of the many taxis waiting conveniently at the curb.[140]

It had been years since I'd dusted off my conversational Spanish, but I made a broken attempt at explaining where we needed to go, which communicated nothing at all. I pulled up our Trip Roadmap and held it up so the driver could see the name and address of our hostel. He took my phone to look more closely — which made me incredibly nervous, because I hadn't yet learned that travel leaves you with no choice but to trust complete strangers — and quoted us a price, which I agreed to immediately because I had no idea how much a taxi should cost.[141] We were on our way!

Forty-five minutes later, we'd circled the wall of Old Town Cartagena about twelve times, and our driver still couldn't find the hostel. He pulled over and

---

140 Thus began a pricey habit of taking taxis instead of using local public transportation that we have never really been able to shake. Taxis are like a beacon of light guiding us in a confusing world, ready to whisk us away to anywhere we need to go — whether we know that destination or not. We have even relied on taxis in multiple destinations in place of ambulances: I still have no idea how to call an ambulance in Colombia, but by this point, I've taken a midnight taxi to the 24-hour pharmacy/clinic *several* times.

141 This can be a helpful thing to research before your trip, but taxi rate information isn't always found online, and often there aren't set amounts. In many places, taxi drivers are free to quote whatever rate they think you'll accept, and you're free to negotiate that rate down, if you like. We're well aware that most taxi drivers in South America charge a "gringo tax," which amounts to maybe a dollar or so more than what they'd likely charge a local; we usually choose not to be bothered by that tax, considering how much further a US dollar stretches for a local family than it does for us back home.

pointed at the address in our phone, doing his best to explain something in Spanish that went right over both of our heads.[142] We stared at him helplessly; we had no idea where we were or what was going on.

Our taxi driver took out his phone to make a call. Jeremy and I stared at each other, wide-eyed with alarm. Was he going to leave us here, on the side of the road, completely lost? Was he calling the cops on us?? Had we unknowingly done something illegal?

The driver spoke into the phone in rapid Spanish. Then, he hung up, handed back my phone (my precious, ancient phone! I was so relieved), and started driving again. Within minutes, we arrived at our hostel, safe and sound.

We realized that the driver must have called our hostel to ask for directions. As he helped us unload, we attempted to pay him more than the rate we'd agreed to, to account for the additional hour it took him to drive around in circles trying to find our hostel. "No," he insisted. We had already agreed to a rate, and that was the rate that we would pay.

We didn't realize it at the time, but that was our very first experience of Travel Magic, a small preview of the innumerable kindnesses we would experience during our trip and the many, many people who would help to point us in the right direction and make sure we were okay.

Sweating in the small lounge room of our hostel, none of that mattered. As our host showed us around and explained how to use the A/C and where to order our included breakfast, all I could think about was the fact that this was it: this was our life now. We had nothing else to return to and no home to go back to.

After stuffing our bags into the lockers next to our dorm room beds, we headed out to sightsee. We were in a brand new place! We had nowhere in particular to go, nowhere we needed to be. The world was wide open to us!

The realization washed over me in an overwhelming wave of shock and dismay. We had nowhere to go. No home to return to. What had we done?

---

142 On our many subsequent trips to Cartagena, we now finally understand what he must have been trying to tell us: the street names that Google uses don't match the ones that are used colloquially. The address, according to Google, is usually a number, something like "Carerra 10," but locals use a specific name for each segment of street or even a single block, like "Calle de San Antonio." This makes navigating using street addresses alone incredibly difficult; we've since learned to also include a screenshot of our accomodation on a map, just to be extra safe.

We walked silently through the hot, chaotic streets of Old Town Cartagena, dodging carts filled with fresh fruit and stacks of striped sombrero vueltiaos, past balconies laden with sweet fuschia flowers and ornate doors marking entrances to brightly colored buildings, jumping out of the way as taxis careened past us down narrow cobblestone alleys. I barely noticed any of it.

Eventually, we made our way to the edge of the city. We stood on crumbling 400-year-old walls, watching the sun set over the vibrantly blue Caribbean sea, and I felt tears stinging my eyes. This should have been a magical moment: we were free, we were here, we had made it. But all I could feel was a deep, welling ache in the pit of my stomach.

I turned to my husband, terrified to confide in him what I was feeling. But the instant I saw those big, green eyes full of concern and comfort — he really has the kindest eyes — I melted into a puddle of tears.[143] I was openly sobbing in the middle of Cartagena.

Through shaking breaths, I choked out my deepest, darkest fear. "I just ruined our lives," I wailed, snot running down my face, "and we're not even having FUN!"

My darling, patient husband wrapped me in his arms. "It's been, like, three hours," he said calmly, as I howled into his chest. "Just give it some time."

We made our way back to the hostel and, at my insistence, squeezed together into my twin-sized bunk bed. We pulled up our computer to put something comforting and familiar on Netflix. And then I had an idea that I knew would make me feel better.

Which is how we ended up messaging Jasper's owners to ask them if we could schedule a video call with their cat.[144]

As it turned out, Jeremy was right (as he usually is): we just needed some time

---

143 Jeremy has this magical ability to look right into a person's soul, ask them, "Hey, are you okay?" and instantly reduce them to a pile of blubbering, vulnerable tears. As a high school teacher, this superpower is incredibly helpful when it comes to building relationships with students (and teachers), but often results in him biting off way more than he can chew.

144 Jeremy insists that he didn't let me actually ask for a video call, and it's been a point of contention for so long that we finally pulled up the message we'd sent them on Nextdoor. It's a pretty obvious cry for help, but we did indeed stop just short of asking specifically for a video call. We did, however, let two people we'd never met know what we cared deeply for their cat, and ask them to send us some photos of him. Understandably, they never responded.

to adjust. Although that very first night in Cartagena wouldn't be the only time during our trip we would find ourselves questioning whether we'd made the right decision, as the days turned into weeks, and then months, we adapted and grew to appreciate the unpredictable rhythms of long-term travel.

After several months and without us noticing, a shift took place: constant travel became our new "normal." We grew intimately familiar with its challenges, learned to expect the unexpected, and found ourselves amused when it inevitably arrived to ruin all of our carefully laid plans. We left behind the burden of anxiety that had hung over us at the beginning of our trip.

To use a term borrowed from Colombia that we've used ever since, we finally found our "tranquilo."

What Actually Happened

Although nothing went exactly as we planned it, our year-long honeymoon was every bit as incredible, amazing, and life-changing as I'd dreamt it would be (just in entirely different ways than I'd anticipated).

We spent five months backpacking through South America before flying home, changing plans, and heading to Europe. We enjoyed nearly two months of European Christmas magic before we dropped everything to fly home and take care of my grandfather in the hospital.

Once we were stateside again, our momentum slowed. We spent a few months couchsurfing around, visiting family and friends and anyone who had a spare room. We were spinning our wheels, with our cash funds running low and no real plan for getting back abroad. This is one of the only parts of our trip that I look back on with any kind of regret: I wish we had booked a cheap flight out of the country to literally anywhere as soon as we realized that my grandfather was okay!

After several aimless months in the USA, we finally booked a flight to Mexico and holed up for a house sitting gig in Puebla. It was exactly what we needed: we spent nearly an entire, glorious month doing nothing but walking the two sweet dogs in our care, going to the local mercado for groceries (Jeremy finally nailed his grandfather's salsa recipe, a long-contested Garcia family mystery), and blogging.

After several months of doing very little, our energy was fully restored. We spent a few weeks backpacking our way down the Riviera Maya and ended our trip with two weeks in Costa Rica. And a few days before our final flight home, I landed in the hospital with an excruciating ear infection: it was the perfect cherry on top of a disastrously wonderful year-long honeymoon.

In total, we visited 15 countries and 56 destinations, in a somewhat random order:

- **Colombia:** Cartagena, Parque Tayrona, Santa Marta, Minca, Cartagena again, Medellín, Salento, San Gil, Bogotá

- **Ecuador:** Quito, the Galapagos, Quito again, Cotopaxi, Latacunga, the Quilotoa Loop (Quilotoa, Chugchilán, Isinlivi, and Sigchos), Latacunga again, Baños, Cuenca, Vilcabamba

- **Perú**: Chachapoyas, Cajamarca, Huanchaco, Huaraz, Lima, Huacachina, Arequipa, Cusco, Ollantaytambo, Aguas Calientes, Cusco again, Arequipa again, Lima again

- **Chile**: Santiago, Valparaiso

- **Argentina**: Mendoza

- **Denmark**: Copenhagen

- **Germany**: Hamburg, Bremen

- **The Netherlands:** Amsterdam

- **Belgium**: Bruges, Antwerp, Brussels

- **France**: Road trip through Nice, Montpellier, Bordeaux, Avignon, Seillans, Nice again

- **Monaco**: We just drove through Monaco (and got a ticket)

- **Spain**: Barcelona

- **USA**: Hermosa Beach, Clearwater, Disney World, Hermosa Beach again, San Francisco, Paso Robles and the Central Coast, Louisville

- **Mexico**: Puebla, Mexico City, Isla Mujeres, Cancun, Tulum

- **Costa Rica:** La Fortuna, Quepos/Manuel Antonio, San José

It's hard to pick favorites, but three of the places we went really stood out to us:

1. We fell in love straight away with our very first stop: Colombia. We loved everything about Colombia: the people, the food, the diversity of things to do, the stunning scenery, the complex history, the music and dancing, the concept of "tranquilo." We loved Colombia so much we've since visited four more times and, on one trip, we even brought a group of Jeremy's high school students with us!

2. The week we spent in the Galapagos Islands was one of the best weeks of our entire trip. We visited three islands by land and spent each day snorkelling, meeting animals (ethically and responsibly), swimming, hiking, and falling in love with these beautiful islands. The fresh seafood,

the beaches filled with unapologetic sea lions and sneezing lizards, the waving palm trees and sandy white beaches — the Galapagos Islands are a magical place, and we can't wait to go back.

3. Of the two months we spent in Europe, Belgium took the top spot as our favorite country. The reason why comes down to two words: chocolate and beer. And waffles. Ok, three words. Oh, and fries. Four words. Oh, and then those spicy little cookies, speculoos. Are you getting the picture yet?!

Honestly, it was a lot more than the food that made us appreciate Belgium: it was a peculiar sense of humor that seemed to permeate everything, the complicated history (and mismatched architecture to reflect the complicated history), the magic and charm and swans of Bruges, and the delightfully ridiculous museums of Brussels. We had no expectations for Belgium, and it completely surprised us.

Over our year-long adventure, we traveled in a variety of different ways, including by bus, chicken bus, mototaxi (my favorite), Willy (Jeremy's favorite), colectivo, rickshaw, rental car, and taxi. Weirdly, we didn't take a single train, even in Europe: it was much cheaper to take the bus or fly.[145]

We stayed in hostels, glamped in luxury tents (also at hostels), slept in hammocks, enjoyed a handful of Airbnbs and a few house sitting gigs, and stayed in exactly two hotels.

As we travelled, we lost many, many things. Three of them still make me upset to think about:

- **We lost Jeremy's prescription sunglasses a mere two weeks into our trip.** They were the first thing we lost, and the most expensive. We aren't sure whether they fell out of our bag or were stolen, but we last saw them in a taxi in Colombia. Jeremy had to squint for an entire year.

- **I left my Kindle Fire on an overnight bus in Peru.** I went back to the station to try to recover it, but it was long gone. I hope you enjoy reading every Harry Potter book in English, lucky new owner of my Kindle!

---

145 Willys are open-air jeeps that only exist in Salento, Colombia, and they are SO much fun (and provide an excellent opportunity for giggling over immature jokes). You can either sit safely inside on a row of seats, or you can stand on the bumper and hang off the back, enjoying the view and hoping your arms don't get tired (this was Jeremy's favorite, of course). The only form of public transportation more fun than Willys, in my opinion, are mototaxis. Riding on the back of a mototaxi through the jungle in Minca, Colombia, is one of my all-time favorite travel adventures!

- **Our hostel lost Jeremy's beloved hiking pants the night before we went to hike the Inca Trail.** This was really an omen that we should have listened to. We had sent them to the laundry the day before our hike, and we never saw them again. Poor Jeremy lived in those pants. Pantsless, he had to hike the Inca Trail in a pair of leggings from the hostel lost & found and his sauna-like rain pants, squinting the entire time. No wonder we didn't make it.

To make up for what we lost, we gained plenty of animal friends, including:

- Lupe the sea lion, who hangs out at the fish market each day in Puerto Ayora.

- Baloo, a giant Saint Bernard who lives at a hostel on the Quilotoa Loop and is best friends with Tito, the resident guard llama

- Caila, an incredibly sweet boxer puppy at a hostel in Arequipa, Peru.

- A bunch of sassy alpacas and llamas at Machu Picchu that we tried to take selfies with.

When we weren't losing things or attempting to befriend llamas, we were usually getting sick or injured. While I was more prone to stomach sickness and other internal illnesses during our trip, poor Jeremy kept doing things like tripping and falling, injuring himself on very sharp rocks while surfing or swimming, and bumping his giant head on everything. We are both the clumsiest people alive, and I'm genuinely concerned about our future offspring.

In between mild head injuries, Jeremy explored his love for high-octane adventure sports, while I developed an extreme dislike for anything even mildly adrenaline-inducing.

Jeremy's Adventure Sports

- **Minca, Colombia:** Cliff diving

- **San Gil, Colombia:** White-water rafting, waterfall rappelling, canyoning, paragliding

- **The Galapagos Islands, Ecuador**: Snorkeling

- **Cotopaxi, Ecuador**: Horseback riding

- **Baños, Ecuador**: Canyoning, white water rafting, ziplining

- **Vilcabamba, Ecuador:** Horseback riding

- **Huanchacho, Peru:** Surfing

- **Huacachina, Peru:** Sandboarding and dune buggying

- **Arequipa, Peru**: White-water rafting

- **Mendoza, Argentina:** White-water rafting

- **Hermosa Beach, California**: Surfing

- **Isla Mujeres, Mexico:** Snorkeling

- **Tulum, Mexico:** Cliff diving

- **La Fortuna, Costa Rica:** Canyoning, cliff diving, white-water rafting

Lia's Adventure Regrets

- **San Gil, Colombia:** White-water rafting *(hated it)*, paragliding *(terrifying)*, waterfall rappelling *(had to be rescued)*

- **The Galapagos Islands, Ecuador:** Snorkeling *(almost ran into a sea lion)*

- **Baños, Ecuador:** Ziplining *(had a panic attack)*

- **Vilcabamba, Ecuador**: Horseback riding *(horse tried to kill me)*

- **Huacachina, Peru**: Dune buggying *(swallowed sand, thought I might die)*

- **Isla Mujeres, Mexico:** Snorkeling *(saw an intimidating fish)*

- **Tulum, Mexico:** Swam in a cenote *(got sick for an entire day)*

- **La Fortuna, Costa Rica:** White-water rafting *(got an ear infection)*

Throughout our many adventures (and just as many misadventures), we learned that the real gifts of long-term travel aren't just the incredible places that you'll go and the wonderful things you'll do there: it's the things you'll learn about yourself, the world, and about human nature in general. Which brings us to the things nobody told us.

The Things Nobody Told Us

It's impossible to predict the myriad ways in which long-term travel will affect you. Honestly, doing so is an exercise in futility: you'll just have to find out for yourself. However, there are a number of things that nobody told us, things that struck as the kind of universal truths that might have been useful to know in advance.

Like, for instance, that Ecuador is filled with tiny trash cans designed to look like clowns.

Or that finding toilet paper in the bathroom is not a universal guarantee, so if you want to use it, you'd better bring some along with you. (And don't assume you can throw it into the toilet, either).[146]

Or that once you've experienced the charm and magic of European Christmas Markets, nothing in the U.S. will ever come close again. (Seriously though, Mariah Carey playing on repeat in a decorated shopping mall is the best we've got?! What have we even been DOING for the last 200 years!?!)

And so we started publishing blog posts about all of the Things Nobody Told Us.[147] They've since become a hallmark of Practical Wanderlust, and I find them the best way to explain all of the weird, not-necessarily-helpful observations that I make during our travels.

And so, here are all of the things nobody tells you about quitting your job to travel:

- **Arriving at the airport is terrifying.**

Sure, you thought the day you quit your job was scary — but actually leaving is so much worse. The minute your plane lands, excitement will give way to immediate terror and regret.

---

146 While we're on the subject, get in the habit of constantly carrying around a little bar of soap or some hand sanitizer, too.

147 We have "Things Nobody Tells You" posts about everything from backpacking through South America to being a full-time blogger to our adopted home city in Oakland! If you'd like to dive into a nice long binge read, you can find them at practicalwanderlust.com/tag/things-no-one-tells-you/

The chaos of landing in a new place, trying to navigate from the airport, suddenly being immersed in a foreign language: the unfamiliarity of it all will overwhelm you.

You'll never feel more homesick on your travels than you will during the first couple of days of your trip, when the magnitude of what you've done finally hits you.

- **After the first few weeks, everything feels so much easier.**

You'll still be emotionally raw for the first couple of weeks as you ease into your new life, and at first, you'll feel totally overwhelmed by your new daily reality. You might mourn your old life and wonder if you've made a huge mistake.

But after the first few weeks, things will start to feel SO much easier. You'll find yourself getting used to the act of constant traveling, enjoying yourself more, and missing home a little less.

Months later, as a weathered, experienced traveler, you'll look back at the nervous, scared selfie you took at the airport and laugh at how naive and carefree you were way back then.

How little you knew then. How young you were.

- **You will take way too many pictures.**

We didn't even have a chance to look through our wedding photos before we'd easily amassed another 20,000 pictures. We took photos of everything: random cute dogs on the street, every plate of food we've eaten for the past 12 months, every time Jeremy got really excited over a new flavor of local ice cream.[148]

I felt a burning need to document everything just in case one day I get desperate and write a blog post like "all the dogs we took pictures of in South America" or "every plate of food we ate for the past twelve months." I kept our photos backed up by syncing our phones to the cloud, uploading all of our photos to Google

---

148 Jeremy set himself the very achievable goal of eating ice cream in every destination we visited. He was thrilled whenever he encountered new flavors, like lúcuma in Peru, a delicious fruit that tastes like caramel. I have about a zillion photos of Jeremy happily enjoying ice cream all over the world, which I saved in a folder on my computer called "Jeremy Eating Ice Cream."

Drive on our Chromebook, so not a single blurry llama selfie was lost.[149] (For what it's worth, I do still treasure all 20,000 of those photos).

- **The concept of "time" will take on new meaning for you.**

Or maybe less of a meaning. We stopped keeping track of things like days of the week, except for when they affected us (like whenever we realized it was Sunday and everything in the entire continent of South America was shut down, leaving us totally screwed for finding something to eat).

At some point, you'll stop bothering to change your watch to the correct time zone. You'll stop doing the math to figure out what time it is "at home."

And forget about waking up or going to sleep at reasonable times: why bother? We woke up whenever we felt like it, and sometimes — like in the dead of winter in Copenhagen — we just slept until there was light outside... at 10am.

- **You'll miss having control over transportation.**

It is so much easier to get from point A to point B when you're not traveling. Whether you own a car, ride your bike, or are just able to read the metro map in the language you actually speak, transportation is so much easier back at home.

But when you're traveling long term, going literally anywhere involves solving a series of confusing riddles.

You have to be wary of scammers and getting overcharged. You have to know which bus to take and where the heck to find it and when it runs and where to get off of it (all in another language, of course). You have to figure out weirdly specific local transit systems (like in the small town of Salento, Colombia, where we were incredibly confused by everyone referring to "Willys" rather than taxis). And, if you're anything like me, you'll spend most of your time in transit feeling nauseous and either sweating or freezing cold.

It's a whole ordeal. How we yearned for the days when we could rent a car or hop on our bikes and just go somewhere!

---

149   Losing photos and other digital data is incredibly common! Back yours up virtually using a service like Google Drive, Google Photos, or Dropbox. If you take giant photo files, like we do now, you might also consider carrying along an external hard drive with an extra terabyte of space — just in case!

- **You'll develop weird cravings for things from home.**

Turns out that when everything is new and unfamiliar, even your most mundane routines can creep up on you with this rose-colored Instagram filter where everything you used to do seems a lot more exciting than it actually was.

We started to miss everything. The minute we realized we couldn't have something, it was all we wanted.

Like the simple joy of sitting on a couch. Or riding the train to work every morning. (Even though our old couch had no legs, and my train commute was nearly two hours long each way.)

The strangest craving we developed was an odd fixation on Cinnamon Toast Crunch. Sure, CT Crunch is the greatest cereal that exists – hands down, no question – but we only eat it like, maybe once a year?

But for some reason, as soon as we realized that we couldn't get it in stores abroad (apparently sugary breakfast cereals are way more of a thing in the States than anywhere else) we craved it like crazy.

We dreamed about it. Every country we visited, we'd check for Cinnamon Toast Crunch in the grocery aisles.

The stupidest part? Now that we're back home again, we don't even really want it anymore.

- **You will crave some semblance of familiarity.**

A few months into our trip, we moved beyond the phase of being excited to try new things, and into the phase of deeply missing and craving familiarity. We went into shopping malls just to feel the warm glow of fluorescent, American capitalism; we reminisced about the good old U.S.A. with fellow travelers, waxing poetic about our rampant addiction to overwork and the shared experience of struggling with student loans and overpriced healthcare.

And we began a new tradition: we started eating at fast food chains, desperate for a taste of something familiar and nostalgic. In each new country, we visited American fast food restaurants and recorded our observations, ranking chains we'd never really liked by how they compared to the "real" versions back home.[150]

- **You'll develop strong opinions about food and drinks.**

Before our trip, my opinion on wine could answer the question "red or white?" and that was it. Beer? Gross, no thank you. Pisco? Literally no idea what that is.

But during our trip, we found out that we love distilleries, breweries, wineries, guided tastings, cooking classes, and food tours — if it combines eating and drinking with travel, we're in. And through our newfound obsession, we became snobby connoisseurs of worldly provisions.

Like wine: we've been wine tasting in four countries — which terroir are you referring to? Beer? Let me tell you about the nine-step pouring ritual for Belgian beer over a glass of Westvleteren. Pisco? We've tasted it straight from the barrel AND learned how to make Pisco Sours from scratch. Belgian waffles? Liege waffles or Brussels waffles; would you like to hear us explain the minute differences between the two?[151]

It's like all of our travel stories converged with our food preferences to turn us into the most irritating, know-it-all dining companions ever.

We also developed preferences for things we'd never even liked before. For instance, while backpacking through South America, we found ourselves completely addicted to agua con gas and constantly craving the bubbly, room-temperature bliss of a grocery store aisle gas water — even though back home, I thought plain sparkling water was gross.

We even became brand snobs: nothing comes close to a crisp bottle of Guitig, which is made in Ecuador from snow-melt filtered through the Andes, naturally

---

150 Argentina, we found, has the best versions of U.S. fast food: their McDonald's serves actual ice cream, plus a delicious burger with sauteed mushrooms and dijon mustard. KFC in Peru was disappointing: they only served chicken with none of the traditional sides, much like the popular chicken "Broaster" restaurants that are ubiquitous throughout Peru. And we found that ketchup varied wildly by country: some were sweeter, others more tangy. Of course, we documented all of our findings with photos and detailed notes; another long-lost blog post that we never ended up writing, complete with countless pictures of Jeremy methodically examining cheeseburgers and chicken nuggets.

151 I can't resist, so: Liege waffles are round, with a dense texture sprinkled with delicious, crunchy caramelized bits of sugar. Brussels waffles are larger and square shaped, with a soft, fluffy crumb and a crispy exterior. Both are delicious, especially when topped with sour cherries and fresh whipped cream. Oh my god, I'm so hungry.

carbonated in mineral caves deep under the earth, and hand-bottled by tiny herds of magical alpacas.

- **You'll wish you could stick to a diet & exercise plan.**

Before we left for this trip, we felt strong and healthy. We cooked all of our own meals to fit whatever millennial diet obsession we were doing that year — gluten-free! Paleo! Keto! Whole 30! — and we worked out three days a week at least.

Then we spent a year eating rice and potatoes in South America and baguettes and beer in Europe and trying every new, delicious food we could. We lost all of our hard-earned muscle and started missing things like salads (sadly, eating raw veggies when you're traveling abroad is usually a bad idea).

As a result, we returned from our Very Big Adventure carrying about thirty extra pounds of weight and not fitting into any of our old clothes. I've long since made my peace with my happy travel weight, and I consider it a long-lasting souvenir from our trip.

Of course, if we REALLY wanted to stick to a diet and exercise plan, I'm sure we could have. But we're naturally lazy people, and a fitness routine would probably have required waking up and getting coffee before noon.

- **You'll fall hopelessly behind on pop culture.**

Long-term travel is the cultural equivalent of spending a year living under a rock. Pretty soon, you'll be behind on everything that's cool back home, from music to movies to pop culture references to memes.

Meanwhile, you'll be discovering brand new artists on your travels that nobody back home has ever heard of. And pretty soon, you'll find yourself operating in the ancillary region of People Who Aren't Hip back at home.

You'll return from your trip and not understand what people are wearing, talking about, or listening to. When did THOSE jeans become cool? What's that meme everyone's quoting?! Did nobody else spend all summer jamming to that new Enrique Iglesias song?!

You're so lost. Oh god. Are you old?!

- **You will develop a weirdly high tolerance for time spent in transit.**

After a zillion miserable 18-hour overnight bus rides on unpaved cliffside roads while watching poorly dubbed Fast and the Furious 18: A Series of Fast & Furious Events and trying desperately not to hurl, anything shorter seems like a walk in the park.

Spending eight hours cramped and thirsty on a budget airplane? Ain't no thing. Bring it on, Ryanair. Six-hour drive to go see some random roadside attraction you found on Atlas Obscura? Reasonable day trip. Your transit time tolerance will be superhuman.

- **You will develop a weirdly low tolerance for doing laundry.**

Back at home it was pretty common for us to re-wear the same pair of jeans for a couple of weeks straight. Now we re-wear everything for weeks on end. Laundry day isn't even the day we run out of underwear anymore: it's several weeks past that.

You may call it gross, but we call it economical — laundry costs money when you're traveling! Precious money that could be otherwise spent on important things, like croissants and beer.

But hey, don't worry: showers are usually free. Usually.

- **The clothes you bring with you will not be the same clothes you return home with.**

I painstakingly packed every piece of clothing carefully with an intended purpose in mind like "this is my Hiking Shirt™" "this is my Casual Dress,™" but then we had to do laundry in sinks and move from hostel to hostel all the time, and somewhere along the way, all of my carefully chosen clothes were lost and replaced with random t-shirts, a giant scarf with an eagle on it, and three pairs of sunglasses I've never seen before in my life.

- **Traveling constantly will become exhausting.**

I've never been a relaxed traveler. I don't do "laying on the beach" well. When Jeremy and I travel, we go out and explore, hike, take tours, have adventures — we don't sit around and relax.

But when you're traveling nonstop, you simply cannot keep up. After a few weeks of constant, daily exploring, you'll be EXHAUSTED. You'll realize that it's not sustainable to travel long-term the same way you used to travel on weekend trips or two-week vacations when time was of the essence. You can't go out and do stuff every single day for months on end. (Plus, all that sightseeing gets fairly expensive.)

Eventually, you'll be so exhausted from constant traveling that you'll just want a day — or a week, or maybe a month — off from traveling. You'll just want to sit inside and do nothing. Maybe mindlessly scroll around on the internet for a good eight hours. Binge watch a TV show or something. You know... boring shit.

You'll crave boring shit like you never thought was possible back when all you craved was adventure.

- **Don't bother complaining to your friends.**

Absolutely nobody wants to hear you complain about your amazing trip, so don't go to your friends for a vent session about how you're just so burnt out on ruins and temples and restaurant meals. They will have zero sympathy for you. "Oh, there are too many exciting things for you to do all the time? You poor thing."

And you know what? They're not wrong. Being exhausted and burnt out sucks. But traveling full time is still a dream come true.

By all means, complain to other travelers about it — your feelings are valid. But if you start to catch yourself feeling too negative, try to identify what's driving your discontent and problem-solve a way to adjust your travel speed or itinerary to accommodate for your needs.

Remember that you chose this — this was your dream! And even if it's not perfect, it's still absolutely amazing.

In the same vein, don't take it personally if your friends back home don't really seem that interested in hearing about all of your incredible amazing travel experiences. Nobody cares about all the wonderful, exciting adventures you're having every day as much as you do, and maybe — if you've lucked out in the parent department — your mom and dad.

We found that it's hard for people back home to even wrap their heads around how MUCH stuff you're doing every single day, how many entirely new and exciting things you've seen and done and experienced. For most folks back at home, there's usually only one or two things to report in response to the question "so what have you been up to?" But on a long-term trip, there's an astronomical, never-ending sea of stories.

Our loved ones are probably still catching up on our travel stories while reading this book (or our blog, or listening to our podcast), and it's not for lack of trying. There's just too much to cover!

Remember: it's not personal. They still love you. And you'll have plenty of time to catch them up on all the wonderful things you did when you're back home again. Savor your experiences for yourself — and be sure to document them in some way so your own faulty human memory is able to relive them in the distant future.[152]

- **You're going to make some awesome new friends that totally get your obsessive love of travel.**

You'll be meeting so many other travelers — in hostel dorms, on tours, in bars, working remotely in the same cafe — and you'll make fast friends with many of them. There's something about travel that speeds up a new relationship (romantic or otherwise) and the people you meet abroad may just end up your friends for life.

Since those new friends will share your obsession with travel (and many will be traveling long-term themselves) they'll just "get" some of the things that your friends back home won't. And you can complain to them about how exhausted you are without them judging you, which is always nice.

- **You'll get tired of talking about your travels to everyone who actually DOES care.**

Meeting brand-new travel buddies who ask "how long are you traveling? Where have you been?" gets tiresome after a while. After the 38th time you've told some-

---

152   I have a terrible memory, so for me, blogging was a way to record our experiences for myself (knowing I'd forget them all later). To this day, when I go back and read my old blog posts from the trip — which I did quite a lot while writing this book — I find myself re-living things I'd completely forgotten, laughing at stories that have long since entirely vanished in my memory (ahem: it's only been a few years, I just have a REALLY terrible memory). Write it all down — every new experience, every bump in the road! You'll be glad you did later.

one you just met about how much you loved the Galapagos and why Colombia and Belgium are your favorite countries and how you had to get rescued off a waterfall that one time, you'll start to feel like a broken record.

- **You'll start to miss spending quality time with people.**

You'll miss friends and family who you feel completely comfortable with. You'll miss inside jokes and feeling totally understood. And you'll miss being able to hang out with people for more than a week at a time before they (or you) move on to the next exciting adventure.

If you're traveling with a companion, you'll start to miss spending time with people who aren't your companion, too.

- **You'll miss stability.**

Moving constantly from place to place will get old fast. You'll get sick of unpacking your stuff just to pack it up a week or so later and make somewhere new your home.

You'll start doing things like finding "your" grocery store or "your" coffee shop in each new location you travel to, and establishing daily little micro-routines to keep you grounded (like watching Netflix every night). Your soul will feel nourished by any small slice of regular life. It will recharge you the way that travel used to recharge you when you were a regular person with a job and a home of your own.

- **You'll develop a burning need to "nest" somewhere, anywhere, everywhere.**

If you travel for long enough, spending three days somewhere will feel like your new home. You'll start doing things like arranging your belongings carefully in your locker.

Anything you can do to make someplace feel like a home, however tiny or temporary, will become The Biggest Deal. Like, whenever there was a shelf in a room where we were staying, we flipped out.

When your travel companion doesn't put their belongings away in the extremely detailed and secret order that you unpacked them, you'll get cranky and say ridiculous things like "you're supposed to put your socks in THIS PILE, not THAT PILE. That's where they BELONG."

Picking up your stuff and moving every few days to go explore a new place is as exhausting as it is exciting, and you may find yourself craving a home base with every travel-spent fiber of your being. We got to the point where we casually browsed apartment listings back at home like we used to browse online looking for our next travel destination.

- **"Museum fatigue" is very real.**[153]

We've always been the sort of travelers who enjoy perusing art museums to learn about local culture and history. So I figured, we'll hit up a lot of art museums. Art museums are great.

But after hitting a museum every week for a month, we were like "Um, can we just Google the local history?"

Nowadays, if it's not free or rated 15/10 on Tripadvisor, it's not happening. In a similar vein: statues, churches, arches, cathedrals that aren't world-famous, and ruins that aren't literally Machu Picchu.[154]

- **The excitement of each new place you go will start to fade.**

After a few months of constant travel, you'll stop getting that tingle of butterflies when you hop on yet another 12-hour overnight bus. That shiny, sparkle-in-your-eye excitement as you groggily step off the bus into the dawn light in a brand new place will give way to an exhausted traveler who's tired, cranky, smelly, slightly nauseous, and dreading the task of haggling with aggressive taxi drivers, walking through plumes of car exhaust, and getting lost just trying to find somewhere to sleep in yet another unfamiliar place.

We learned that we needed to travel slower and stay in each place longer just to scrounge up the mental energy to look forward to going somewhere new.

- **Your "travel" habits will replace your regular habits.**

There's the "unable to wake up before 9am" thing. There's also the "made plans, but didn't feel like doing them, so instead I bought plane tickets to a different country" habit that many long-term travelers (including us) develop.

---

153 I didn't coin this term: museum fatigue is an academic phenomenon that's been studied since the 1910's. You'll hear travelers in Asia talk about "temple fatigue," or "cathedral fatigue" in Europe, and so on. It is a real thing!

154 A notable exception to the museum rule is Brussels, Belgium, where we BINGED on museums. Brussels has rad museums.

And then there's a Boy Scout-esque thing travelers do, where you feel like you have to prepare for every possible situation each day "just in case." Every day, each of us carried a fully packed day bag, as if we were always going on a hike to somewhere that has WiFi and outlets. We'd find ourselves standing in a grocery store or a bank or some other totally ordinary place with giant packs on our backs like "Why the hell did we bring all this crap?"

Things Nobody Tells You About Long-Term Travel as a Couple

When you're traveling with a romantic partner, long-term travel will affect your relationship in strange and unexpected ways.

- **Pick one: intimacy or spending cash.**

When traveling long-term on a budget, privacy is a luxury — and you can't always afford to sleep in the same bed. All I have to say about that is, welcome to our marriage, 12 total strangers! We're ALL sharing the bedroom now.[155]

- **Your relationship will age by several years longer than your actual trip.**

Through various incredibly scientific calculations, we deduced that the amount of time we spent together as newlyweds (all day, every day, for a full year) versus most normal people who have other things to do (jobs, friends, errands to run on their own, lives, etc.) gave us the equivalent of roughly five years of marriage in a one-year span.

I can count on one hand the number of times we were apart during our year-long honeymoon, and it shows. When we started the trip, we were that sickeningly cute couple that did obnoxious stuff like play-fight over when to hang up or who got to eat the last bite.

By the end of our trip we were like a sad, mid-40s couple who has run out of things to say and is so exhausted by raising children and paying bills that conversation is actually too much of a hassle to even bother. All of our conversations started out like "How was your day? … Never mind, I was there."

---

155 We highly recommend booking a private room every so often, just to keep things romantic.

Speaking of which, spending every single second of every single day glued to each other's sides doesn't make for thrilling dinnertime conversation. If one of you so much as leaves the room without the other person, suddenly there will be so much more to catch up on than usual. "How was the bathroom?" will be a new exciting conversation starter.

- **You'll miss each other way more than is normal for extremely short periods of time spent apart.**

Ventured out on a journey to the store alone? You'll feel yourself irrationally missing your other half and excitedly sharing inane details upon your grand reunion, like the kinds of cheeses you found and how much they cost.

Also: if you go to the store and don't bring back a fun snack for your partner, I'd call a lawyer, because those are grounds for divorce.[156]

- **You'll have the same songs stuck in your collective head for weeks on end and neither of you will even know the name of the song... or any of the words.**

The worst offenders for us were cumbia hits by artists we've never heard of, whose words we were unable to grasp except for "corazon," which is in every popular song in South America — so we couldn't even Google the song to put ourselves out of our misery.

We found ourselves humming the same repetitive notes for days. And days. And days...

- **You'll eventually stop feeling like two different people and begin to feel and act as one conjoined human.**

Your partner will feel like an extra limb, like an extension of yourself. Which is kinda romantic, but it also quickly verges from romanticism into weirdness. Like when you catch a glimpse of yourself in the mirror and accidentally call yourself by your partner's name before realizing that's actually your own reflection.

- **You'll accidentally wear matching outfits. All the time.**

Even if you didn't intentionally bring all of the same clothes, you'll still somehow end up looking eerily alike. If you're like us and happen to own a lot of the

---

156 This is the second most serious grounds for divorce in our marriage, the first one being watching "your" TV show without your partner. No relationship can pass that test.

HOW TO QUIT YOUR JOB & TRAVEL

same clothes already, you'll inevitably find yourself getting dressed — only to turn around to find your partner wearing the exact same outfit.

- **99% of your arguments will involve hunger, exhaustion, or feeling overwhelmed. Watch out if all three hit at once.**

You'll learn to interpret your partner's crankiness, like "Oh, that's your hunger sass. Let's get you a snack." You'll also learn to ask your partner three questions so you can solve them as quickly as possible and get your companion back: "Are you hungry? Are you tired? Are you feeling overwhelmed?"

In those moments, a snack, some coffee, or just spending a few moments sitting quietly can work miracles. If you let those feelings take over, you'll soon find yourself in full-on meltdown mode, screaming at each other in the street while complete strangers stare at you. (Listen: we've all been that couple.)

- **You'll learn not to take those arguments personally.**

Travel is full of challenges, and no couple is safe from the occasional fight. They are inevitable. You'll learn not to take it personally when your partner snaps at you because they're cranky, hungry, tired, homesick, or just overwhelmed. Not taking it personally means fewer fights and fewer "I'm sorry for what I said when I was hungry" conversations. Instead, you'll be able to just say "That's OK, it just means next time I'M cranky, you can't say shit!"

This is so much easier said than done, but once you get there most of your arguments will stop being disruptive, which means you can go back to your regularly planned adventures faster.

Tricks of the Trade

As we travelled, we picked up habits that we came to think of as "tricks of the trade," age-old traveler's lore and helpful habits during our trip. Our favorite bit of travel lore, of course, is Travel Magic: we encountered Travel Magic everywhere we went, from the kindness of strangers to fortuitous happenstance that seemed to have come from the universe itself. Like, for instance, when we found ourselves hiking so slowly on the stunning Valle de Cocora hike[157] that we were terrified we'd miss the last Willy of the evening and end up stranded — only to realize that even worse, we were totally out of cash.

But Travel Magic came to our rescue: we caught the last Willy, thanks to a faster hiker who asked the driver to wait. The Willy driver was happy to take us to the only ATM in town to replenish our cash supplies. But in another weird twist, the ATM wasn't working; in fact, the entire town was mysteriously out of power.[158]

No matter: our driver cheerfully returned us to our hostel and talked to the front desk, who paid him out and added the extra amount to our hostel bill. We were left totally "tranquilo," free to enjoy a freezing cold, pitch-black shower and a candlelit, family-style dinner: it ended up being one of the most magical evenings of our entire trip.

Although you'll develop your own favorite travel tricks as you go, here are a few tips we've picked up over the years to get you started.

Travel Safety: Staying Safe & Avoiding Theft

As anxious travelers, travel safety was a major concern during our trip. What if we got robbed? What if we got lost? What if we got kidnapped by guerillas in a jungle and nobody even noticed we were gone until our faces showed up in the news?!

---

157 Hiking is perhaps an exaggeration. We spent most of our time trying not to fall in knee-deep mud, attempting to extricate ourselves out of knee-deep mud, and at one point, cheerfully sipping hot chocolate and eating cheese while watching wild hummingbirds. You can read all about this adventure in our post: Hiking Valle De Cocora in Salento, Colombi.

158 You'll get used to random and unexpected power outages; in many places, they're fairly common. Learn to expect the power to go out when it would be most inconvenient, because that's always when outages occur.

We may have particularly active imaginations, but leaving the comforts of home and exploring a foreign country is undeniably a little scary. Still, letting your fear keep you from traveling would be a real shame.

That said, some of the most obnoxious advice we've gotten from seasoned travelers is to "not worry about it." Not worry about it?! As if! Worry leads to preparation, and preparation makes you less vulnerable.

But there's a nice middle ground between "Don't worry about it, you'll be fine" and worrying so much you never leave the house, and that middle ground is where you take reasonable precautions and prepare yourself to face any of those scary circumstances that can pop up on a trip. With a few basic travel safety tips, you'll feel more like an informed, prepared traveler — and not like a walking target.

Besides, travel mishaps either aren't as bad as your imagination makes them out to be, or aren't as likely as the news — and your overly concerned parents — would have you believe.

For example, everyone's heard horror stories of being mugged and left stranded while traveling abroad. In my personal experience, however, most theft while traveling abroad is an opportunistic crime: make one rookie mistake and you become an easy mark.

And it's not just traveling abroad, either. I was robbed at least three times in three months when I moved from Kentucky to the big city of San Francisco: I had my phone and ID stolen twice, and my purse was stolen out of a locked locker at a gym (stupid cheap lock). I even had a man attempt to mug me in broad daylight on a crowded street at 5pm in front of my office!

Am I just a walking disaster magnet? Yes. But also, I can point to a few things I could have done in each instance to make it a little less easy to steal from me:

- The first time I had my phone and ID stolen, they were sitting in my purse in plain sight on the floor of a restaurant, with easy access to the door. Nowadays at a restaurant, I keep my purse underneath me or the table where it can't be easily accessed.

- The second time I had my phone and ID stolen, they were in my jacket pocket... but I took my jacket off at a club, stuck it in the corner, and hit the dance floor. I wasn't watching them, so I never saw them get taken. I don't do that anymore.

- The locked locker was kind of a fluke — although I no longer use cheap locks — and I've learned to keep things in the trunk of my car instead. (Never on the backseat — we've had too many car windows broken into to make that mistake again!)

- My attempted mugging? My mistake was that I was staring at my phone while walking down the street instead of paying attention to my surroundings. (My second mistake was that I fought off the guy who tried to mug me — that's a really dumb move. Don't do that. Phones are replaceable).

Now that I've wised up and developed city-slicker street smarts, I have not been robbed a single time since — at home or abroad.

But that's not all: combined with the other precautions I take, I know that even if I am robbed while traveling, I have a way to access money, insurance to replace my belongings or cover me in case of injury, a network of people who know where I am at all times, and copies of the necessary legal documents to return home. That brings me incredible peace of mind so that I can actually enjoy my trip!

Learn from my mistakes and use these basic safety tips for travelers to protect yourself and prevent theft.

- **Research and prepare before you leave.**

Travel safety starts before you even get on the plane: it begins when you're pulling together your Trip Roadmap. Ensure you've done sufficient research on your destination: what are common safety risks and what scams are prevalent in that country? Which neighborhoods are considered unsafe for tourists? Read reviews on the places you'll be visiting and the hostels you're staying at.

Google "[Your Destination] Common Scams" or "Is [Your Destination] Safe?" to find suggestions and experiences that will help you to prepare. (But try not to let it make you too anxious! You want to be prepared, not terrified).

Doing research will help you to feel more comfortable and confident when traveling to a new country... and to not buy that train ticket from that pushy French guy at the airport metro station in Paris who just happened to be sitting around waiting for a crowd of tourists to help him offload his definitely-not-fake $20 train ticket. I nearly fell for this on my first trip to Paris, by the way!

It's also crucial to take the safety steps outlined in Part Two, including pulling together physical and digital copies of all of your important documents, sending out details of your trip itinerary to your family and friends, and buying a travel insurance policy to cover your trip.

- **Be mindful and take extra precautions during transit and in crowds.**

One of the times you're at your most vulnerable during a trip is in transit. A bus station or airport is like a pickpocket buffet: there are large crowds of confused, overwhelmed people carrying all of their belongings while completely preoccupied. If I was going to embark on a life of crime, I'd probably start there.[159]

It's all too easy to bump into someone and quickly grab something, without them noticing, when everyone is bumping into everyone else. This is doubly true for a crowded bus or subway when you can be standing elbow-to-elbow with hundreds of people.

Pickpockets are looking for your attention to be diverted so that you don't feel something being slipped out of your pocket or purse — don't give them the chance. Avoid keeping things in your back pocket — it's an easy target.

When you find yourself in a crowd, keep your hands on or in any pocket that you're keeping something in, and over any openings in a purse. If you can, wear your purse across your body and tucked under your arm so that its opening is towards your body and inaccessible. And never wear a purse that cannot be zipped, fastened, or covered![160]

On transit days, I also put my passport in a zippered passport holder with my

---

159 My next book is called "How to Do Crime: A Practical Approach to Taking Advantage of Tourists, Who Never See It Coming."

160 Or, join me in creating a purse-free world. Together, we'll have sweaty boob cash, actual-sized pockets, and *freedom*. It will be so beautiful! ... At the very least, just get a bra pocket or money belt and a few pieces of clothing with hidden, zippered pockets.

phone, which is fastened firmly across my body and never comes off, even when I'm fast asleep on a bus or plane.[161] It's also a good idea to wear your backpack or daybag in the front when walking through crowded streets.

And always, always maintain eye contact with your belongings. When your back is turned, your stuff is easy to snatch. That includes absolutely everything: sunglasses, phone, purse, even your drink. If it's not in your hand, keep it within eyesight!

- **Keep your money in multiple locations, and always have an emergency credit card.**

This is so important: Never, EVER travel with all your money in one location! Get in the habit of stashing emergency money and credit cards throughout your luggage and on your body in separate places. This way, even if you're robbed while out and about, there's a good chance you'll still have a card and some cash tucked away in a sock or rolled into an empty mini M&M's container somewhere.[162]

In the vein of not putting all your eggs in one basket, it's also a good idea to have a few backup cards spread out across different banks. If your bank freezes a card or you lose one, some banks will freeze all of your cards, which is super unhelpful and leaves you without access to money. Play it safe and stuff a random, no-annual-fee credit card deep in your bag.

- **Be careful when using your phone on a city bus, train, or while walking down the street.**

Protecting yourself from theft while traveling means being constantly aware of your surroundings. If you're zoning out on your phone, you're not aware of what's going on around you!

Buses and trains that are frequently stopping to let people on and off are hotbeds of phone theft. It's easy for an opportunistic thief to snatch the phone out of your hand and bolt for the door, disappearing before you even realize what just happened.

---

161 My tiny zippered passport pouch is the closest I get to wearing a purse these days. Just say no to purses!

162 We keep an empty plastic tube (upcycled from its former life holding pills, I think) stuffed with a wad of $20 bills, buried in a forgotten pocket deep in our bags. U.S. dollars can always be exchanged for foreign currency as needed, and are widely accepted worldwide in a pinch! We've only needed to dip into our emergency cash a few times (almost always because we didn't pull out enough at the ATM — or ended up somewhere without an ATM — and ran out of the local currency.)

The same applies to walking down the street: your phone is like a target that is all too easy to grab and run away with. I learned this lesson at home in San Francisco, where a good half of my friends — and myself — have had multiple phones stolen.

- **Deter thieves with locks on your bags.**

Whenever possible, lock your bag. Backpacks and luggage should always be locked during transit, even when stowed away. If someone next to you on a crowded bus can quietly slip their hand in your purse, they absolutely will. If your purse isn't zipped and lockable or doesn't have a flap that covers its opening, it's not good for travel (or anything, really; maybe just throw it away).

That said, a determined thief doesn't care if you've put a lock on your bag, but a casual or opportunistic thief will typically go for an easier target. Personally, I prefer non-TSA travel locks because it's easy for thieves to get a TSA universal lock key, but if you're checking your bag you'll need a TSA-approved travel lock.

- **Watch your back when using ATMs.**

ATMs have long been an easy place for thieves to swipe information from unsuspecting travelers — but they're also typically the most convenient and low-cost place to get money in foreign currencies while traveling.

So while we DO recommend using ATMs, we also encourage you to be cautious! When at an ATM, always cover your card with your hand when entering your pin and wiggle the card reader a little to ensure there are no signs of tampering. Also, ensure that the person behind you isn't too close, and if they are, politely ask them to give you some fucking space.

- **Keep valuables on you at all times while in transit.**

We've heard too many stories about bags hidden away under a bus or checked at the airport getting rifled through by opportunistic employees. So when we travel on a train, bus, or plane, we pull out all of our electronics, important documents, and other valuables and keep them on us in a locked bag that we never let out of our sight or off our person. That way, even if our backpacks get rifled through, all they'll find is clothing — the important stuff is safe with us!

And, as we talked about in Part Two, keep your eye on those bags filled with valuables at all times!

- **Don't bring anything with you that is irreplaceable or that it would break your heart to have lost or stolen.**

Bringing something expensive on a long-term trip is basically like signing a contract that says "This item will serve as a sacrifice to the Travel Gods."

Whenever you can, bring a cheaper version of your most prized possessions: a (slightly) older smartphone, travel-friendly wedding rings,[163] clothing that is cheap enough to accidentally lose, and so on. Leave your treasured family heirlooms safe at home.

- **Develop a healthy sense of skepticism around new people.**

I know, I know: we've mentioned the kindness of strangers like, a million times. Strangers are great. But strangers can also steal the truffles you made at the local chocolate-making class out of the hostel fridge before you even have a chance to eat them. Or worse!

Before you leave your valuables with the new best friend you just met five minutes ago at the bar, or go off to take a shower in your hostel while leaving your locker wide open, err on the side of caution and get into the habit of being street smart. If you're traveling solo, think before you share too much of your travel information with someone you've just met.

That said, don't be afraid to meet locals and make friends with other travelers. Healthy skepticism can keep you safe, but at the same time, mistrusting everyone can prevent you from making connections!

- **Watch your drinks!**

At all times, no matter what the circumstances, always watch your drink. It's easy for someone to slip a pill into it when you aren't looking. If you've been offered

---

163 The responsibility of an expensive piece of jewelry made me anxious, so when we purchased wedding rings for one another, we agreed to a $100 limit. That said, mine did eventually turn my finger green, so I have since upgraded to a slightly more pricey gold ring that I found at an antique market, which I am fully prepared to inevitably lose. A durable silicon ring, like the ones made by GrooveLife, probably would have been a better choice. And remember: rings are just symbols imbued with meaning by their wearer!

a drink from someone you've just met at the bar, make sure you can see it being poured and watch the bartender to ensure that it hasn't been spiked. If you or someone you're with gets "too drunk" after only having just one or two normal-strength drinks at the bar, it can be a sign that their drink has been spiked.

If you can, use the buddy system so that someone is watching out for you and makes sure you get home safely. And watch out for your fellow travelers: if a total stranger is trying to hustle someone you know who's suddenly incredibly drunk into a taxi to "take them home safely," your red flags should go way, way up. Men, you too — this is not a female-specific tip! Use the buddy system and watch out for your friends, too.

And while we're speaking of drinking: have a good time, but be extra careful when drinking and partying in a foreign country. People prey on travelers who are drunk or walking down a dark alley alone in the early hours of the morning. Drink responsibly, preferably with a buddy or a group.[164]

- **If you've got it, try not to flaunt it.**

Traveling is like the opposite of social media: the goal is to look like you're not living the good life. Blending into a crowd and looking like a schlubby backpacker can be an effective way to deter theft! Wearing flashy clothing or jewelry will also cost you more as you travel: it's an invitation for vendors to charge you more, since it looks like you have money.[165]

- **Always wear a helmet.**

One of our favorite methods of transportation is on the back of a motorbike! If you're riding a scooter or moto-taxi, whether you're the driver or passenger, always

---

164 This is doubly important when it comes to drugs. If you choose to experiment with drugs abroad, know that you are putting yourself at high risk. There's no way to verify that the drugs you're taking are what you think they are, or that the people you're partying with will be able to keep you safe if they're partaking, too. You may also be running afoul of local laws, which can land you in legal trouble. Take as many precautions as you can to keep yourself safe, and if you do choose to partake, do so as responsibly as you possibly can. (Although my inner mom really wants you to just say no to drugs!)

165 We learned this the hard way after getting stuck with a "free upgrade" on a rental Mercedes in Tulum, Mexico. It was a nice car, but we were still backpackers — and we couldn't afford the massively inflated rates we were charged by everyone from parking attendants to tour guides just because we pulled up in a nice rental car. Our car also attracted policemen, who pulled us over looking for bribes. Yikes! Make that another travel safety tip: don't accept a free fancy rental car upgrade! They've brought us nothing but trouble.

wear a helmet. In countries where motorbike rentals are common, we've seen all too many tourists with giant road rashes or worse from scooter accidents — it's all too common.

Remember that you or your driver may be in control, but the person driving straight for you may not be, and a helmet can save your life. Before hopping on the back of a moto-taxi, ask for a helmet and say no if the driver can't provide you with one.

- **Know what's safe to eat and drink.**

Ahhh, the inevitable traveler's diarrhea. Listen, it happens to all of us — but it can be mostly avoidable if you know what to look for. We've talked about the importance of purifying your water already, but it bears repeating: never drink tap water (and always ask whether a restaurant's ice is made from purified water).

It's also helpful to be a little cautious about what you eat. In countries where the water is not drinkable, you'll want to avoid salads and other raw vegetables, as they will often be washed in water that you can't drink. (Fruits with a thick, removable skin are perfectly safe.) Likewise, street food is delicious, but it's typically safer to buy from a vendor who you can see preparing the food right in front of you instead of purchasing a chicken kebab that has been sitting in the hot sun for hours. (That said, we've taken the risk for many a delicious bus snack, and lived to tell the tale.)

When it comes down to it, a little awareness and vigilance goes a long way. Do your best not to make yourself a target, don't put yourself in harm's way, and take a few reasonable precautions. The rest, more or less, just comes down to luck!

Ways to Save Money While Traveling

There are a few tricks of the trade that can help you stretch your hard-earned cash on your travels.

You'll want to make sure you're not paying more than you think you are. As I mentioned in Part Two, foreign transaction fees and currency conversions can rack up quickly — it's usually best to withdraw cash directly from ATMs if you can, and avoid exchanging money at airports, where conversion fees are usually much higher.

Another sneaky fee you might not realize you're paying is the conversion fee that gets tacked on when you choose to pay for something in USD (and many vendors will give you that choice at point of sale). Never pay in anything other than the local currency.

During our trip, we encountered a particularly sneaky setup in Tulum Mexico, on the main tourist strip. Everything was priced in USD: the price tags on products hung in gorgeous open-air boutiques, the fee for the only nearby parking lot, and even the bill for our meal. When we insisted on paying in Mexican pesos, we were given a corrected bill — calculated without the whopping 50% upcharge for paying in USD — but informed that the restaurant would not accept a payment in pesos by card. Since we didn't have enough cash on hand, we asked where to find the nearest ATM. "There's an ATM next door," we were informed, "but it only gives out US dollars."

Never, in nearly a year of traveling abroad, had we encountered an ATM that only gave out US dollars. But sure enough, they were telling the truth: there was no option to take out Mexican pesos, only dollars — at an unbelievably high exchange rate.[166]

Cutting down on your food costs by cooking meals regularly and stocking up on snacks at grocery stores and markets is another great way to save money. But you should also take advantage of inexpensive deals that still allow you to enjoy the local cuisine, like street food, buying prepared meals at a market, and budget-friendly set menus that can be found in certain countries, such as prix-fixe multi-course lunches in South America and Europe.[167]

In general, tourist areas are typically pricier. If you're on a tight budget, always find a restaurant outside of the touristy parts of town to make sure you're getting a deal (and look for restaurants filled with locals to know the food is good).

This rule also holds true for accomodations: the more popular a neighborhood is with tourists, the more expensive it will be to stay directly in that neighbor-

---

166   We're petty, so Jeremy hopped in our overpriced rental car and drove all the way back into town to find a regular ATM and avoid the outrageous upcharge.

167   In South America, these budget lunch deals are called *"almuerzos,"* which confuses me to no end because we learned in Spanish class that *"almuerzo"* just means "lunch." How can you distinguish between a multi-course set menu *almuerzo,* and, like, a sandwich that you just happen to be eating for *almuerzo?* This question keeps me up at night.

hood.[168] Consider staying in a different area and visiting the tourist attractions on foot or via transit instead.

When it comes to transportation, although I have a deep appreciation for helpful taxi drivers (and their language-practicing assistance), taxis are not always the cheapest option. Depending on the destination, it may be cheaper to take transit or rent a bike (or motorbike). Walking, of course, is always the cheapest option: the more you can walk, the less you'll spend on getting yourself around.

To save money on activities, check whether a museum or popular tourist attraction offers off-peak deals. Often, if you show up near closing or on a certain day of the week, you'll be able to score a deal.

For accommodations and tours, while some destinations are cheaper when you book in advance, others are far more inexpensive if you show up and pay in person. We found that booking ahead saved us money in Europe and the USA, while negotiating a price on the spot saved us money in South and Central America.

For many destinations, there are specific tricks for saving money that only in-the-know travelers and locals are aware of. Spent some time lurking on local forums, Googling "how to save money in [destination]," or ask in a Facebook Group or subreddit for location-specific tips!

---

168   The same rule also extends to more popular cities and regions. For example, this is why the island of Bali is a zillion times more expensive than the rest of much cheaper Indonesia! Stick to less visited parts of these areas to find better deals. (In the case of Bali, you'll save money by spending more time enjoying the beaches of sleepy Amed, which few tourists visit, and less time in the pricey, trendy town of Ubud).

My Money Ran Out ...
What Now?

Scrimping, saving, and budgeting can get you pretty far: all the way to another country, even. But at some point, chances are you'll find your savings running uncomfortably low.[169]

Even if you saved up the amount you'd intended to, travel can come with unexpected (and expensive) surprises. We ended up spending significantly more than we had planned to during our trip. But if you take away the accommodations we paid for with credit card points and miles, the reimbursed flights home for the holidays that we accepted as a gift from our family, three weeks of shacking up near Grandpa Bob to take care of him in the hospital (also reimbursed by my grateful family), the number goes back down to slightly more manageable amount: $35,000 total for the full year for both of us.

We spent everything I'd saved, and then some. Ouch.

But honestly, considering how screwy our plans got and how much time we spent in the pricey USA during our year abroad, plus that unplanned stint in Europe — where a night at a hostel is significantly more expensive than in South America — it could have been a LOT worse.

All told, we averaged out to around $50 per day for each of us. We even managed to stick to our $1000/month each budget for our first two months in Colombia and Ecuador... which I know, because I was meticulously tracking EVERY cash purchase on Mint. (You can't use credit cards all the time in South America, so I more or less gave up tracking every dollar around month three.)

We were lucky to have a bit of extra cushion to dip into and, by the tail end of the trip, our travel blog was helping to offset some costs. But the anxiety of watching our savings dip lower and lower affected our willingness to spend money. We spent months couchsurfing with family and friends in the United States because we wanted to save cash — but we spent just as little during our month-long house sitting gig in Mexico. Sleeping in your dad's guest room and living in Mexico are

---

169 If you set yourself an "oh shit" number back in Part One, this is the signal that it's time to stop moving around and hole up in one place to build your savings back up.

two very different kinds of experiences, and only one of them fits into the vision I had for our year-long honeymoon.

So before you buy a flight home and end up stuck in your parents' house for months on end, I've pulled together a list of suggestions for working in exchange for accommodation, and for working while traveling and earning money online. You don't have to stop traveling just because you're out of money!

How to Find a Place to Stay for Free

There are many ways to find a place to stay for free or in exchange for work. Once you're settled, you can embrace slow travel and live "like a local" for a stint, all while saving on expenses.

House Sitting

Looking after someone's home is an excellent way to stay in one area for an extended period of time — it's almost like borrowing someone else's life. House sitting gives you the opportunity to live like a local and experience the country in a whole different way, and can provide quite luxurious accommodation (a villa in Tuscany? Yes, please!), which can last anywhere from a couple of days to a full year. For most house sitting gigs, you will need to pet sit, care for plants, or even do a little bit of outdoor gardening.

Our month in Puebla, Mexico, was the first time we ever tried house sitting, and we landed the job through a fellow blogger on an online forum. It turned out to be one of our favorite (and most relaxing) ways to travel! Now that we're settled again, we rely on house sitters to take care of our home, plants, and our beloved dog, Mulan.

There are multiple platforms that match potential house sitters with house sitting opportunities around the world. However, be aware that house sitting can be quite competitive, especially in popular destinations. Take care when setting up your profile, and apply as early as you can to give yourself a leg up.

These days, we prefer to use Trusted Housesitters. You will need to pay an annual fee to become a "member," but we've found that the fee pays for itself after your first house sitting gig. There are a few cheaper programs, including Australian-run

HouseCarers, European based Nomador, and MindMyHouse, which has lots of listings in Latin America. We like having the security of having an actual company to vet its users and help us out if there are problems (plus, we can read reviews from other house sitters), but there are also plenty of unofficial house sitting groups on Facebook — just be a little more careful with those.

Before you apply for a house sitting job, make sure to consider whether your visa is valid for the duration of your intended stay. You should also be prepared to stay in the same area (meaning no long weekends or even days away from the house without first getting approval from the owners) and be comfortable with the homeowners and duties requested.

Once you land your house sitting assignment, try to spend at least one day with the homeowners before they leave so that they can walk you through all the duties, provide you with community contacts, as well as share more information about the local area. This is one of the highlights of house sitting — you are immediately connected with other locals and given insights on the best places to eat and things to see around your temporary home.

Working in Exchange for Accommodation

Working abroad in exchange for accommodation (and sometimes meals too) can be a meaningful way to connect and learn from local communities. You can harvest lavender on an organic farm, help out at an NGO, teach at a local school or even learn new skills while working on a boat!

- Worldwide Opportunities on Organic Farming (WWOOF): first started in the 1970s, WWOOF connects volunteers (WWOOFers) with organic farmers to 'promote a cultural and educational exchange, and build a global community conscious of ecological farming and sustainability practices.' There are over 12,000 WWOOF hosts in over 130 countries to choose from, ranging from organic Italian vineyards to plum orchards in Korea. As a WWOOFer you will participate in daily life on the farm, learn about sustainability and eco-friendly farming practices, and receive free accomodation and food during your stay.

- Workaway: Workaway is a cultural exchange platform that connects you with hosts all around the world. You offer a few hours of work and the host provides you with free accommodation and food in exchange. You can volunteer as a single person, as a couple, or even as a family or group of friends. Workaway charges a small membership fee to join the platform but provides you with 24/7 support and a range of placement options. Some placements may require a minimum stay and a certain amount of hours of volunteering each week. Host placement opportunities include volunteering with an NGO, helping at a local school, staying with a family for a cultural and language exchange, and sustainable farming.

- Worldpackers: Worldpackers is another collaborative platform that connects you with hosts from over 170 countries where you can exchange your skills for accommodation (some hosts may also provide food). Host projects include ecological projects, permaculture farms, and volunteering at local hostels. Worldpackers plans start around $49 and also include insurance and support before, during, and after your placement.

Local Homestays

While not always free, living with a local family can cut down on your costs and is one of the best ways to immerse yourself in the local culture. You can learn how to make naan bread from an Indian family, go to a local festival with your Australian hosts, or experience just how beautiful the midnight sun is around a fire in Norway. Staying with a host family for a small fee can also help give back to the local community.

We recommend finding a host family through an established program or online platform that connects travelers with host families. Make sure to read through the reviews and do your own research into the family and location when looking for a homestay placement. Homestay platforms to help you with your search include HomeStay, Lingoo (which specializes in language-focused homestays), and HomeStayIn.[170]

Working/Volunteering at a Hostel

Many hostels around the world rely on travelers who are willing to work in exchange for a place to stay.[171] These volunteers help out with everything from run-

---

170 If you'll be traveling in Nepal, CommunityHomestay.com is an excellent source for finding ethical, community-led homestays throughout the country!

171 Ethical travel note — while this is a great opportunity for travelers, it can also mean taking paid jobs away from locals who would otherwise be gainfully employed.

ning the front desk, fire watch (basically staying awake overnight to make sure no fire breaks out), maintenance, and housekeeping.

You can sometimes land a volunteer gig by just asking if there are any opportunities at the hostel you're staying at, or looking for postings on their websites. Or you can use Hosteljobs.Net, a job platform that specializes in hostel placement.

How to Find a Job While Traveling

Something I realized about myself during our trip is that I actually enjoy working. I like having a project that I'm focused on, and being productive each day makes me feel good. Idle time drives me a little nuts. I missed checking things off of to-do lists and fiddling with spreadsheets.

So, I threw myself into travel blogging like it was my new job. Soon, I was working 30 hours a week for almost no pay. What a dream!

It certainly kept my mind occupied, but if your goal is to replenish your cash supplies you'll probably want to look for a job with an hourly rate.

Working abroad in a paid position not only allows you to travel more slowly and immerse yourself in a single place, but it also helps you replenish your savings so you can continue your trip. However, before you jump right in, you will need to get a work visa if you want to work in a paid position overseas — and obtaining a working visa is much easier in some countries than others.

Working holiday visas are usually limited to travelers 35 years old and younger, and can last up to 24 months. You also don't need to have already secured a job before applying: once you have the visa, you can find a job as you are travelling when and where needed. Common working holiday jobs include:

- **Cafes and Restaurants**: Many local restaurants and cafes are always looking for extra help — just ask.

- **Bartending**: If you've got some bartending skills (or at least know the basics of pouring backpackers drinks), inquire at your favorite pub or hostel bar. When you factor in tips, this can be a quite lucrative job!

- **Seasonal Farm Work**: Many countries, such as Australia, rely heavily on working holiday backpackers from the U.S. and Europe to help with fruit and vegetable harvests. Be aware that this can be hard physical work, but on the upside your accommodation is often included.

- **Tourism Industry**: English proficiency is a major plus in the tourism industry. You might work as a tour guide, at a hotel front desk, on a cruise, or at other places catering to travelers. If you have a specialized skill set, you can even land teaching yoga classes or as a scuba diving instructor or ski instructor.

Once you've got your visa in hand, you can pick up a job as needed for a few days or a few weeks, pocket some extra cash and then move on.

U.S. citizens can obtain working holiday visas in six countries: Australia, New Zealand, South Korea, Singapore, Canada, and Ireland. You'll want to find out whether you'll need to apply for a working holiday visa before you arrive in the country, or whether it is possible to apply once you are already there.

If you hold a non-U.S. passport, you may have more options for working holiday visas: for instance, Canadians can work in many European countries, select South and Central American countries, and some Asian countries. Just Google 'working holiday visas for [insert your land of citizenship]' to find out how and where you can get such a visa.

You can look for a wide variety of jobs all over the world on websites like SeasonalJobs, CoolWorks, SeasonWorkers, and SummerJobs.

In the "Resources" section, you'll find a table with information about obtaining working holiday visas for U.S. citizens, and you can also check with consulates for more information on applying for working holiday visas.

Getting a Work Visa through an Employer

While working holiday visas are a great option for younger travelers, depending on your skill set, you can also get a traditional work visa regardless of your age. Work visas are usually contingent on employment, meaning that you will first need to find an employer who is allowed to 'sponsor' your visa. You can apply for a work visa from abroad or as you are traveling; however, you are not allowed to officially start working until your host country has issued your work visa. Check out country-specific requirements and their skill shortage lists to see whether it may be easy for you to get a work visa.

One good option to look into is teaching English as a second language. This is a fantastic option for English speakers who have teaching experience! To teach English abroad, you may be required to hold Teaching English as a Foreign Language (TEFL) accreditation. Obtaining a TEFL certificate does take some time and costs around $300, so if you'd like to explore this option, start early. Once you have completed your TEFL program, you can look for English language teaching jobs — along with other teaching positions — on job platforms such as TEFL. org, GoOverseas, and TeachAway.

Taxes and Getting Paid Abroad

Although you may find a job that pays you in cash and doesn't ask any questions, many paid positions abroad will require some finagling to get the money you need into your account where you can access it. The easiest solution is to use a service designed for overseas transactions, like Transferwise, which allows you to set up foreign banks in multiple currencies that you can easily transfer back into your home currency with low transaction fees.[172]

If you're on a work or working holiday visa, you will likely have local taxes deducted from your paycheck, but you should receive a large portion of that back once you leave and file your tax return in that country.

In many countries, your employer may also pay into social security plans and other retirement or social programs. You will receive most, if not all, of these funds when you leave the country and submit your foreign tax returns and social security paperwork. Ask your employer for all necessary tax-related documents before you leave the country.

Technically, under U.S. law, you will also need to report any foreign earnings in your U.S. tax filings. However, unless you were making significant money (around six figures or so) or abroad for under 330 days, you should not have to pay any additional U.S. taxes.[173]

---

172 U.S. citizens should be mindful of IRS regulations when using this option; if the total value of your foreign bank account is over $10,000, you are required to file a *Report of Foreign Bank and Financial Accounts* (FBAR) with the IRS if you are a U.S. citizen. The FBAR is just an informational form, though, so you don't have to worry about taxes (although interest earned on accounts with an aggregate value of $10,000 may be taxable). More information can be found here.

173 The 330 day rule is an oddly specific tax law called Foreign Earned Income Exclusion. If you come back 329 days after you leave, you'll have to pay all kinds of taxes; but spend another 24 hours abroad and you're all good. The Foreign Earned Income Exclusion website explains all of the minutiae and details, including when the clock starts and ends (it's all incredibly specific).

That said, I am not an accountant, and laws are constantly changing. So please check with a tax professional if you have any questions, especially when it comes to how to file your foriegn income earnings when doing your U.S. tax return!

What is a Digital Nomad?

A "digital nomad" is someone who works online while they're traveling. Armed with a laptop and WiFi, digital nomads can be found typing away everywhere from the beaches of Bali to the cafes of Amsterdam. Driven by advances in technology and shifts in traditional work environments, digital nomadism is a growing worldwide phenomenon.[174]

In recent years, several countries have even created specific visas that establish an official path for what was previously a bit of a legal grey area. For remote workers and long-term travelers who will be gainfully employed back home as they travel, this is a fantastic option. You can find remote-work-friendly visas in Dubai, the Czech Republic, Spain, Estonia, Barbados, Bermuda, Mexico, Iceland, Germany, the Cayman Islands, Antigua & Barbuda, and Georgia. And more countries are developing these new visas each year!

Digital nomads vary: some work part-time and some full-time, many are self-employed, and still others work remotely for an employer elsewhere. But it's not necessarily a life of luxury: although digital nomads can work from anywhere, they need to balance working online with travel. That means traveling slowly, carefully arranging travel plans around work projects or reliable WiFi, and navigating time differences abroad.[175] But the trade-off is a reliable source of income that allows you to travel for as long as you like.

---

174 A 2018 MBO Partners study estimated that there are over 4.8 million digital nomads working around the globe — and that number is dramatically increasing each year. These location-independent workers come from a variety of professions and backgrounds, including creative jobs, IT, and marketing. 54% of digital nomads are over 38 years old, and there's a pretty even split between full-time and part-time jobs. Digital nomadism also doesn't pay too shabbily, either: one in six digital nomads earns more than $75,000 annually.

175 Several of our team members at Practical Wanderlust are digital nomads. It makes scheduling team meetings a little challenging, and occasionally team members on faraway continents are up late, working past midnight even as I'm still drinking my coffee in the morning. Time zone challenges get even trickier when I'm on the road, too! I've found that setting clear expectations and communication around working hours, avoiding last-minute deadlines, and keeping in touch using remote-work-friendly tools like Slack and Asana help us all stay organized.

If you like your job and much of your work is done on the computer, you may be able to convince your employer to let you work remotely rather than quitting outright. In the wake of the COVID-19 pandemic of 2020, many businesses pivoted to flexible work models and are now more open to remote workers.

Before asking whether you can transition to remote work, it helps to set the stage well before you make your request by setting yourself apart as an indispensable member of your team, so that your boss really doesn't want to lose you. When the time comes, take all the guesswork out of your remote work request by hammering out all the details. How do you plan on working effectively while abroad? What hours would you work? How will you communicate with colleagues? Do you need any special technology or will a laptop be sufficient?

In many cases, it comes down to a question of WiFi. When I offered to go remote at the job I quit to take my year-long honeymoon, I wasn't able to guarantee that I'd have access to reliable, high-speed WiFi — which I would have needed to do my job — because I hadn't planned my trip around it. If remote work is an opportunity you'll be exploring with your employer, do so well in advance — before you book everything.

Many jobs don't need much more than an ordinary WiFi connection, and WiFi is globally ubiquitous. Here are a few tips in staying connected no matter where you are in the world:

- **Use a WiFi finder app**: In our digitized world, we now even have apps to find free WiFi! Check out Wefi or another WiFi finder app to search out the most reliable free WiFi spots.

- **Pick accommodation with strong WiFi**: Before booking a hotel or hostel, read through reviews and take note of mentions about the reliability of the WiFi. Also check if the WiFi is only in shared spaces or in your room, as there may be times that you will need a quiet place to attend meetings.

- **Use your phone's hotspot or purchase a mobile WiFi router**: If your international plan or prepaid SIM card provides enough data, you can connect your computer via your device's hotspot. You can also use a local prepaid SIM card in a MiFi device, a mobile WiFi router, if you can't use your phone to hotspot.

- **Get creative**: Public libraries often offer WiFi, as well as large global chains like McDonald's and Starbucks. However, while local cafes may have WiFi, some cultures look down on working for extended periods of time in these spaces — especially if you are taking calls and conducting meetings.

- **Check out local co-working spaces:** Many co-working spaces abroad cater to digital nomads. You can purchase a one-day 'hotdesk' membership at a local co-working space, or look into longer memberships across a range of partner co-working spaces. This can also be a great way to meet and network with other digital nomads on your travels!

How to Make Money Online

Back in my day — which was about 10 years ago — "making money online" meant filling out long, specific surveys for a dollar or two a pop, or watching advertisements and idly clicking through websites for a few cents an hour. It took a very long time to make anything more than pocket cash, although it could be quite fun. In college, I ran a blog called "The Broke Student's Guide" and dove deep into the depths of online money-making schemes.[176]

Things are much, much easier now.

The beauty of living in our modern, digitalized world is that there are a plethora of options to take your random skills online as a freelancer. You can market your existing skill set — such as formatting Excel tables or developing business plans — or you can try something new, like becoming a voice-over artist or writing social media captions.

To give you an idea of the breadth of gigs out there on freelancing platforms, here are a few actual job postings on one freelancing platform:

- Write for a blog about raising chickens

- Compile a list of local cleaning services

- Help with making a LinkedIn profile

---

176   This was my second blog of three total, and one of many online businesses I've run over the years. Other online hustles included a "cartoon dolls" website when I was 12, a fashion blog when I was 16, and an online jewelry e-commerce website that I ran from age 16-23, which I considered my business baby before Practical Wanderlust was born.

Making money online has never been easier, and all you need to get started is to create a profile online and start putting in applications.

When you're just starting out, using online platforms gives you more access to potential clients and a higher degree of legal and financial protection as well. There are a variety of online platforms that can connect you with clients, manage job contracts, provide payment guarantees and even offer mediation services. Most platforms charge an administration fee as a percentage of your earnings, and there is sometimes a small fee to apply for jobs as well. The platform manages all payments and makes reporting your taxable earnings easy.

I've used freelance platforms as both a freelancer myself and as someone who hires freelancers. There are three platforms I recommend:

- Upwork: Upwork is one of the largest flexible work platforms with hundreds of new jobs posted daily. You must be accepted as a freelancer on Upwork, so take your time creating a strong profile and outlining your niche skills. Once you are accepted, you can submit proposals to posted jobs that interest you. Potential clients can also seek you out based on your skill set and ask you to apply to a job. Upwork charges a sliding service fee based on how much work you do with a client, and the platform facilitates all contracts, payments, and communications with your clients, making it a user-friendly option. Once you find a client you like, you can always take things off of the platform too.

- Fiverr: Fiverr is a freelance marketplace that allows you to post almost any service (as long as it's legal!) as a Fiverr 'gig.' You can offer to write a blog post about the environment, design a logo or make silly videos. On Fiverr's platform and user-friendly app, you can include examples of your work and additional add-on services, like rush completion or additional customization. Fiverr charges a 20% commission fee on any gigs that you sell.

- Work for Impact: Work for Impact is a relatively new platform that specializes in work for social organizations, such as non-profits or inclusive for-profit businesses. Client jobs range from helping create strategic plans to conducting GHG emission inventories. Work for Impact offers to 'verify' your skills — either through a skill test or manually reviewing your work — to provide additional social proof to potential clients of your skill set. Another attractive feature: Work for Impact only charges a 10% service fee.

To learn more about how to land your first online freelancing gig, check out the resources section of your chosen freelancing platform. Upwork, for example, offers loads of tips on how to create a profile that stands out to clients and best practice guidelines to writing winning proposals.

You may choose to start a freelancing business independently, such as offering services to other small business owners as a virtual assistant or an online business manager. Many small businesses, including bloggers, rely on part-time freelancers to complete clerical or administrative tasks, assist with social media management, and even write or edit articles. At the time of publication, the best way to find those types of jobs is through online groups on Facebook or by word of mouth. Consider creating a website to showcase your skills, post client testimonials, and bundle your services as set packages.

Since you'll be traveling, you might try pitching a few articles to travel publications and blogs as a travel writer. Earning money as a travel writer can pay anywhere from a few cents to as much as a dollar per word, depending on the publication and your reputation or other bylines. Finding the right publication and crafting the perfect pitch can be a challenge, but once you've landed a few commissioned pieces for the same publication, you should have an easier time writing for them moving forward. My favorite resource for landing paid work as a travel writer is Dream of Travel Writing, which I've used to help land a few bylines.

Enjoy teaching or have a specific subject that you are passionate about? Tutoring can be a flexible way to make some money online while you are traveling! You can tutor on a wide range of subjects, from basic English for young children to pre-law for graduate students. You'll be able to schedule your tutoring sessions around your travel schedule.

Tutoring can be competitive, but it's a good option if you're a subject matter expert; you will need to put together a strong application and will most likely need to hold a bachelor's degree to be accepted. Once you are accepted and begin receiving tutoring requests, expect to make around $15-20 per hour. There are tons of tutoring platforms out there to choose from — apply to several to increase your chances of landing your first tutoring job.

- QKids: Qkids is a language learning platform with over 800,000+ students that matches native English speakers with Chinese students between 4 and 12 years old. You do not need a TEFL certificate to teach English on QKids, just an undergraduate degree and at least six hours of availability each week. Expect to make between $16-20 per hour.

- Preply: Focusing primarily on language tutoring, Preply supplies a built-in video platform and allows tutors to set their own rates, hours, and availability. The service is free to join but charges a commission.

- Wyzant: Wyzant allows tutors to set their own rates. The platform charges a service fee but handles all the matching, payment, contract, and other logistics. An average Wyzant tutor provides two tutoring sessions per week and is paid between $18-36 per hour after commission.

- TutorMe: TutorMe looks for tutors in over 300 different subjects. TutorMe provides tutoring matches, 24/7 support, and pays tutors $16 per hour (in five-minute increments) regardless of subject. You tutor students through TutorMe's bespoke learning platform, including a virtual whiteboard, text editor, and lesson archives. You do not need a college degree to work as a tutor, but you should be able to prove a high level of mastery of the subject(s) you are tutoring.

- Chelsea International Education: Chelsea International Education is a great option if you are already a teacher and have 2+ years of experience. You can make anywhere between $15-150 per hour depending on the subject, but you'll need to go through a pretty stringent screening process (including a background check) before you are accepted onto the platform.

Before you throw yourself into new business ventures, I have one last piece of advice: be wary of roping your travel companion into your online money-making schemes unless you're sure they really want to be your new co-worker. Otherwise, there's a good chance you'll start to have work-related arguments on top of your travel-related arguments — and work-related arguments can't usually be resolved with snacks. Keeping your expectations low will keep the peace between you and your travel partner.

What About Travel Blogging & Content Creation?

One glaring absence in this list of ways to make money online is travel blogging. It might sound odd, considering the fact that I personally earn a living as a travel blogger, but I actually don't recommend starting a blog (or Instagram, or YouTube, or TikTok, or Podcast…) as a way to earn money while you travel long-term.

It's not that you shouldn't start them at all; truth be told, if it weren't for starting a travel blog and working on it during my year-long trip, I would never be a full-time blogger today!

But the honest truth is that blogging and content creation is not a good way to make money in the short term. It takes a very long time to earn money from a blog or as a content creator — the average is about a year, and most don't even make it past the year mark.

I intentionally chose to focus on options that have a more immediate and concrete payoff, meaning jobs where you set an hourly rate and are then paid that amount by a client or employer — jobs that come with a guaranteed and actual income.

Blogging and content creation, on the other hand, come with absolutely no guarantee of income. Earning money as a blogger is incredibly difficult, growing an audience big enough to attract the attention of sponsors can take a very long time, and sponsorship rates vary widely from definitely-not-worth-it to lucrative, all depending on your chosen niche, your audience, your engagement, and a zillion other factors that are difficult to control until you've got some experience under your belt.

Blogging (and content creation in general) is an excellent hobby, and can be a wonderful full-time job. But it is not easy to turn into a stable income.

That said, I want to be entirely transparent: during my year-long trip, Practical Wanderlust grew very quickly from a brand-new baby blog to a gangly adolescent blog, with about 80,000 monthly readers.

Its quick growth was thanks to a few crucial and lucky facts: first, Practical Wanderlust was my third online blog and fifth online business, so I'd already made many of the mistakes that the difficult first year typically teaches an aspiring blogger. Second, I concentrated my efforts on traffic-building methods that I was already familiar with, like Google keyword research and Pinterest, which helped save time as I skipped over a steep learning curve. And third, I spent around 30 hours per week during our year-long honeymoon working on the blog and growing our readership, treating our blog as if it were already the full-time job it would one day become.

But despite unusually fast growth, Practical Wanderlust wasn't a reliable source of income during our trip, and I didn't begin thinking of it as a potential job until after we returned back home.

During our year-long honeymoon, I earned a grand total of $10,000 in actual cash from the blog, along with about a thousand dollars worth of "comps" — tours or hotels that were provided free of charge in exchange for blog coverage. It's certainly nothing to sneeze at, but some context is helpful: the vast majority of that income came from a handful of sponsored campaigns with tourism boards back in the USA on the very tail end of our trip. It wasn't until the blog was nearly nine months old that I began averaging more than $100 of income per month.

Of course, this story ends on a high note: Practical Wanderlust is now one of the most popular travel blogs in the world, reaching an audience of millions each year.[177] And without the opportunity to spend a full year focusing solely on growing the blog — along with a constant stream of new places to write about — I would not be here today.

But the blog did not pay for our year-long trip, and it would have been risky to expect it to.

So: if you have a blog already, or you're hoping to begin one during your travels, I highly encourage you to start now. Start immediately. Start as soon as the idea crosses your mind. (It took me two years after I had the idea for Practical Wanderlust to actually publish my first blog post, during which time I broke the site, let the domain lapse, lost interest, forgot all about it, and then finally dusted it off and tried again right before we left for our trip).

The earlier you begin, the sooner you might be able to make a steady income from your blog (or podcast or social media channels).

177 If you're curious about how much money the blog earns (and how we monetize our blog in general), you can read a few detailed income reports that I published during the first year we hit six figures in annual revenue on (you guessed it) PracticalWanderlust.com.

But it won't be easy: it will likely take a lot of hard work and a very long time. So I do recommend exploring some of the other opportunities in this chapter to supplement your income as you travel!

What Else Could Go Wrong?

If you think I'm an anxiety case, you might be surprised to know that Jeremy is actually much, much more anxious than I am. (Again: I worry deeply for our future offspring.)

Jeremy's inner monologue is a constantly running mental list of worst-case scenarios, which he stays up nights obsessing over. Some of the scenarios he mulled over while lying in a hostel dorm bed at around 2am included:

- What if we get robbed?
- What if someone steals our credit cards and we have no way to access our money?
- What if we don't get out enough cash and can't find a working ATM?
- What if we lose our passports?
- What if we miss a flight?
- What if our phones get stolen?
- What if we lose our bags in transit?
- What if a hostel loses our reservation?
- What if one of us gets seriously injured?
- What if someone in our hostel dorm room is belligerent?
- What if you go snorkelling and run into a mildly intimidating fish?
- What if the entire world shuts down because of a pandemic?

With all the wisdom and maturity that a year of long-term travel and the many, many trips I've taken since, I have only this insight to offer you: you're going to be fine.

I mean, listen: one of those things is definitely going to happen. Maybe even a fun combination of several of them! But with each new calamity, you'll learn how to navigate the unexpected and confusing world of finding help in an unfamiliar place, and you'll grow to be a stronger, more capable person because of it.

I know, I know. I sound like those very same seasoned travelers I once hated before my trip. How am I supposed to be fine, exactly? What are the specific steps that I will take in order to achieve "fine"?? And if I don't worry constantly, how will I avoid horrible things happening to me while I travel?!

The uncomfortable truth is that no matter how much you worry and how much you prepare, at a certain point, things are just out of your control. And while that's terrifying, there's nothing you can do about it. So you're going to have to learn to live with it. Look, as a seasoned control freak, this is my least favorite advice to give or receive. But it's true!

From a strange man climbing into my dorm bunk in Amsterdam at 2am, to a trip to the police station to report a stolen cell phone in Cartagena during an international field trip with Jeremy's students (while simultaneously juggling three students with missing luggage), to destroying the headlight on a rental BMW in France, each new disaster we've faced brought with it an improved ability to problem-solve — and a fantastic story to tell when we returned home.

When — not if — one of these nightmare scenarios happens to you, you'll rely on the kindness of total strangers to help you. You'll ask the friendly staff at the front desk to direct you to the police station, your travel insurance provider will help you find the nearest hospital, your embassy or consulate will help you replace a stolen or lost passport, your bank will overnight you a new debit card, and a taxi driver will happily drive you as far as you need to get to an ATM.

You'll also get a little more savvy: you'll develop a habit of double-checking your flights so you don't show up on the wrong day and allow yourself more time than you need the get to the airport, you'll start putting a spare set of clothes in your carry-on luggage just in case your suitcase goes missing, you'll find ways to adapt and cope and prepare better for next time.

Take it from someone who is forever (and ever) making mistakes: these disasters are how you learn and grow. They are, in some ways, the entire point of long-term travel, which is, after all, just a series of incredibly difficult challenges that you will, eventually, figure out how to overcome.

Do the best you can to take reasonable precautions, don't put yourself in harm's way if you can help it, and always ask for help when you need it.

I promise: everything will work out just fine.

No matter what bumps in the road you inevitably encounter, you're going to have an amazing, incredible, once-in-a-lifetime adventure — and, mishaps and all, it will be totally, entirely, completely worth it.

PART FOUR:
THE RETURN

Actually, THIS is the Hardest Part

Travelling long term will be one of the most life-changing things you ever do, but it will be hard to fully wrap your mind around the ways it has affected you until you come back home and try to slide back into your old life, only to realize that you don't quite fit like you used to (in my case, both literally and figuratively).

Although I hadn't embarked on a year-long trip with the intention of "finding myself," to my own surprise, I returned home fundamentally altered.

For one thing, I'd gained a newfound appreciation for life's smallest luxuries. A year of sleeping on uncomfortable twin beds surrounded by snoring backpackers gave me a deep appreciation for the joy of sharing a soft mattress with my husband. The concept of "ice" as something you could easily create at home, for free, stuck with me deeply — I no longer take ice (or clean drinking water) for granted.

And, although I'd believed myself to be a fairly minimalist person before our trip, when I returned I found myself both more and less minimalistic. I craved material comforts. A couch was at the top of my bucket list, followed by shelving. We even went shopping for holiday decor for the first time in our lives after returning from our trip — before it had seemed so silly and wasteful, but now it seemed exciting and momentous.

But I no longer craved convenience, and I was well versed in the joy of making do with less. Reimmersion in the consumerist culture of the USA, with its massive convenience stores and shopping malls, shocked me. I found myself overwhelmed by the amount of products in grocery stores and their insanely high prices (was the U.S. always that expensive?!), unable to remember how I used to make simple decisions like which kind of milk to buy. It had been so long since I'd had choices about which kind of milk to buy!

I'd also forgotten how easy everything was. Tasks that were once an adventure, like buying Ban-Aids, were now just a car ride away, or a simple click of a button. It made everything seem less special, and I didn't want to lose my starry-eyed wonder and newfound sense of appreciation and gratitude.

So, we intentionally rejected convenience. We gave away our microwave — a gateway drug into conveniences we didn't want to be tempted by — and committed to working towards a more sustainable, zero-waste household. Even though we did end up with a car, we still refused to drive to most errands, choosing instead to walk, bike, or take transit whenever possible, loading our groceries into backpacks and enjoying the nostalgia we now associated with schlepping a heavy bag. And we savored everything, doing our best to seek adventure and excitement wherever we could.

But despite our best efforts to reintegrate smoothly, the change was jolting.

We'd been thrust back into the USA, with all of its ease — and all of its capitalism and greed and expensive healthcare and a culture focused on working at the expense of everything else.

It was overwhelming. We had reverse culture shock. For months, things felt very, very weird.

It didn't help that when we'd so lovingly packed away our old lives, we'd given ourselves boxes full of rubbish to dispose of. Why did we think we'd be excited to reunite with an old jar lid?!

It felt like the chapter of our lives we'd thoroughly, satisfyingly closed at the beginning of our trip had been reopened again, and we didn't really want to go back.[178]

Even as we settled back down, we had a creeping feeling that we should be picking up and moving again soon. While we were traveling, feeling bored with our routine was a sign that it was time to move on to the next place. But in regular life, you can't just pick up and move every few months, and we'd long since forgotten how to handle monotony.

It felt like I was still in "travel mode" for months after we'd officially settled back down. I couldn't shake the habit of wearing the same six pairs of clothes and pack-

---

178 There was one notable exception: our beloved neighborhood cat friend, Jasper! We took the first opportunity to return to our old neighborhood and say hello. Although he was very old by then and clearly had trouble walking, he was so excited to see us and limped right over for cuddles. We sat on his owners' driveway petting him until they came outside, at which point we very awkwardly explained that we were the couple who'd sent them a message on Nextdoor. His owners knew exactly who we were and kindly told us that of all Jasper's neighborhood homes, he'd always spent the most time with us. We continued visiting Jasper over the next few years until we found out, through Nextdoor, that he had passed away peacefully of old age. I have never cried harder in my entire life. I loved that drooly, cranky old cat so much.

ing a daybag every time I left the house. Every so often, we'd sit down to dinner and this weird feeling would come over me like: wait, this is temporary. After six months of settling back down in the U.S., we took a trip abroad, and when we arrived, I realized that those six months had felt like a vacation, and that unpacking my backpack in our little hostel in Prague felt like a return to real life. Had I totally lost my grip on reality?

I tried to talk to friends about it, or strike up conversations with strangers — I couldn't shake the habit of greeting everyone I passed on the street with "buenos!" for months — but few people shared my desire to marvel at how wide the streets were, the luxury of parking lots, or how many THINGS were sold in stores. Nobody was terribly interested in deep conversations about how easy it was to acquire things, yet how hard to find the time to enjoy things that mattered.

I was not much fun at parties.

Another jarring realization was the time trick our minds had played on us: for everyone else, it had just been an ordinary year that, as usual, had passed in the blink of an eye — "Is it already the holidays? Time flies!"

But my year had been several years. It had been a decade of years, filled with a lifetime of stories and experiences. It was hard to explain how much I'd seen and done to people who had barely even noticed I'd left.

I felt like I was living in an episode of the Twilight Zone, or the end of Interstellar.

Although everyone politely asked about my trip, what most people really wanted to hear was that it was a lot of fun, and not much more. They weren't interested in the realizations I'd had about myself and our culture and society. They weren't interested in hearing about our adventures and disasters and new foods and cultures that I'd experienced. (And they definitely weren't interested in my theories on time relativity and travel.)

It wasn't that they weren't interested or supportive, exactly... it was just that it was a lot to explain, and I was more excited to talk about it than most people were to listen.[179]

---

179 If at any point while reading this book, you found yourself skimming through one of my travel stories, wishing I would stop going on and on about my trip and get back to the point, you know exactly how it feels to care less about someone else's travel stories than they do. I've long since learned not to take it personally — but given the opportunity, I will tell travel stories for hours and hours and hours. (Which, incidentally, is exactly why we have a blog … and a podcast.)

But in addition to a lack of enthusiasm, we faced pushback upon our return that felt similar to what we'd experienced when we first announced our plans to travel long term. We struggled through more difficult conversations with passive-aggressive or just plain unsupportive friends and family members. We couldn't win: if we shared our trip's highlights we were bragging; if we were being honest about the challenges we'd faced, we were complaining.[180] Honestly, they just didn't really want to hear about it. And since we could never say the right thing, we ended up just avoiding talking about our trip.

Worst of all, we lost friends during our trip for reasons we still don't know. People disappeared from our Facebook friends list. People who were close to us; people who were in our wedding. Perhaps seeing our photos each day of the adventures we were having and hearing our tales of excitement and joy was a realization for those people that they really didn't want to see us happy after all.

It took a few years, but I no longer miss those people in my life.

Ultimately, this is the hardest part of long-term travel: coming home. Trying to fit back into your old life. Trying to play the part of whoever you were before the trip, and realizing that the person you have become no longer wants to play that part. Seeing your loved ones' eyes glaze over as you start yet another story with "when we were in…" and trying not to take it personally.

And worst of all, swallowing down the monotony of regular life again — after you fought tooth and nail to reject it. You'd escaped, but now you're back. Are you stuck again, forever?

Here's what I can tell you: the first year is by far the hardest. But I promise you, it DOES get better. It gets SO much better.

You will adapt. You will grow and change, and your life and your values and the people you surround yourself with will grow and change with you.

You will find a career that doesn't make you fantasize about leaving it every single day — because you have seen how worthwhile it is to be free.

You will find receptive ears for all of your stories, and grow closer to the wonderful

---

180 I also struggle with striking the tightrope-wire balance between honesty and positivity on my blog. When I verge too much onto either side, angry comments pour in telling me I'm either "ungrateful" and "negative" or "too privileged." I don't think I'll ever really be able to let them roll off my back.

loved ones in your life who really, truly care.

You will carve out a life for yourself that matches your values, because you will be unwilling to compromise after how hard you worked to upend your old life that didn't serve you.

And you are not stuck forever. Because you've figured out how to escape the monotony of daily life once, you can do it again, whenever you need to. This was not your only life-changing trip or exciting adventure; it was only the first.

Designing the Life You Want

When you first started dreaming about your long-term trip, way back in Part One, before the spreadsheets and the planning — what was it that made you want to risk everything you had, to leave it all behind to start an adventure?

A true sense of adventure for adventure's sake is a beautiful thing. But in many cases, the desire to travel long term stems from a sense of unhappiness and dissatisfaction. Something about the life you lived wasn't serving you; something wasn't meeting your needs.

In those cases, returning from your trip and trying to pick your life back up again exactly where you left off will feel like opening up a wound that had finally healed over. It will hurt. And it can feel like an undoing of all of your hard work.

But it doesn't have to be that way. The real gift of long-term travel is a chance to start again — but you won't be starting over from scratch. In the process of taking a long-term trip, you'll have developed a particular set of skills:

- You will have learned how to unapologetically listen to your gut and chase after your dreams.

- You will have become an expert at constant problem-solving and figuring out your next move.

- You will have fully mastered the art of thriving outside your comfort zone.

As difficult as returning home will be and as lost as you may feel, remember this: your adventures (and misadventures) have taught you to adapt and overcome a never-ending set of challenges. Those skills will help you for the rest of your life.

Taking advantage of the unique opportunity of hitting "pause" on your life means re-assessing the things that were serving you, and finding ways to adapt to or change the things that weren't.

For many of you, and for me, the biggest cause of my dissatisfaction was also where I spent most of my waking hours: my job.

But to figure out those things, you have to get in touch with the real you. So who are you?

Returning to Work

The first priority for us when we returned from our trip was to get back to work ASAP. We were broke; we'd spent all of our savings and then some. We needed to replenish our coffers again, and fast.

For Jeremy, the drive to return to work wasn't just a matter of finances. During our trip, he'd experienced an unexpected shift in his feelings about his work.

As a teacher, my husband works long hours and is often overworked and under-paid. It's all too easy to become jaded by a system that takes advantage of caring teachers while under-serving students in need. Many teachers reach this point a few years in; Jeremy was no exception.

But taking a year off renewed his commitment to teaching. He missed his kids and his coworkers. He missed his classroom. And most of all, he missed the feel-ings of satisfaction, pride, and fulfillment that come from watching a student learn and grow.

As we stared out the window on long bus rides, I wrote long blog posts in my head. And Jeremy? Jeremy was writing lesson plans.

Only one problem: once he'd left, his teaching position had been filled.

We had a few options; he could find a position at a new school, take more time off and work at a coffee shop until he found a new position, or return to substitute teaching. There was also an exciting new opportunity: during our trip, Jeremy had applied for and been accepted to a Masters of Education program at New York University. Could our new chapter in life take us to New York instead of back home to San Francisco?

The idea was enticing, but expensive. Paying for a Master's degree and an apart-ment in New York City was beyond our already-overstretched budget.

We needed a paycheck coming in, and fast. So we got creative coming up with ideas for positions within Jeremy's old school that he could potentially fill: an in-house substitute; coaching and mentoring; a substitute teacher coordinator. Could we convince the school administration to find a way to hire Jeremy back?

In the end, we got incredibly lucky. The teacher who was hired for Jeremy's role left after only one school year, and the school immediately offered Jeremy the opportunity to return. The idea of a steady salary easily won out over an expensive Master's degree, and Jeremy returned to his old classroom just two months after we returned, full of newfound excitement and passion — not to mention a vastly improved mastery of the Spanish language.

For Jeremy, taking a sabbatical year was exactly what he needed to realize that he was in the right place all along. Time off from work answered the questions that had been swirling around in his head before our trip: Is education the right career for me? Am I making the right decisions for myself and my happiness?

With his career concerns quelled, Jeremy happily returned to his old job. Four years later, he's still teaching at the same school, in the same classroom — and he has no regrets about his decision.

Changing Careers

I watched with mixed feelings as Jeremy happily skipped his way back to his old job. I was thrilled for him, as well as relieved: now that we had a source of income, we could stop couchsurfing and house sitting and actually sign a lease.[181]

But I also felt a little bit jealous. I mean, I liked my old job, too, but I wasn't sure how eager I was to return.

I scheduled a meeting with my old boss, just to feel things out. We'd left on good terms and stayed in contact during my trip, so perhaps I could slide back into my old life, too?

Driving back to my old office felt eerie, like I was in the wrong reality. Walking

---

181 For three months after we returned, we were still living out of our suitcases, renting rooms and house sitting — even after Jeremy started working again. Even though we were "back," we didn't feel settled until we were able to sign a lease and ship all of our stuff back across the country, several months after our trip officially ended.

past cubicles and offices that looked exactly the same as they had one year ago — down to the same half-drunk coffee mugs and post-it notes stuck to computer monitors — I had the distinct feeling that time here had stalled. It felt as if I could sit down at my desk and turn on my computer, and literally nothing would have changed — as if the past year had never happened.

It wasn't just me, either: a friendly co-worker stopped to say hello, assuming I was back at work. "Back already! How long has it been? A few months?" she asked, smiling. "Welcome back!"

My stomach churned. I wasn't back. It had been a year — a LONG year — and I wasn't even the same person! I'd changed so much! "I —" but she was already gone.

I backed away from my old desk, as if it was the source of the time shift problems.

Lunch with my old boss went well, all things considered. She was happy I was home safe, but she couldn't make any promises. Times were tough and it was out of her hands, really, but she'd talk to some higher-ups and let me know.

I peeled out of the parking lot. Whatever Jeremy had felt walking back into his old school, I felt the exact opposite: I couldn't possibly go back.

But that left me with a lot of question marks. If my old job wasn't the right fit for me, what was? Was my problem with the role itself, or with the company? I'd come to look back with fondness on my old job, with its casual corporate culture, Silicon-Valley-esque perks, and low turnover that meant most of my coworkers had been happily working together for decades. All things considered, it was a great place to work — the problem was definitely me.

I spent a few weeks soul- and job-searching. I looked at other positions I was qualified for in my industry, and I did a few interviews.

But in my heart, I wasn't sure I could return to corporate fashion again. I'd removed the lens of consumerism from my eyes, and I no longer wanted to tell people that their problems could be solved by buying new clothing.

I expanded my search to include other industries, but I found that I really wasn't qualified for most roles in Silicon Valley. Besides, did I really want to work in the tech industry?

So I took a deep breath and expanded my search to other cities.

And then, I found it: The Perfect Job. It was a senior-level role at one of my favorite ethical retailers; a company that sells products to help people spend more time enjoying the outdoors. Selling sustainably made products that promoted travel and outdoor adventure didn't feel like icky consumerism, it felt like it aligned with the values I'd discovered about myself during my trip. Could this be the solution to my career conundrum?

During the interview process, I was delighted to find that my year-long work break wasn't as much of a question mark as I feared it would be: everyone I interviewed with seemed to understand why I'd want to take a year off to travel. I discovered other things that were now important to me: the offices were moving towards being zero-waste, and the company even gave paid time off for travel and outdoor adventure, with a generous vacation policy meant to encourage employees to spend their time out-of-office, testing out the store's products. Plus, we would be relocating! We would have a whole new city to explore, in a new region surrounded by mountains and beautiful wilderness.

It was perfect.

Well, almost. It also meant that we would be picking up and relocating just months after settling back down, and moving to an unfamiliar place where we didn't know anyone. And then there was the question of the job Jeremy had just returned to. Would we need to live separately until the end of the school year?

I was torn. On paper, it was the perfect career move: a pay raise, great benefits, and a step up on the career ladder. But deep down, I wasn't sure if returning to my old career was what I really wanted.

I was at a fork in the road with a critical decision to make, so I did the only thing I could think of: I made a spreadsheet.

The Life Decision Spreadsheet catalogued everything that was important to us in a place to live: cost of living, proximity to friends and family, weekend trip and hiking opportunities, and so on.[182] Each quality was assigned a numeric value from 1-5, which was then weighted by how important it was to each of us. After we plugged in all of the data, the numbers told us exactly what the right decision was for each of us: we would stay in Oakland, and instead of returning to the

---

182 You can access a copy of this spreadsheet to make your very own Life Decisions at practical-wanderlust.com/quit-your-job-book (the password is *verybigadventure*)

career I'd spent five years building, I would blog full-time.

Honestly, if it was just me, I think I probably would have taken the job and given it a try. But I couldn't pull Jeremy away from the school he was so excited to return to. And while starting over in a new city where we didn't know anybody was exciting, we were actually ready for familiarity and comfort.

Mind you, the blog was not earning very much — but it was earning something. And I thought with more time and permission to really focus on it, I could grow that something.

We wouldn't be rich, and I wouldn't have "senior" in my job title — but I realized that I didn't care. We would each be spending our time and energy working on something that felt meaningful to us, deep down. We would be fulfilled.

After all, we had the luxuries of ice and our very own couch, what more could we possibly need?

And so, we lived happily ever after.

No, I'm just kidding. Nothing is that easy! We couldn't really afford to be a single-income household any longer, so I took a temp role at an entry-level position in my old industry to save up some money.

I worked there for a couple of months and then quit. They offered me a full-time role; I turned it down. I finally knew what I wanted, and spending a few months back in the corporate world — even as a contractor — cemented my decision. This life wasn't for me anymore.

And so, six months after returning from our year-long honeymoon, I quit my job again: this time, to work for myself. My new career might not have paid much, but by then we were comfortable with making compromises in our lifestyle to accommodate chasing after our dreams.

And to my surprise, giving myself permission to whole-heartedly chase after my passion project was exactly what I needed to turn my little travel blog into a real business. I was able to replace my old corporate paycheck within that first year.

Four years later, Practical Wanderlust is one of the most popular travel blogs in the world. I have moved from a solo-preneuer into the role of CEO, with a growing team of wonderful freelance contractors working alongside me, each chasing after their own dreams in various countries and continents all across the world. I've created exactly the kind of company I was so eager to work for: one that values time and experiences over productivity and work, that encourages work-life balance and discourages working nights and weekends, and whose driving goal above all is to have a positive impact. I wake up most days feeling invigorated by my work and energized by the intoxicating feeling of following my true passion; and on the days that I don't, I give myself permission to not be productive.

It's an impractically happy ending, and one I never expected or could have guessed when I first quit my job all those years ago. Jeremy and I have managed to craft a life together that aligns with both of our values and meets all of our needs, and in doing so, we have achieved my personal definition of success.

That said: becoming self-employed as a travel blogger isn't exactly a realistic option for everyone (especially because most blogs don't earn very much money in the first year, or ever). And self-employment comes with its own set of challenges, like a lack of financial stability or health insurance.

If returning to your old job isn't an option or just doesn't feel like a good fit, and you're struggling to figure out what does feel right, home in on what really matters to you. Is time off to travel your top priority? Or the ability to leave work behind when you go home for the day, so that you can spend your hours away from work mentally unchained to your job? Is being fulfilled by your job worth sacrificing time off or a pay reduction? Or is a high salary most important of all?

For Jeremy, fulfillment was a worthy goal that he was willing to make some sacrifices for. He rarely works under 40 hours a week, but it feels like a choice he's made rather than a life he fell into unwillingly.

For me, the chance to travel while exploring my own creativity was exciting, as was the idea of working for myself with nobody to answer to, and the opportunity to make a positive impact on other people. For those gifts, I was willing to give up a reliable paycheck and benefits, as well as abandoning my climb up the corporate ladder. It was a risk that has ultimately paid off for me, but even before my blog was earning much, the happiness and satisfaction I felt working on building something of my very own was worth all the corporate titles and salaries in the world.

But your work does not need to bring you joy, or to be a significant part of who you are. Maybe your job is just a way to pay the bills so that you can spend your time on the things that really do matter to you, whatever they may be. Thinking of your job as a means to an end, rather than as something that defines you, can open you up to career opportunities that you may not have imagined in the past.

For instance, if your priority is being able to continue to integrate travel into your life, you might explore career options that make travel possible. That could mean thinking outside the 9-5 box, looking for remote work, or seeking out a job that allows for spending weeks or months each year traveling, such as seasonal work. Just because you began this journey by quitting your job to travel doesn't mean that the end of your journey should be getting a job again and no longer travelling.

But regardless of whether you return to work only because you have to pay your bills and feed your travel obsession, or with a renewed sense of passion and excitement for your chosen vocation, you'll have more opportunities to shape your life into something that fits you. The real you. The "new" you.

The real question is, after you come back, who will you be?

The "New" You

I never became the person I really wanted to during the trip. I wanted long-term travel to magically turn me into a Morning Person, who does sunrise yoga and hikes several miles and drinks smoothie bowls and meditates — all before 10am. But I'm just not that person. I never have been, and I probably never will be.[183]

That said, I'm also not the same person that I was all those years ago, bending over backwards to fit myself into a rigid corporate mold, endlessly waiting for my life to really begin.

My long-term trip didn't change who I was, but it helped me accept who I really am. It illuminated my "real" self. The "real" me who sleeps in late and watches TV every night, who makes the same dumb mistakes over and over again, who's almost always filled with anxiety, and who never stops dreaming about all the places she's been and the infinite places she's yet to go.

The person I discovered during the trip appreciates life's little joys, like coffee in the morning with Jeremy and watching the birds in our little birdfeeder.[184] I found out how much I love getting from place to place on foot, and I've carved out a few hours each day to go on long, aimless walks, discovering new neighborhoods and identifying local flora and fauna. I've learned that the excitement of a new place doesn't have to take me far away from home: I'm just as invigorated by exploring a foreign country as I am walking through a new neighborhood or visiting a nearby town. I've grown to see the world through a new lens, filled with appreciation and gratitude for the smallest, simple things. The convenience of ice has still never ceased to amaze me.

Our trip taught me other lessons, too. It taught me to always pack a daybag, and that I really hate purses. It taught me that I prefer being comfortable even more than expressing myself creatively through clothing and makeup. It helped me realize that I can be both fat and athletic; that I love the feeling of being strong, and that I really do love hiking, even if I am very, very slow.

---

183 Every single night of my life, I go to bed thinking that maybe tomorrow will be the day I wake up and transform into a Morning Person. The closest I get is usually from jet lag, but I'll never give up hope.

184 Every time I get excited about a bird I can feel yet another cell of my body turning into my mother. In a few years, maybe I, too, will wear binoculars on a harness and wake up before dawn to go on early morning birding capers. But hey, at least I'll finally be a Morning Person, right?

Long-term travel taught me to sit with my discomfort — and at the same time, to advocate for my needs. It taught me to relish the difficulty of tackling a challenge head-on and I've grown to love being really terrible at new things. I've even learned that the willingness to venture beyond my comfort zone and try something terrifying is well worth it, even if only for the sake of a good story.

Then there was the lesson that took so long — and so many mistakes — to finally sink in: the need to slow down. To sit still. To replenish my energy by the wonderful act of doing absolutely nothing, the joy of being totally unproductive.

I also discovered that I have a superpower: when I catch myself getting caught up in the breakneck pace of everyday life, I have the ability to slow down time just by tricking my brain with new experiences.

I've even learned to enjoy the deep, aching longing that comes with falling in love with places. I once felt that a long-term trip would cure me of my ache to travel once and for all, but now I know that I'll never not want to travel. I've now learned to savor that lack of satisfaction: the anticipation for my next trip is as sweet as the trip itself.

Most of all, long-term travel gave me a deep sense of gratitude. I realized that the things I once took for granted are the most exciting of all: convenience, ease, stability, and routine. Those are treasured luxuries that I'd never stopped to truly appreciate.

I know, it sounds a little lame. I mean, we traveled around the world for a year, living out of backpacks, hitchhiking through the Andes, catching rides on chicken trucks to cross borders, road tripping through French wine country, and living the dream life — and it made us realize that what we really want is a house, a couch, and Netflix. Long, boring walks at twilight. A daily gym habit. A regular coffee shop where they know our order. Wine glasses. Pieces of reclaimed wood with decoupaged maps and inspirational quotes plastered all over our walls. Were we always this basic?[185]

Somewhere along the way, our needs had shifted. After our crazy, amazing, exhausting adventure was over, we were ready to settle down. We even started dreaming about the kinds of deep commitment that once terrified us: getting a dog, having some kids, taking those kids on weekend trips and family vacations,

---

185   There is a very good chance that we were, indeed, always this basic.

and then — once they're all grown up and we've had a good, long rest — packing up our old, worn-out backpacks and doing it all over again.

Whoever you discover you are once you come back from your trip, know that you are in a constant state of discovering who you "really" are, and that the "new" you will be ever-changing.

Self-discovery doesn't happen just once — and you don't need to take a Very Big Adventure to change your life. You will reinvent yourself over and over throughout your life.

And when, yet again, you feel as though the life you're living isn't meeting your needs, ask yourself: what do I value? And how do the things I value match up with how I'm spending my time and energy?

Remember: if you can achieve the monumental, insanely difficult, ridiculously amazing task of quitting your job to travel, you've already proven that you can do anything you set your mind to.

Changing and adapting your life to fit your needs doesn't have to start and end with your job. It also extends to the place where you live, your friends and close personal relationships, the vision of your future that you're working towards, the things in your life that bring you fulfillment and meaning, and the ways you spend your time. Identifying your values and bringing your life into alignment with them is a constant practice, and the best time to start is today.

If you're anything like me, you will probably always feel a pull to go elsewhere and be somewhere other than where you are — a constant travel ache, a wanderlust. That feeling isn't a problem that needs to be solved: it's a passion for learning, adventure and exploration that will always live deep inside of you. Try to sit with it, and whenever you can, nurture it by learning something new. Seek to incorporate a little bit of adventure into your everyday life, even in the smallest ways: cooking a new cuisine, learning a language, picking up a hobby, going for a walk in a new place.

And of course, take as many trips as you possibly can. Because there is always somewhere new to explore, some fantastic adventure to have, and some ridiculous story yet to be told.

And hey, maybe I'll bump into you on the road sometime.

Resources

In this section, you'll find all of the businesses, resources, and tools mentioned throughout the book, organized in an indexed list of Websites by Part. You'll also find a Reference section containing helpful tables and checklists, as well as a Bibliography and further reading recommendations.

For an online, clickable Resources section please visit **practicalwanderlust.com/ quit-your-job-book**

and enter the password: *verybigadventure*

Websites

Part One: The Dream

Where Are You Going?

- Google MyMaps
- Google Flights

Finances

Calculating the Cost of your Trip

- BudgetYourTrip
- Rome2Rio
- Travel.State.gov

How to Create a Budget

- Budgeting Services
- Mint

- PocketGuard
- Wally
- PadMapper
- Car Sharing
- ZipCar
- GetAround
- Enterprise
- Paying off Debts
- Suze Orman Debt Roll-Down Calculator
- U.S. Federal Loan Repayment Programs
- SoFi
- National Foundation for Credit Counseling
- Financial Counseling Association of America

- Savings Accounts
- SmartyPig
- Ally

Crafty Ways to Earn Extra Money

- Mystery Shopping
- Market Force
- Intelli-Shop
- Sinclair Customer Metrics
- Best Mark
- Sharing Economy Services
- GetAround
- Airbnb
- HipCamp
- Tentrr
- Neighbor
- PeerSpace
- Repairing Your Credit Score
- TransUnion
- Equifax
- Experian
- CreditKarma
- Credit Card Churning
- /r/churning subreddit
- The Points Guy
- NerdWallet
- Upwork
- Fiverr
- TEFL
- UserFeel

Travel Scholarships and Stipends

- Hostelling International USA
- World Nomads
- Volunteer HQ
- Packs Light

Footnote Mentions

- Eco Hostel Yuluka
- Secret Garden Cotopaxi
- Curb Free with Cory Lee
- HostelWorld

Practical Wanderlust Blog Posts Mentioned

- Parque Tayrona, Colombia: How to Get There & Where to Stay
- The Best Hostels in Colombia
- 1 Month Colombia Itinerary
- 1 Month Ecuador Itinerary
- How to Visit the Galapagos Islands (without a Cruise)
- The Mono Hot Springs Camping Incident

Part Two: The Plan

Planning & Booking Your Trip

Creating Your Trip Roadmap

- Microsoft OneNote

Trip Planning Resources

- Booking Flights
- Google Flights
- Skyscanner
- Kayak
- Accommodations
- Booking.com
- Hostelworld
- Airbnb
- TrustedHousesitters
- Tours
- Viator
- GetYourGuide
- Luggage Storage
- Stasher
- LuggageHero

Ethical & Responsible Travel

- BookDifferent
- EcoHotels
- GreenDestinations
- Global Sustainable Tourism Council
- Norwegian Airlines
- Native Land
- TreadRight
- VisitNative
- Cool Effect
- Sustainable Travel
- Impact Travel Alliance

Crossing Your I's and Dotting Your T's

Get a Passport

- Passport Acceptance Facility Search Page
- U.S. Passports — Travel.state.gov
- Smart Traveler Enrollment Program

Apply for Entry Visas

- Country Information — Travel.state.gov

Buy Travel Insurance

- World Nomads
- SafetyWing
- International Association for Medical Assistance to Travelers

Visit Your Doctor

- CDC Travel Website
- Routine Vaccines — CDC Travel Advice
- CDC Travel Destinations List
- International Society of Travel Medicine Online Clinic Directory

Collect Important Documents

- DropBox
- DoYourOwnWill.com Living Will Templates
- PowerofAttorney.com — Free Forms
- AAA Notary Services
- International Driving Permit

Prepare Your Cell Phone

- Global SIM Card Companies
- WorldSIM
- OneSimCard
- Telestial
- Google Fi
- Communication Apps
- Google Voice
- Skype

- WhatsApp
- Google Translate
- Helpful Travel Apps
- TripIt
- TrailWallet
- Globe Convert

Request an Absentee Ballot

- U.S. Absentee Voter Process

Fee-Free Bank Accounts and Credit Cards

- Charles Schwab
- Capital One 360
- Transferwise Debit Card
- Chase Sapphire cards
- Capital One Venture Rewards
- Capital One Venture One

Putting Everything On Hold

Mail

- Data & Marketing Association
- Online Mail Management
- Traveling Mailbox
- Earth Class Mail
- US Global Mail
- USPS Change-of-Address Form
- Opening a USPS P.O. Box

Bills & Loans

- Federal Student Loan Deferment
- U.S. Student Aid — Income-Driven Repayment Plans

Your Stuff

- Getting Rid of Stuff
- BuyNothing
- Facebook Marketplace
- Nextdoor
- Letgo
- Craigslist
- eBay
- DeCluttr
- PoshMark
- thredUP
- PickUp Please
- Habitat for Humanity ReStore
- GreenDrop
- Goodwill
- Salvation Army
- Unpakt
- Move

Your Car

- Neighbor

Your Home

- National Association of Residential Property Manager
- Vacasa

- TurnKey
- Airbnb
- VRBO
- Trusted HouseSitters

Difficult Conversations

- BetterHelp

Footnote Mentions

- LifeStraw Water Bottle
- LUSH Cosmetics
- Aviator USA Comfort Skinny in Jet Black
- VivoBarefoot Winter Boots

Practical Wanderlust Blog Posts

- How to Plan a Trip
- The Complete Guide to Minca, Colombia
- 4-Day Quilotoa Loop Hike in Ecuador
- Packing Guides
- The Ultimate Guide to Beauty & Makeup for Travel
- What to Pack for South America
- Backpacking Essentials for Hot Climates
- Travel Essentials for Cold Weather

Part Three: The Trip

The Things Nobody Tells You

Digital Backups

- Google Drive
- Chromebook
- Google Photos
- iCloud

My Money Ran Out ... What Now?

How to Find a Place to Stay for Free

- House Sitting
- Trusted HouseSitters
- HouseCarers
- Nomador
- MindMyHouse
- Working in Exchange for Accommodation
- Worldwide Opportunities on Organic Farms (WWOOF)
- Workaway
- Worldpackers
- Local Homestays

- HomeStay
- Lingoo
- HomeStayIn
- Homestay.com
- CommunityHomestay.com

How to Find a Job While Traveling

- HostelJobs
- SeasonalJobs
- CoolWorks
- SeasonWorkers
- SummerJobs
- Getting a Work Visa through an Employer
- TEFL.org
- GoOverseas
- TeachAway
- Taxes and Getting Paid Abroad
- Transferwise
- IRS (FBAR)
- Foreign Earned Income Exclusion
- MBO Partners Study

What is a Digital Nomad?

- Wefi
- MiFi

How to Make Money Online

- Upwork
- Fiverr
- Work for Impact
- Dream of Travel Writing
- Tutoring
- QKids
- Preply
- Wyzant
- TutorMe
- Chelsea International Education

Footnote Mentions

- GrooveLife Silicone Rings
- Slack
- Asana

Practical Wanderlust Blog Posts

- The Year-Long Honeymoon
- "Things Nobody Tells You" posts
- Hiking Valle De Cocora in Salento, Colombia

Part Four: The Return

- The Life Decision Spreadsheet: accessible online at practicalwanderlust. com/quit-your-job-book (password: *verybigadventure*)

Reference

For a printable version of this section, please visit
practicalwanderlust.com/quit-your-job-book

and enter the password: *verybigadventure*

Backpacking Trail Highlights

Below are some of the highlights of the two most popular (and most affordable) backpacker routes, the Banana Pancake Trail and the Gringo Trail. I recommend setting aside an evening, throwing on your comfiest pajamas, pouring yourself a nice cup of something, and indulging in a nice long research-fest! (Which is, in all honesty, my favorite way to spend a Friday night.) You'll want to read up on — and drool over photos of — all of these.

Highlights of the Banana Pancake Trail	
Thailand	Bangkok, Chiang Mai, Koh Phi Phi, Krabi, and Ko Pha Ngan
Laos	Luang Prabang, Vientiane, Vang Vieng, Si Phan Don Islands, and Huay Xai (including the Bokeo Nature Reserve)
Vietnam	Hoi An, Ho Chi Minh City, Sapa, Halong Bay, and Hanoi
Cambodia	Phnom Penh, Siem Reap (including Angkor Wat), Kirirom National Park, Koh Rong Samloem Island, and Kep

Highlights of Central America and Mexico	
Mexico	Mexico City, Mérida, Oaxaca, Guanajuato, San Miguel de Allende, Sayulita, Valladolid, and Isla Holbox
El Salvador	Joya de Cerén, Atacó, Cerro Verde National Park (including the Santa Ana Volcano), Tazumal, Suchitoto, and El Tunco
Guatemala	Tikal, Lake Atitlan, Antigua, Semuc Champey, and Pacific Beaches of Monterrico and Paredon
Belize	Belize Barrier Reef, Placencia, San Ignacio, Caracol, and Hopkins
Nicaragua	Granada, Léon, San Juan del Sur, Lake Nicaragua, and Corn Islands
Costa Rica	Monteverde, Tamarindo, Manuel Antonio, Corcovado National Park, and La Fortuna
Panama	San Blas Islands/Guna Yala, Panama City, and Bocas del Toro

Highlights of South America	
Colombia	Cartagena, Playa Blanca, Parque Tayrona, Minca, the Amazon, San Gil, Medellín, Guatapé, and the Valle de Cocora
Ecuador	Quito, The Galapagos Islands, Baños, The Quilotoa Loop, Cotopaxi, Mindo
Peru	Machu Picchu, Cusco, Lima, Huacachina, Huaraz
Bolivia	Uyuni Salt Flats, La Paz and the Valley of the Moon, Lake Titicaca and Copacabana, and Sucre
Chile	Atacama Desert, Valparaiso, Easter Island, Santiago, and Patagonia
Argentina	Mendoza, Patagonia, Buenos Aires, Iguazu Falls, Salta, and Ushuaia
Brazil	Rio de Janeiro, Iguaçu Waterfalls, Salvador, São Paulo, and Bonito

Sample Itinerary & Budget Spreadsheet

Below is a sample of a budget-planning spreadsheet to help you estimate and track the cost of your trip as you plan your itinerary. We filled in cost estimates by looking up flights and accomodations online, used Rome2Rio to find bus and transit costs, and estimated the rest based on research. (*Note that the actual cost numbers in this example are out of date — this is the budget spreadsheet I created for the first month of our trip, back in 2016!)*

Category	Destination	Description	Cost
Flight	Cartagena	SFO to Cartagena	$496
Accomodation	Cartagena	2 beds, 2 nights in a dorm room	$70
Accomodation	Santa Marta	1 night	$20
Tour	La Ciudad Perdida	6-day guided jungle trek	$600
Accomodation	Parque Tayrona	Park entrance fee & 2 nights in a hammock dorm	$40
Accomodation	Minca	Hammock dorm	$26
Accomodation	Cartagena	2 nights, dorm	$60
Tour	Cartagena	Day trip to Playa Blanca	$20
Flight	Medellin	Cartagena to Medellin on Avianca	$70
Accomodation	Medellin	4 nights, dorm	$69
Transit	Salento	Bus from Medellin to Salento	$24
Accomodation	Salento	Glamping, canvas tent 3 nights	$76
Transit	Bogotá	Bus from Salento to Bogotá	$30
Transit	Bogotá	Bus from Bogotá to San Gil	$40
Accomodation	San Gil	6 nights in a dorm	$150
Tours	San Gil	Rafting, paragliding, rappelling, etc	$150
Transit	Bogotá	Bus from San Gil to Bogotá	$24
Accomodation	Bogotá	5 nights	$128
Flight	Bogotá	Flight from Bogotá to Quito	$140
Food	Colombia	$5 per person per day	$300
Transit	Colombia	Taxis, colectivos, mototaxis, etc	$100
Total	**Colombia**	**Estimated Total Cost**	**$2,633***

*This was fairly accurate to what we spent! Total expenses for both of us for our month in Colombia ended up at around $2,000 (we didn't end up hiking to La Ciudad Perdida, which saved us $600).

Common Vaccine Checklist

Below is a basic overview of common vaccines recommended at the time of publication. Check the CDC travel website for the most up-to-date information, organized by country.

Vaccine	Area or countries	When to Get Them
Hepatitis B	Some countries in Eastern Europe, Asia, Africa, Central and South America	At least 8-12 weeks before your departure date
Cholera	Many Caribbean, Africa, and South-east Asia countries	Approximately 1 week before
Polio	Afghanistan, Democratic Republic of the Congo, Nigeria, Pakistan, Somalia, Syria	If you have never been vaccinated against polio, then a full course may take up to 12 months
Rabies	All over the world, some countries with higher prevalence	At least 4 weeks before
Yellow Fever	Many African, South and Central American countries	At least 10 days before
Typhoid	Some countries in Africa, Asia, South and Central America	Approximately 1 week before
Meningococcal	Some Sub-Saharan countries	At least 1 week before

Anti-Malarial Medication

The below table was adapted from the CDC and compares some of the common antimalarial drugs. Figure out which one best fits your needs, and ask your doctor for it specifically.

Anti-Malarial	Dosage	Pros	Cons
Doxycycline	Daily	Inexpensive Fast acting — dosage starts 1-2 days before traveling to an high risk area	Must be taken daily Increased risk of sun sensitivity Must be taken for 4 weeks after travel May cause an upset stomach (especially if taken on an empty stomach) Cannot be used by pregnant women
Malarone (Atovaquone/Proguanil)	Daily	Well tolerated medication — little to no side effects Good for short trips as it only needs to be taken 7 days after travel Fast acting — dosage starts 1-2 days before traveling	Bit more expensive Must be taken daily Cannot be used by pregnant women
Chloroquine	Weekly	Only needs to be taken weekly — good for longer trips Can be taken by pregnant women	Cannot be used in areas with chloroquine or mefloquine resistance Dosage starts 1-2 weeks before traveling Must be taken for 4 weeks after travel

| Mefloquine | Weekly | Only needs to be taken weekly — good for longer trips

Can be taken by pregnant women | Dosage starts at least 2 weeks before traveling

Must be taken for 4 weeks after travel

Cannot be used in areas with mefloquine resistance

Cannot be used in patients with cardiac conduction abnormalities, certain psychiatric conditions, or with a seizure disorder |

Important Documentation Checklist

Hard Copies to Bring	Digital Copies to Upload*	File Before Trip
☐ Passport	☐ Passport	☐ Living Will
☐ Driver's License	☐ Driver's License	☐ Other Advance Directives
☐ International Driving Permit	☐ Birth certificate	☐ Power of Attorney (*Medical*)
☐ Yellow Fever Card	☐ Marriage license	☐ Power of Attorney (*Financial*)
☐ Proof of Vaccination (as needed)	☐ Social security card	
☐ Signed doctor's note	☐ Travel Insurance policy	
	☐ Login details as needed	
	☐ Trip Roadmap	

Make sure you're uploading these to a secure, password-protected and encrypted shared drive, such as on Dropbox.

Long-Term Travel Packing Checklist

Stuff to Put Stuff In	
☐ Backpack (or suitcase)	☐ Laundry/wet bag
☐ Day bag	☐ Shoe bag
☐ Packing cubes	☐ Toiletry bag

First Aid Kit	
☐ Dramamine/Motion sickness	☐ Band-Aids
☐ Imodium/Anti-diarrheals	☐ Alcohol pads
☐ Emergen-C/Immune support	☐ Hand sanitizer
☐ Tylenol/Pain relievers	☐ Anti-Malarial
☐ Melatonin/sleep aids	☐ Altitude sickness medication
☐ Allergy meds	☐ Prescription medications, as needed
☐ Moleskin blister pads	

Toiletries	
☐ Shampoo & Conditioner	☐ Tweezers
☐ Moisturizer (face & body)	☐ Folding scissors
☐ Chapstick	☐ Beauty & hair necessities
☐ Deodorant	☐ Toothbrush & toothpaste
☐ Baby wipes (for face, etc)	☐ Menstrual cup/supplies
☐ Bar of soap (& carrying case)	☐ Travel towel (Full-Sized)
☐ Sewing kit	☐ Travel laundry wash

General Essentials	
☐ Water bottle	☐ Travel Clothesline
☐ Water purification tool	☐ Sunglasses
☐ Smartphone (unlocked)	☐ Mineral sunscreen
☐ Bug repellant	☐ Lightweight umbrella
☐ Money belt/bra pocket	☐ Camera
☐ Locks for bags	☐ Passport
☐ Sink stopper	☐ Drivers License

Hostel Necessities	
☐ Small flashlight	☐ Spices (for cooking)
☐ Laptop	☐ Tupperware (for leftovers)
☐ Plug adapters	☐ Lightweight slippers
☐ Outlet splitter	☐ Lightweight robe/ large travel towel
☐ Phone chargers	☐ Ear plugs
☐ Kindle, books, cards, etc	☐ Sleeping mask
☐ Locks for lockers	

Digital Nomad Necessities	
☐ Computer	☐ Laptop stand
☐ Ergonomic mouse	☐ VPN
☐ Ergonomic keyboard	☐ Mobile router or portable WiFi

Clothing (For Her)	Clothing (For Him)
☐ 7 Pairs of underwear	☐ 7 Pairs of underwear
☐ 5-7 Pairs of socks	☐ 7 Pairs of socks
☐ 1 Swimsuit	☐ 1 Swimsuit
☐ 1 Pair jeans	☐ 1 Pair jeans
☐ 1 Pair shorts	☐ 1 Pair shorts
☐ 1 Pair hiking pants	☐ 1 Pair hiking pants
☐ 1 Pair lounge pants	☐ 1 Pair lounge pant
☐ 1-3 Cozy dresses or skirts	☐ 3-5 T-Shirts
☐ 3-5 T-Shirts & tank tops	☐ 2-3 Long-sleeve tops
☐ 1-3 Long-sleeve tops	☐ 1 Sweatshirt or sweater
☐ 1 Cardigan	☐ 1 Hiking outfit
☐ 1 Hoodie/sweatshirt	☐ 1 Lightweight jacket
☐ 1 Lightweight jacket	☐ 1 Lightweight rain jacket
☐ 1 Lightweight rain jacket	☐ 1 Packable down jacket
☐ 1 Packable down jacket	☐ 1 pair sandals
☐ 1 pair sandals	☐ 1 pair hiking shoes
☐ 1 pair hiking shoes	☐ 1 pair everyday shoes
☐ 1 pair everyday shoes	☐ 1 warm hat
☐ 1 warm hat	☐ 1 pair gloves
☐ 1 pair gloves	☐ 1 scarf
☐ 1 scarf	

Lia's Favourite Travel Items	
☐ Steri-Pen	☐ Aviator USA Jeans
☐ Permethrin Spray	☐ Vivobarefoot Winter Boots
☐ Picaridin Bug Repellant	☐ AllBirds Tree Skippers Walking Shoes
☐ Bra Pocket	☐ Teva Sandals
	☐ Outdoor Voices Lounge Pants
	☐ prAna Zion pants and Halle pants

Working Visas for U.S. Citizens

Working Holiday Visas

Country	Visa Duration	Age Restrictions	Specific Requirements	Relevant Job Boards
Canada	12 — 24 months	18 — 35yrs	Health insurance Proof of savings equivalent of at least $2,500 CAD	Indeed Canada Glassdoor
Australia	12 months; 24 months if you work in a remote area for part of the time	18 — 30yrs	Proof of savings the equivalent of $5000 AUD	Gumtree Seek
New Zealand	12 months	18 — 30yrs	A return ticket or enough funds to purchase a return ticket	SeasonalJobs WorktheSeasons
South Korea	12 months	18 — 30yrs	Criminal record check Proof of sufficient funds	Xpatjobs JobKorea
Singapore	6 months	18 — 25yrs	Hold a degree or enrolled in university	JobStreet Gumtree Singapore
Ireland	12 months	Enrolled or within one year of graduating from university	Proof of savings the equivalent of €3000	IrishJobs

Freelance, Remote Work & Digital Nomad Visas

Country	Visa Duration	Cost	Specific requirements
Anguilla	12 months	$1000 — $2000	Proof of employment or business incorporation certificate and a police record (with a validity of not more than six months)
Aruba	90 days	Approx. $30	Must purchase Aruba's travel insurance and stay in designated accommodation, Book a packaged stay through Aruba's One Happy Workation and compliance with Aruba's traveler health requirements
Barbados	12 months	$2,000	Income declaration that you expect to earn an income of $50,000 or more over the next 12 months and/or have the means to support yourself during the 12 months in Barbados
Bermuda	12 months	$263	Proof of employment with a legitimate company or your own company registered and operating outside of Bermuda
Cayman Islands	24 months	$1,469	Proof of employment with a minimum annual income of $100,000; proof of legal existence of employer or company; health insurance; police clearance; bank reference
Costa Rica	24 months	$250	Show income of $2,500 per month for two years or make a $60,000 deposit in a Costa Rican bank
Dubai	12 months	$287 + processing fees	Proof of employment with a minimum of $5,000 per month and at least one-year contract validity) or business incorporation certificate; health insurance with UAE coverage validity
Estonia	12 months	€80 — €100	Proof of employment with a company registered outside of Estonia, business incorporation certificate (registered abroad, or work as a freelancer for clients mostly outside of Estonia; proof of income with a minimum threshold (currently €3504) during the six months preceding the application

Germany	Up to 3 years	€60 — €260	Portfolio of previous work, professional licenses and/or diplomas, freelance plan, recommendation letters from previous employers, letters of commitment from future customers, health insurance, and evidence of means of subsidence
Georgia	12 months	N/A	Proof of you own a location independent business or proof of employment with a company based outside of Georgia; proof of means of subsidence (earn at least $2,000 per month); health insurance
Iceland	6 months	$70	Proof of annual income of at least $88,000

Responsible Travel: Further Reading

Books

- **Going Local: Experiences and Encounters on the Road by Nicholas Kontis**

This enjoyable read lays out the how-tos of responsible and experiential travel, from choosing ethical tour operators to sharing meals with locals. The book also contains case studies, expert interviews and information on how to place protecting local societies and the environment at the forefront of any trip.

Sharing personal travel stories throughout the book, author Nicholas Kontis demonstrates how travel can be so much more than checking a destination off a bucket list — it is an immersive experience that should lead to greater understanding between people and places.

- **Overbooked: The Exploding Business of Travel and Tourism by Elizabeth Becker**

Elizabeth Becker, a former New York Times journalist and NPR editor, delivered a disturbing exposé of the dark side of the travel industry and how this growing industry produces ripple effects across the global economy, the environment, and culture. Employing approximately one out of twelve people in the world, the tourism industry is booming but must evolve to protect the world's irreplaceable sites and spaces. Elizabeth Becker draws from her own travels and meticulous research to illuminate case studies of this evolution and offers examples of how to tread more lightly while traveling.

Academic Studies

- Commodification, Culture and Tourism" by Shepherd R. Tourist Studies. (2002);2(2):183-201. doi:10.1177/146879702761936653

- "The Phenomena of Overtourism: A Review" by Dodds, R. and Butler, R. International Journal of Tourism Cities (2019), Vol. 5 No. 4, pp. 519-528.

- "A Causation Theory of Visitor-Resident Irritants; Methodology and Research Inferences" by Doxey, G.V. In: Travel and Tourism Research Association Sixth Annual Conference Proceedings, San Diego (September 1975), pp. 195-98.

- "Environmental Effects of Tourism." Islam, Faijul. American Journal of Environment, Energy and Power Research (2013).

- "Tourism and Indigenous Peoples" by MacCarthy, M. Oxford Research Encyclopedia of Anthropology (2020).

- "When in Rome ... Learn Why the Romans Do What They Do: How Multicultural Learning Experiences Facilitate Creativity" by Maddux, W. W., Adam, H. and Galinsky, A. D. (2010) Personality and Social Psychology Bulletin. 36(6), pp. 731–741. doi: 10.1177/0146167210367786.

- "Tourism Impacts: Evidence of Impacts on employment, gender, income" by Lemma, Alberto (2014) Overseas Development Institute, Economics and Private Sector Professional Evidence and Applied Knowledge Services

- "When Culture is for Sale: Tourism and Indigenous Identity in the Andean and Amazonian Regions of Peru (Unpublished master's thesis)." Ross, J. (2016). New York University.

- "Leakage, economic tourism." By Jönsson C. (2015) In: Jafari J., Xiao H. (eds) Encyclopedia of Tourism. Springer, Cham. doi:10.1007/978-3-319-01669-6_527-1.

What Did You Think of How to Quit Your Job & Travel?

First of all, thank you for purchasing How to Quit Your Job & Travel. I know you could have picked any number of books to read, but you picked this book and for that I am extremely grateful.

Did this book help you in some way? If so, I'd like to hear about it! Your feedback and support will help me improve my writing craft, and make this book even better. (Also, it *really* makes my day.)

I would love you to review How to Quit Your Job & Travel on Amazon or Goodreads.

I hope that you enjoyed reading it, and that it inspired you to take your own Very Big Adventure. If so, I would love for you to share this book with your friends and family by posting to Facebook, Instagram, and Twitter. And please tag us! I'd love to see your post.

All the best and happy travels,

Lia Garcia

About the Author

After her year-long honeymoon, Lia Garcia returned home to Oakland, California, where she currently lives with her husband and dog. Through the Practical Wanderlust blog and podcast, she helps millions of travelers each year embark on life-changing travel experiences. Her travel advice and writing has been featured in Forbes, Travel + Leisure, Lonely Planet, The Washington Post, Vice, Fodor's, and more. You can follow along with her (mis)adventures at PracticalWanderlust.com.

Printed in Great Britain
by Amazon

16371093R10153